# Global Capital and Social Difference



This volume offers insights into ongoing global socioeconomic transformations by directing attention to the significance of labour, work, craft, community, social institutions, social movements and emergent subjectivities in different parts of the world. This is in contrast to theories that project globalisation as a process driven exclusively by global capital and technology, a scheme in which some parts of the world forever will be 'peripheries' supplying labour and natural resources, the lives and work of those people purged of originality, meaning and value by the very construct that describes them. Together the chapters in the book present a non-essentialist and non-linear reading of global transformations by examining the relations and adaptations between economy, polity and society, which remains a fundamentally unresolved question in the social sciences.

Combining a wealth of conceptual and empirical investigations, this book will be of interest to scholars and researchers of sociology, globalisation studies, anthropology, economics, development studies and area studies.

**V. Sujatha** is Professor at the Centre for the Study of Social Systems, School of Social Sciences, Jawaharlal Nehru University, New Delhi, India. She specialises in the fields of sociology of knowledge and sociology of health and medicine. Her research focuses on the dynamic interface between scientific knowledge, state policy and societal perspectives. Her publications are, *Health by the people* (2003), *Medical pluralism in Contemporary India* (Ed. With Leena Abraham; 2012), *Sociology of health and medicine. New perspectives* (2014) and *Globalization of South Asian medicines. Knowledge, power, structure and sustainability (Ed. 2020).*

# Global Capital and Social Difference

Edited by V. Sujatha

Routledge
Taylor & Francis Group
LONDON AND NEW YORK

First published 2021
by Routledge
2 Park Square, Milton Park, Abingdon, Oxon OX14 4RN

and by Routledge
52 Vanderbilt Avenue, New York, NY 10017

*Routledge is an imprint of the Taylor & Francis Group, an informa business*



*British Library Cataloguing-in-Publication Data*
A catalogue record for this book is available from the British Library

*Library of Congress Cataloging-in-Publication Data*
Names: Sujatha, V., editor.
Title: Global capital and social difference / edited by V. Sujatha.
Description: Abingdon, Oxon ; New York, NY : Routledge, 2021. | Includes bibliographical references and index.
Identifiers: LCCN 2020016426 (print) | LCCN 2020016427 (ebook)
Subjects: LCSH: Capitalism—Social aspects. | Globalization—Economic aspects. | Globalization—Social aspects.
Classification: LCC HB501 .G547 2021 (print) | LCC HB501 (ebook) | DDC 306.3—dc23
LC record available at https://lccn.loc.gov/2020016426
LC ebook record available at https://lccn.loc.gov/2020016427

ISBN: 978-0-8153-6049-0 (hbk)
ISBN: 978-0-367-54687-8 (pbk)
ISBN: 978-1-003-09013-7 (ebk)

Typeset in Sabon
by Apex CoVantage, LLC

# Contents

# Contributors

**Suraj Beri** is Assistant Professor at the Department of Sociology, Indraprastha College for Women, Delhi University. He works in the field of political sociology and emerging forms of social inequalities in contemporary India. His research interests include social theory, class analysis, social mobility, cultural identity formation in neoliberal capitalism and the changing nature of urban space and its relation to power. He was a visiting research fellow at Humboldt University Berlin in 2014.

**Manuela Boatcă** is Professor of Sociology and Head of School of the Global Studies Programme at the Albert-Ludwigs University of Freiburg, Germany. Her work deals with world-systems analysis, postcolonial and decolonial perspectives, gender in modernity/coloniality and the geopolitics of knowledge production in Eastern Europe and Latin America. She is the author of *Global Inequalities beyond Occidentalism* (2016).

**Lucas G. Christel** is Director of Political Science BA at National University of San Martín (UNSAM), Argentina, and Lecturer at the Latin American School of Social Sciences (FLACSO), Argentina. He is a postdoctoral fellow of The National Scientific and Technical Research Council (CONICET), Argentina. His research interests include collective action dynamics, environmental politics and biodiversity issues. He has a PhD in Political Science from the National University of San Martín (UNSAM), Argentina.

**J. Devika** is a feminist researcher and teacher at Centre for Development Studies, Kerala, India. She has contributed to the understanding of the history of gender, development, politics and culture of modern Kerala. Her work is interdisciplinary, and she brings to bear her training as a historian on contemporary issues. She is interested in opening up the boundaries between academic, public and pedagogic discourses; the social sciences and humanities and English and Malayalam.

**Patricia Ferrante** is a political scientist and researcher at FLACSO, Guatemala, and the National Pedagogical University (UNIPE), Argentina, where she also teaches different courses regarding media and globalisation and digital media and education. Her research interests involve digital culture, teaching and learning in the digital age, intellectual property regulation, TV and cinema on the internet and data literacies.

**Gaston Fulquet** has a PhD in Social Sciences from FLACSO, Argentina. He was previously a Fellow with the National Council of Scientific and Technical Research (CONICET). He served for several years as a consultant to the Ministry of Environment and Sustainable Development of the Nation on issues of environmental water management. He is currently coordinating a regional programme for the conservation and restoration of the wetland system of the Paraná-Paraguay corridor at Fundación Humedales/Wetlands International LAC. His research interests include regional integration, global governance, international political economy and environmental policy.

**Faisal Garba** is Lecturer at the Department of Sociology, University of Cape Town, South Africa, and is affiliated to the Institut Fuer Soziologie Albert Ludwigs Universitaet, Freiburg, Germany. His research interests include migration and social change, social movements, globalisation and inequality and historical sociology. His recent publications include *Masons and Maids: Class, Gender and Ethnicity in Migrant Experiences*, edited with Bruno Monteiro (2019).

**Aarti Kawlra** is Academic Director of the *Humanities across Borders: Asia and Africa in the World* programme of the International Institute of Asian Studies (IIAS) in Leiden, The Netherlands. Her research focuses on colonial, postcolonial and global discourses of culture, heritage, education, nation and development. She has published numerous articles and book chapters.

**Ratheesh Kumar** is Assistant Professor at the Centre for the Study of Social Systems, School of Social Sciences, Jawaharlal Nehru University, New Delhi, India. He has previously taught at the Department of Anthropology, University of Hyderabad, India, and at the School of Interdisciplinary and Trans-disciplinary Studies, Indira Gandhi National Open University (IGNOU), New Delhi. His teaching and research interests are in the areas of popular culture, sound studies, sport and society, media anthropology, sociology of education, critical pedagogy and debates in ethnography.

**Pía Marchegiani** is a PhD Candidate at the Latin American School of Social Sciences (FLACSO), Argentina, and Environmental Policy Director at FARN (Fundación Ambiente y Recursos Naturales), Argentina. She is a lecturer at FLACSO (Global Studies Programme) and at the University of Buenos Aires Law School (Environmental Law Legal Clinic), Argentina. Her research interests include environmental and social dimensions of lithium mining in Argentina.

**Aditya Nigam** works at the Centre for the Study of Developing Societies, Delhi, India. His work focuses on the decolonisation of social and political theory. He is the author of *The Insurrection of Little Selves: The Crisis of Secular Nationalism in India* (2006); *Power and Contestation: India Since 1989*, with Nivedita Menon (2007); *After Utopia: Modernity, Socialism and the Postcolony* (2010) and *Desire Named Development* (2011). He also comments on contemporary political issues on the blog kafila.online.

**Alejandro Pelfini** is Director of the Global Studies Programme at FLACSO-Argentina and Director for Postgraduate Studies at the Faculty of Social Sciences at the Universidad del Salvador in Buenos Aires, Argentina. He was Professor of Sociology at the Universidad Alberto Hurtado in Santiago de Chile. His research areas are social theory, environmental sociology and political sociology, particularly the topics of populism, collective learning processes and the public sphere (elites and public goods).

**Boike Rehbein** is Professor for the Study of Transformation and Society in Asia and Africa at Humboldt University Berlin, Germany. His areas of specialisation include social theory, inequality, globalisation and Southeast Asia. He has published 25 books and over 100 articles. His recent publications include *Inequality in Economics and Sociology*, edited with Gilberto Antonelli (2018), and *Inequality in Capitalist Societies*, with Surinder S. Jodhka and Jessé Souza (2017).

**Julia Roth** is Professor for American Studies with a focus on Gender Studies and Inter-American Studies at Bielefeld University, Germany. Her research focuses on postcolonial and gender approaches, intersectionality and global inequalities. Her work currently focuses on anti-racist feminist knowledge from the Caribbean, intersectionality theorising and rightwing populism and gender. Her recent publications include *Right-Wing Populism and Gender: European Perspectives and Beyond*, edited with Gabriele Dietze (forthcoming), and *Can Feminism Trump Populism? Right-Wing Trends and Intersectional Contestations in the Americas* (forthcoming).

**Sudha Vasan** is currently Associate Professor at the Department of Sociology, Delhi School of Economics, University of Delhi, India. Her research interests include political ecology with a focus on issues of gender, caste, class and *adivasi* issues as they intersect with ecology and environmentalism. She is the author of *Living with Diversity: Forestry Institutions in the Western Himalaya* (2007).

# Preface

The trajectory of the term *globalisation* tells us something about the phenomenon it is referring to. It is such a widely used term in popular parlance to refer to any international link that, like many of its kind, it has lost its precise meaning. But as a concept referring to a process of transformation, it is not so widely used among scholars and writers in the global South, especially those from South East Asia and Africa, as much as in the global North and by the non-resident scholars of Asia, Africa and Latin America. In other words, it seems that the observed social and economic transformation in some regions of the global South is not adequately accounted for by the concept and not all processes of change could be related causally to global players and forces. This point would often come up in our curriculum and teaching of what is known as the Global Studies Program (GSP), of which I was a part for more than a decade and subsequently the co-ordinator for my centre for four years. The Global Studies Program, started in 2003, is a longstanding intercultural academic programme connecting academic institutions from four continents (Asia, Africa, Latin America and Europe), through a postgraduate programme in the social sciences. A (global) batch of 30–35 students from different countries study one semester in every continent to complete the two-year programme. The partner institutions are Jawaharlal Nehru University (New Delhi) and Chulalongkorn University (Bangkok) from Asia, Albert-Ludwigs University, (Freiburg) and Humboldt University (Berlin) from Europe, FLACSO (Buenos Aires) and University of Cape Town (South Africa). GSP is designed to combine the rigors of a structured curriculum with the liberties of regional and institutional diversity. It offers an opportunity for students anywhere in the world to learn from different cultures of studying and living. The centrality of globalisation as a concept varied in the curriculum and the bibliographies in different institutional locations and itself became a point of discussion.

Global teaching programs also provide fodder for research. This volume is the outcome of an international conference organised by Jawaharlal Nehru University (JNU), New Delhi, India, in October 2016 under the Global Studies Program with the aim of bringing the thoughts within the GSP team together with those of other scholars in India. Globalisation discourses often place heavy emphasis on the quantum of capital as the sole factor in socioeconomic processes, reducing labour, craft and social experience of resource-poor societies to a one-way relationship at the receiving end. The essays in this volume unpack social aspects of the transformation in different regions of the world and in various domains of life. In this rendering, global capital is contextualised as one possible factor among many. The many routes taken by the papers have been organised as themes in my introduction.

I am thankful to the participants and contributors to this volume for their valuable inputs during the conference and after. I must mention the important role of two dynamic research scholars, Ankita Mookherjee and Rai Ganguly, in assisting with the logistics of the volume, writing to the authors, reading the drafts and checking the proofs. I am thankful to Ankita and Rai for their enthusiasm and initiative in making this volume possible.

To Vilasini, I owe the very inspiration for this effort.

# Introduction

## Global capital and social difference: beyond dialectics and embeddedness

*V. Sujatha*

Globalisation is a well-explored concept with a rich body of work on its distinct characteristics as a process and a lot more debate on whether it represents a state of affairs that is desirable. In Dhanagare's view (2003: 4), 'no other concept, with perhaps the solitary exception of "gender", has stirred a major discourse in social sciences as the term "globalisation" did', in the past few decades. While economists have presented statistical figures about the volume of external trade and exports, mobility of capital, growth of transnational corporations and integration of national economies into global circuits of demand and supply, scholars on polity point to the emergence of institutions of global governance and world trade as confirmation of independent supra-national political structures above the arena of nation states. Anthropologists have brought to light the cultural mixes and hybridisation created by migration of people and the movement of their material culture and practices. In sociology, globalisation is postulated as a concept, a construct referring to a process leading to 'global society', or a state of global cosmopolitanism.

The mobility of capital across national boundaries and the technological achievements in transportation, air travel and world wide web have integrated the vast globe into a finite space that can be traversed with ease. Face-to-face interaction has been surpassed by social media technologies that offer numerous networks outside the here and now of our life, blurring spatial boundaries; all these developments have been central to the sociological understanding of globalisation. Globalisation is defined as 'the widening, deepening and speeding of worldwide connectedness in all aspects of contemporary life from the cultural to the criminal, the financial to the spiritual. The computer programmers in India now deliver services in real time to their employers in Europe and the United States while the cultivation of poppies in Burma can be linked to drug abuse in Berlin or Belfast', thus connecting communities in one corner of the world to another (Held et al. 1999: 2).

As a concept denoting a process of expansion and diffusion, the term globalisation appeared in the seventies. However, the processes themselves have a long history spanning thousands of centuries. This has led to profound debates on the forces that led to extension, expansion and worldwide spread in the previous eras and those in the contemporary epoch. Hence one of the pressing questions about globalisation has been whether it is new and distinct in character, an extension of existing politico-economic processes like colonialism or a new label for the same old processes. Economists have engaged with this question in terms of parameters like trade flows, foreign direct investment and volume of imports in the period before World War I and the early seventies and have argued about the extent of global integration of markets (Nayyar 2006; Nayar 2007). Going beyond these numerical indicators, mainstream sociology, however, has postulated certain qualitative and substantive characteristics of contemporary globalisation in terms of how the experience of time and space has been drastically altered now so as to produce an unprecedented intensity and velocity of social connections. Whether it is viewed as time-space compression (Harvey 1989 c.f. Inda and Rosaldo 2002) or as time-space distantiation (Giddens 1990 c.f. Inda and Rosaldo 2002), there is no doubt that there is a re-ordering of time-space coordinates of social networks in a very fundamental way.

Globalisation theories often go on to assert that the intensity and velocity of social interaction in current times is something that never existed in previous epochs anywhere in the world (Held et al. 1999). Our first dispute here is not about the altered character of networks in time and space but about networks becoming synonymous with society. Sociological approaches to globalisation are making larger claims with greater certainty about the social realm. Social networks and their forms may not exhaust the social. Second, far-reaching market linkages in themselves cannot cause global social consciousness, and the causal relationship between capital investment, technology and society that is assumed in these statements may not withstand the scrutiny of sociological data from different parts of the world. This is especially so because the claims are not backed by any sociohistorical analysis of trajectories around the world; they are but retrospective application of a theory of the present.

Another line of debate is whether globalisation is desirable; here, again, there are strong views expressed on either side about the outcomes of globalisation. Without getting into the normative discussion, this volume focuses on the relationships postulated between economy, society, polity and culture in the understanding of globalisation as a process of transformation.

## Social difference and the centrality of labour

First, the idea is to problematise the manner in which global capitalism is assumed to cause social change everywhere in the world, something like a universal constant. The sociological concept of globalisation assumes that economic integration, global institutions of governance and communication technologies can seamlessly cause social structure and relations to change in a particular direction. *It is pertinent to ask how social differences in a region deflect, refract, predispose, accommodate or deviate to produce manifold forms of capital or lack of capital.* The relations between economy, polity and society and the way in which they influence each other is a fundamentally unresolved question in the social sciences, and the concept of globalisation carries this ambiguity at its very core. This reminds us of the old debate between Weber and Marx on whether it is the Protestant ethic of a specific Calvinist denomination that predisposed Europe to capitalism or the advent of industrial system of commodity production.

Second, the cardinal importance given to capital over labour in both the Marxist and liberal interpretations of the economy is another issue. It is also possible to reinterpret Marx, as many have tried to. In Uberoi's view (2012), Marx's masterly story of political economy begins in the economic and political manuscripts with labour as a basic quality of the human species and as the unifying force for the human eye, mind and hand, giving rise to knowledge of nature and the material basis of the world in the unalienated subject. Language and labour emanate from the act of producing. Here labour is intricately woven into production as mode of livelihood. When this posited unity is broken by the contradictions of capitalism, estrangement occurs. 'The real and true purpose of labour, as clearly explained by Marx, is the self-aware objectification of man's species life through his free conscious activity, but which the present capitalist system tears away from him and makes a mere means to his individual physical existence' (2012: 74). The starting point of production is human labour, which generates surplus. 'The apparent firm conclusion of Marx then is that private property is evidently a result and consequence, of alienated labour, and not that alienated or estranged labour is a result of the system of private property, and that consequently the science of "political economy has merely formulated the laws of estranged labour"' (Uberoi 2012: 74). Uberoi (2012: 80) observes that whenever Marx considered the 'organisation of labour he was optimistic about the future', but when he considered 'the system of property on the other side he became pessimistic and gloomy and foresaw only doom and class conflict, exploitation and downfall'. Yet 'Marx often made history progress by what he called its dark side', and Uberoi suggests that we should now take a new look at the brighter side of human work, labour and usage rather than simply the concept of property as ownership' (ibid.).

Studies on what is known as the informal economy affirm that there is a realm of economic action in the sense of earning livelihood through self-employment that represents the 'outside' of capital (Sanyal and Bhattacharya 2009), nevertheless income generating and life sustaining. Considering forms of labour and work as the baseline of the economy would probably make it possible to develop a framework that is truly global in perspective and can account for social difference.

## Linear causality in the concept of globalisation

By virtue of hinging on the history of capital, globalisation as a concept evokes a very specific notion of time. It is a process in linear time in which all societies move at their own pace but towards the inevitable and also the cherished destination of new global order. Held et al. (1999: 11) explain that sociohistoric approaches like that of Giddens and Rosenau consider globalisation as 'a process which has no single fixed or determinate historical "destination" '. In their work, globalisation is conceived as a contingent, open-ended process which is not based on linear models. But subsequently, Held et al. summarise the causal explanations for contemporary globalisation and observe that writings converge on the point that capitalism and new technologies of communication and connectivity are the fundamental causes. Other plausible causes cited by multi-causal approaches are political decisions, ideology and market forces (Held et al. 1999). However, the perception of capital and modern technology as independent variables for all the changes happening in the world tends to insert linearity such that societies tend to be classified and ranked according to the magnitude of capital and every process as one of plausible incorporation into the circuit of global capitalism.

Held et al. argue that all pre-modern forms of globalisation everywhere in the world were fragile, limited in scope, with just a few sporadic interactions beyond regions, without any institutional structure for interregional encounters, and were characterised by slow and unmechanised forms of transport and communication. There were more one-off encounters, and the cultural networks were mostly between elites (ibid.). By contrast, contemporary globalisation is characterised by extraordinary innovations in the infrastructure of transport and communication that not only have social networks intensified, they are also characterised by instant and high-speed connectivity across time and spatial barriers. There is then the unparalleled density of regulatory institutive forms of governance in the contemporary world that was never present in the earlier epochs.

While the achievements of capital investment and machine technologies have indeed been quite major, the very framing of contemporary globalisation as a unique Western emergence associated with capitalism and technological prowess leaves very little for multiple trajectories and therefore is far from being open ended. In this framework, the large majority of regions of the world with low surplus will forever be 'peripheries' supplying labour and natural resources, their lives and work purged of originality, meaning and value by the very construct that describes them. This is a serious problem about globalisation as a concept that involves a double reduction of the contemporary existential experience – double reductionism because it limits the varied nature of social experiences both in space and in time. The permutation and combinations of the economy, society and polity relationship that are played out differently across space and the role of labour, craft, artisanship and knowledge are subordinated to the history of capital. It also tends to compress multiple simultaneities into linear time by postulating a sequential model of movement of societies. This is true of both the protagonists and critiques of globalisation.

If social difference is foregrounded here, I should also admit that the argument about the social embedding of markets has long been made in the embeddedness approach (Granovetter 1985). Granovetter clearly pointed out that he does not believe that non-market societies display greater embeddedness than market societies. By embeddedness, he refers to the fact that, 'Actors do not behave or decide as atoms outside a social context, nor do they adhere slavishly to a script written for them by the particular intersection of social categories that they happen to occupy. Their attempts at purposive action are instead embedded in concrete, ongoing systems of social relations' (1985: 487). While this phenomenon is confirmed by many studies included in this volume, the embeddedness approach focusing on proximate social causes and interactions is yet to yield a macro-perspective on how divergent social structures and relational forms interact in a global arena. In Granovetter's words: 'I should add that the level of causal analysis adopted in the embeddedness argument is a rather proximate one. I have had little to say about what broad historical or macrostructural circumstances have led systems to display the social-structural characteristics they have, so I make no claims for this analysis to answer large-scale questions about the nature of modern society or the sources of economic and political change. But the focus on proximate causes is intentional, for these broader questions cannot be satisfactorily addressed without more detailed understanding of the mechanisms by which sweeping change has its effects' (Granovetter 1985: 506).

As we shall see in the chapters, not just social networks, entire social strata or communities become the agents of economic action. Further, as social, cultural and economic agents all in one, it is not analytically sound to put their economic action as prior or as the cause of their social existence. Nor can those agents be reduced to 'local' factors, as they had already set the ball of market rolling by building infrastructure and networks and have been the key players in regions much before globalisation started.

## Form and content of 'the social'

Also at stake here is what is understood as constituting the global realm. While there could be descriptive consensus about the processes underway, such as the integration of markets and the emergence of global governance, the question remains as to whether this could be interpreted as constituting 'the global' realm as an autonomous social reality. Sassen, in her sociology of globalisation, answers in the affirmative and foregrounds the formation of explicitly global institutions like the World Trade Organization (WTO), global financial markets and international war crimes tribunals to show that

'Although they are partly enacted at a national scale, they are to a large extent novel and self-evidently global formations' (Sassen 2007: 5). Hitherto, she points out, the social sciences assumed the nation-state to be the container of social processes. Today's social formations like the global capital market and the international human rights regime are starkly different in form and substance from those of previous era. There are then processes 'deep inside territories' but part of globalisation, as they involve transboundary networks, and this include civil society organisations, state policies and institutional modifications made by nation-states to accommodate global demands. In her view, globalisation has a multiscalar character in that a financial centre in a given global city is also part of a globally scaled electronic market. The global/local binary collapses, and the task of sociology is to detect 'the presence of globalising dynamics in thick social environments that mix national and non-national elements' (2007: 5). She recommends that sociology focus on new spaces and concepts that are global in their very constitution such as 'transnational communities, global cities, commodity chains, and space-time compression'.

Sassen's call to take sociology beyond national borders will not be a surprise to those parts of the world that are still trying to fit their civilisational breadth and cultural diversity into the model of the nation-state, quite often unsuccessfully. Her careful elucidation of the truly global character of emerging institutions, spaces and practices focuses on the structural form of linkages and networks. But content and culture could often be counteracting forces and may not be subject to the same logic as things, places, material elements and institutional protocols that constitute just one dimension of social reality.

The unique quality of contemporary globalisation in Sassen's rendering is to be found in the global city, represented by London, New York and Tokyo, which are the spaces inhabited by transnational communities, highly mobile finance capital, commodity chains and cutting-edge technologies. While her work foregrounds the significance of global metropolises to speculative financial networks, Mayaram (2013: 5) argues that 'it almost negates the prior and present existence of *other* global cities' based on labour, craft, financial and population flows, creating not just a 'transnational homogenous economic space alone, but a cross-regional heterogeneous politico-cultural space'. Her own emphasis is on multiple indices of globality that include state and empire, sect and science, knowledge and culture. By this token, Mayaram points out that Byzantium/Constantinople/Istanbul was a global city for fifteen centuries, and Istanbul was the base of the Naqshbandiyya Sufi order connecting the three regions of Ottoman Turkey, India and Central Asia. While global cities today are, in fact, the hub of finance capital and cutting-edge technologies, the conceptual imperative to delineate the uniqueness of the contemporary global city is achieved by lumping all 'pre-modern' formations outside of finance capital, ignoring the religious, political, moral and aesthetic functions of global cities in the rest of the world. A comparative social history of globality of cities based on more than one characteristic would be required to make generalised sociological statements about the scale and dynamics of the global cities that are more adequate at the level of meaning and causality.

Arjun Appadurai (1990) is more attentive to multiple global flows that include not just finance and technology but people as bearers of culture, ideologies and images. He suggests that these flows are not isomorphic and that there is a disjuncture and difference in the global cultural economy between the political, economic and the cultural which world systems analysis has not come to terms with and which cannot be explained by centre-periphery models. Drawing on Lash and Urry's (1987 c.f. Appadurai 1990: 295) notion of 'disorganised capitalism', Appadurai (1990: 296) argues that, 'The complexity of the current global economy has to do with certain fundamental disjuncture between economy, culture and politics which we have barely begun to theorise'. There is a tension between cultural homogenisation and cultural heterogenisation. Not all global cultural processes of homogenisation need to be seen as Americanisation or Westernisation. For the people of Irian Jaya, Indonesianisation may seem more fearsome than Americanisation, just as Japanisation could be more fearsome for the Koreans and Russianisation to Armenians. Appadurai argues that there is a scalar dynamic to cultural processes which cannot be fitted into linear models. While democratic institutions may have taken root, 'the political narratives that govern communication between elites and followers in different parts of the world involve problems of both semantic and pragmatic in nature' (1990: 300). Political conventions also vary based on the communicative genres, such as newspapers versus cinema, employed in a cultural zone. The relationship of reading to hearing and seeing may vary in crucial ways in national and transnational contexts so that democracy as a master term sits at the centre of several pragmatic reformulations that may roughly translate the 'vocabulary of the Enlightenment' (ibid.).

If social theorists saw globalisation as a process of diffusion of Western modernity through the transplantation of its institutions and values, Appadurai's cultural analysis shows how this acculturation process is culturally mediated and received by localities. As Held et al. (1999: 12) put it, 'At stake in this debate is a rather fundamental issue: whether globalisation today has to be understood as something more than simply the expanding reach of Western power and influence'. Even in the open-ended approaches, globalisation is about how peripheries or the rest of the world is influenced by the metropolis; this unidirectional and irreversible manner of postulating the relationship blocks the perception of independent reverse flows from the global South.

## Invisibilisation of reverse flows

A good part of the New Age health movements of the postmodern West is driven by products, body practices and knowledge from Asia, South America and Africa. The chemical-weary populations in the Anglo Saxon world are clamouring for natural and traditional foods from the rest of the world through the market mechanism, having lost all their practices of natural cultivation at the altar of industry and technology. The global health movement around 'organic' foods has brought traditional food and therapeutic substances of many indigenous communities, including quinoa, coloured rice, herbs and spices, as commodities to the supermarkets in the West. The global appeal of 'hatha' yoga practices and the booming industry around yoga is another field of study in itself. The commodification of otherworldly Asian practices and indigenous healing substances in the West is crucial to the emergence of the alternative subjectivity of late modernity (Csordas (2009) c.f. Sujatha 2020). 'Transcendental experiences such as trance and intoxication have been banished from modern Western cosmology and labelled as psychosis with no escape from the here and given. Buddhist meditation practices afford a mode of non-being that could co-exist in the rational and materialist world offering brief forays away from space-time' (Obeyesekere (2003) c.f. Sujatha 2020: 15). It is important to note here that the assimilation of health knowledge and healing practices and substances by the Anglo Saxon world predates the arrival of the world wide web and has been a critical factor in shaping the postmodern condition. Whether or not we see this as going back to the future, reverse flows are conspicuous by their absence in the mainstream globalisation discourse (Sujatha 2020).

## Can there be global society?

Interrogating the received definitions of globalisation as a process that 'intensifies consciousness of the world as a whole' (Robertson 1992 c.f. Dhanagare 2003: 5) and the idea that it is open ended, Dhanagare cautions that triumphalist claims about globalisation have to be thoroughly scrutinised, as there are several overstatements about the global reach, and cites longitudinal studies that show most of the world's large business corporations continued operations within national boundaries, and three-quarters of their business linkages were domiciled in the same territory. He concludes that even if a global production system were to be in place, economic integration cannot be transferred to the realm of social integration. In other words, he would think that social and cultural integration in a region may usher in economic connections as in past civilisations, but not the other way round.

> Often the domineering presence of MNCs in a national economic space is taken as an unassailable proof that global productive system has come to stay. Economic, mainly financial, integration through the market may have accelerated the pace of exchanges between nation-states and their principal corporate actors. However, to assume that such frequent exchanges necessarily lead to the shaping of a new global

> society – civil, economic and political – appears to be a far-fetched idea. It is as much an unattainable idea as it is an ahistorical viewpoint simply because a community or society needs a shared vision, values and sentiments. Just shared economic interests, pursued with the calculus of balance of payments, trade deficits and profits, do not suffice. That shared vision is possible only when commonality of interests transcends pure economic interests or financial integration. As things stand today, centrifugal tendencies do operate quite visibly even within the EU and other formations like the Group 7/16/20, Commonwealth, ASEAN, SAARC and similar other regional formations. 'Fear of the other' seems to be a common running undercurrent of all centrifugal activities and initiatives within such formations.

Truly enough, Dhanagare's concerns expressed in 2003 are not unfounded. In the past few years, we have seen Britain opting to exit from the EU on precisely immigration-related issues, while the US experienced a shift of leadership to the right wing on similar fears about immigrants taking away jobs. Most regional political blocks are saddled with contrary impulses of integration into the common market and protection of domestic producers and other interest groups at home. Studies in Africa also show how economic inequality between nations has increased labour migration within the continent in the direction of richer nations that are closing their borders for a variety of reasons including fear of immigrants and criminal activities (Akokpari 2000). Thus there is growth of global capital and income, but it is accompanied by exclusions through citizenship.

Tracing the concept of citizenship from the work of Max Weber, Boatcă (2015) sets out how citizenship was thought of as an associational status group, coterminous with the medieval European city. Other world cities had only four out of five features that Weber identified for the city, namely fortification, market, autonomous justice, associative structure and autocephaly; they did not have the 'associational character of the Occidental city, modelled on and mediated by the Christian congregation, that had brought forth the modern concept of the citizen' (Boatcă 2015: 78). Thus the uniqueness of Christianity lies in its quality of underplaying clan ties and replacing the ritual aspects of religious affiliation with the principle of voluntarism. But Boatcă finds that the idea of citizenship as a trait that one inherits by being born in a place called a nation and handed over to subsequent generations is very much an ascribed status. 'In a global perspective, citizenship is a powerful instrument of social closure, shielding prosperous states from the migrant poor' (Brubaker 1992 c.f. Boatcă 2015: 185). It is in this manner, Boatcă argues, that citizenship becomes a crucial explanatory factor for global inequality. Citizenship by birth or by marriage functions as a kind of inheritance that restricts membership in rich countries to a small part of the world population. Drawing on the work of Shachar (2009), Boatcă shows how inherited property and inherited citizenship often go together, benefitting selected few in the global market. Sachar argues that a girl born in Mali, struggling to find nutrition and education, will miss by sheer accident of birth the benefits enjoyed by her counterpart in the United States. The recent trends toward commodification of citizenship in which governments extend citizenship rights on the basis of monetary payments or investments only exacerbates the inequality. Rich clients opting for citizenship are referred to as global investors, expats and the like, while the poor are termed immigrant and exiles. Thus the associational character of citizenship within the modern nation-state is called into question.

The globalisation discourse rests on the assumption that the global market and global institutions of governance constitute a domain of supranational organisations that were not found in earlier epochs of trans-regionalism. But global institutions like the United Nations (UN), International Monetary Fund (IMF) and World Bank are not benign forces of global participation and are not devoid of power exercised by rich nations. Trying to understand their global character only in terms of structural form will be an injustice because the content of their policies and their activities often shows them to be carrying out the interests of powerful economic blocs and rich countries at the expense of the poor and weak. It is common knowledge that the IMF, UN and World Bank do not represent 'global' interests, as no such thing exists. Nor can governments unconditionally move towards global integration. Though global markets continue to expand, in 1995 and 1998, popular mandate in these nations voted the governments that followed IMF policies out of power, indicating that alternative programmes would be welcome (Patnaik and Chandrasekhar 2007). Ake (1996) discusses in detail how the African nations that were ushered into the structural adjustment programme (SAP) suffered due to inadequate external aid that was tied to impossible conditions and failed to reach developmental goals. They then embarked on the pathways to self-reliance.

Patnaik and Chandrasekhar (2007) show how post-independent India was a classic case of *dirigiste*, that is, state-driven economy with a sizeable public sector. The economic policy erected during the freedom struggle displaced metropolitan capital in favour of state-sponsored industrialisation under the 'mixed economy model'. This model faced difficulties, and in the nineties, import liberalisation was adopted to cope with the balance of payments crisis. The authors observe that in the mainstream discourses around liberalisation and globalisation, there is complete silence on the role of the domestic investment effort in explaining growth performance, for which overwhelming evidence exists.

It is quite clear that we do not find much affirmation about the uniqueness of contemporary globalisation among the social science scholars of the global South. Even as the term *globalisation* is used, it is often used as a descriptor rather than as a concept. Apart from those discussed previously, there are other reasons for the fact that the theory of globalisation as the triumphant march of capital and technology does not have much purchase in many parts of the global South. Global markets generate proactive as well as counteractive influences that make it impossible to make categorical assertions about direction of change. Globalisation is envisaged as a flow of capital, people, things and ideas across national boundaries, but it is not true that all kinds of flows happen with equal ease in the global arena. Cultural products, even the exotic and unusual, could be commodified and floated in the global market as a niche or ethnic product, and they get accepted. But real human beings as labour, immigrants or refugees who carry a specific culture and identity will find it difficult to gain acceptance and integration. People as bearers of regional identities organise themselves as members of distinct social groups to enter economies of scale or attain political recognition at higher levels, as they will not be able to make it as individual bearers of capacities and qualifications.

Even as we observe how digital interconnectedness extends social networks beyond the immediate and face-to-face relationship, we also encounter with equal force dismantling of social and cultural practices, relationships and artefacts as they get commodified. It seems that the developmental and social gains attained by some countries a few decades ago are lost in the present that is vitiated by various political and religious separatist movements. While social and cultural differences often get augmented in the political sphere, labour participation and economic mobility erase some identities. Similarly, the explosion of social media and worldwide connectivity both augments cultural difference in some ways while blurring them in others. 'When difference is permitted – sometimes even flaunted – under the signs of diversity and multiculturalism, it only comes into being within a prior consensual framework. The ungovernable difference, or the non-consensual, is what becomes subject to violence and coercion in one form or the other' (Kaur and Wahlberg 2014: 3). There are forces of integration and counterforces of disconnect such that it is difficult to sustain the thesis of consistent and progressive global integration based only on internet connectivity.

The essays in this volume do not address all the issues raised in the foregoing discussion but only some of them; however, they seek to examine the relation between economy, society, polity and culture through non-linear approaches. The title of the volume is hence *Global Capital and Social Difference*. This volume is the outcome of an international conference organised under the aegis of the Global Studies Programme, an academic experiment in teaching sociology from four different continents, namely Asia, Africa, Latin America and Europe, to the same batch of postgraduate students who move every semester to a different institution. The conference was a forum for the GSP faculty to interact and mutually share research findings with researchers in India. In this volume based on the conference proceedings and some invited papers, contributors from different parts of the world deal with a diverse range of subjects around the idea of global capital and social difference. The chapters have been organised under five themes, namely the question of temporal sequence in social transformation, the role of community in capital formation, the substitution and shuffling of institutions and new social movements, questions of citizenship and emergent subjectivities from new media technologies.

## Social change and temporality: interrogating linear time and sequentiality in the social sciences

One of the challenges in conceptualising social transformation is dealing with the question of temporality and sequence. This is true to an extent of the concept of globalisation. Despite the deployment of terms such as *glocalisation*, *global flows* and *multicentricity* which seek to broaden the scope of the concept, we saw how capitalism and modernity are inevitably tied to the history of contemporary globalisation and debates are centred around the question: How much of capitalism and modernity have been attained by various societies to rise and be included in history (Nandy 1995)?

Capitalism and modernity have constituted the fulcrum of social theory since its very inception. In fact, social sciences like sociology owe their birth to these forces and have grown up with them such that they have not been able to extricate themselves from the conditions of their genesis for more than a century of its emergence. Terms like 'pre-capitalist' and 'pre-modern' are used to subsume many centuries of social life, emptying them of their substantive and existential reality that is contemporary. Nigam's chapter in this volume interrogates the twin categories of capitalism and modernity which form the basis of the conceptualisation of globalisation. Arguing that even the vociferous critiques of capitalism like the Marxists and Neo-Marxists believed that it is something that must happen and interpreted other social formations only as incomplete capitalism, Nigam points out that such an approach crucially contributed to the linear view of societal change. Modernity, a sociological category intimately associated with capitalism, entailed secularism and individualism as civilisational characteristics and was seen as representing a higher stage of evolution where men emerged from animism and savagery. In this transition, 'The heterogeneity of Time would now come to an end as it were, as "backward" societies like India too would now be able to step into the "common" global present' (Nigam, this volume). He then sets out on the challenging task of disentangling capitalism and modernity, in the process critically examining the works of subaltern scholars Dipesh Chakrabarty and Sudipta Kaviraj. Nigam finds that while Kaviraj concedes that there could be many trajectories of modernity, he attributes it to the 'logic of self-differentiation within modernity', eventually succumbing to the singular view of modernity as a given and the sequentiality of the world in arriving at this modernity.

Another issue relating to the sequentiality question is the idea of developmental stages. How do we think about the processes associated with democracy and development in Africa, Asia or Latin America? Are they 'unfinished stages' of history or emergent experiments in their own right with varying combinations and dynamics? The actual experience of many parts of the world does not necessarily show patterned sequential unfolding or evolution but back-and-forth movement, some gains and many losses.

Garba's chapter in this volume is on the African situation; it compares how the alliance between capital, state and religious affiliations in society is played out differently in Nigeria and South Africa, presenting two different trajectories of development after centuries of excruciating colonialism. Garba discusses how the European colonial administration not only systematically left out provincial elites from the process of accumulation in Nigeria but they also instrumentalised ethnic and religious identities to their political and economic ends. The first few decades of independence did see advancements in healthcare, education and public transportation with the programme of import substitution and funds from the IMF. But the huge burden of debt and pressure from the IMF led to cuts in publicly financed services. The many waves of outmigration that followed this crisis included a significant section of the population migrating to other better-developed African countries, nations like South Africa, where the White elites were well established with a small section of the newly emergent Black elites who viewed the working-class immigrants with suspicion and wanted a closure on citizenship. With a concluding note on capital's contradictory generation of difference, Garba's chapter demonstrates that global financial institutions do not behave any differently from the colonial powers, nor does integration into the global market produce cumulative trends of growth, development and global consciousness.

As we mentioned before, xenophobia accompanies global economic integration in most parts of the world, including Europe and the United States. Social identity is a deeper barrier restraining global economic integration than has been acknowledged in sociological theories of globalisation.

## Capital, class and community

The conventional antagonism between capital and community and the sociological wisdom that the growth of capitalism and modernity will completely replace traditional communities is not borne out by the historical experience of many a society. In his chapter on global capitalism, Rehbein draws upon the work of Picketty to outline the importance of the wealth possessed by traditional elites. Questioning the role of market as an impartial leveller and as a ubiquitous force, Rehbein argues that the so-called capitalist class is actually very small if we consider the magnitude of capital that could be globally significant. A good part of it is constituted by the traditional elites, who are also the socially dominant status groups. This is explained by comparing the case of Germany and Brazil, and Rehbein concludes that global and national forces will be in contradiction because the interests and priorities of the dominant social classes lead to both trends of globalisation and anti-globalisation.

In the Indian context, the significance of provincial capital generated by hitherto middling peasant and occupational communities provides another challenge to the conventional one-way understanding of global capitalism influencing local realities. That the rural and agrarian classes could fashion products and services to capture the market at many levels is something that the Marxists also did not foresee. There was overwhelming focus on commercial money lenders and industrialists in understanding surplus generation in the South Asian context. This arises because of a structural and static view of class. Drawing on Thompson's argument that 'class' is a social and cultural formation finding institutional expression that can only be understood in relation to other classes, Parthasarathy offers a powerful critique of globalisation theories that view labour issues in India in relation to global capital without examining the dynamics of provincial capital. 'Whether it is the issue of agrarian crisis, food security, and rural indebtedness, or problems of exclusionary urbanism and infrastructure development, or the over-dependence of the Indian economy on the informal sector, it is imperative to comprehend and address the role of provincial capital in enabling or thwarting economic development and welfare policies of the state, in facilitating or constraining the capital working of domestic and global markets and flows' (Parthasarathy 2015: 817).

Part of the problems in conceptualising the capitalist class in India is the neglect of erstwhile peasant communities and their turn to business enterprise in postcolonial India and the significance of farmer-capitalists and regional capital in theorising dominant classes in India. In Parthasarathy's view (2015: 817), the critiques of globalisation theory also consider global capital and markets the main problem in causing distress and impoverishment, overlooking the semi-feudal structures and enterprises that fuel economic growth in the region. Critique of globalisation has become 'a central trope in the social sciences that it has begun to obscure many other modes of inquiry and streams of theorisation that hold promise for comprehending historical trajectories in the long run, and India's economic change in the recent past' (ibid.: 817). Rural and urban, agrarian and industrial, peasant and capitalist have been constructed as binaries, and 'the local gets directly linked analytically to the global without an understanding of mediating agencies, structures, and institutions; causality of distress is always explained as originating from above and from outside' (ibid.: 818). Marxist scholars and other critics of neoliberalism alike 'make globalisation into this great, disembodied spectre. Forces of globalisation and global capital are seen to haunt critical studies of farmers' suicides and agrarian distress, land grabs for Special Economic Zones and infrastructure projects, and the privatisation of social and physical infrastructure and services' (ibid.). On the other hand, the changes in agrarian relations in rural society; the nature of ongoing processes of peasant differentiation; rural-urban connections; networks; conflicts; regional patterns of social mobility and the overwhelming scale of movement of people, goods and services across diverse regions within the country rarely count.

New forms of rent-seeking behaviour by peasants and new strategies of surplus generation by crafts and weaving communities reflect the conceptual reality of the caste and class dynamic and political action in India today, and this is true of South Asian societies in general. The excessive stress on the enormity of global capital in the globalisation discourse overshadows the rich ethnographic and archival research in the economic history of provincial capital and its role in state formation.

The failure of dominant peasant communities to enter the domain of capital also has repercussions. Two essays in this volume address fascinating aspects of success and setback through case studies from different regions of India. Aarti Kawlra's ethnographic study shows how the Padmasaliyar, a community of silk weavers from South India that in the previous century was weaving silk to cater to the needs of a small upper-caste segment, rose to become globally renowned producers of silk sarees and fabric, in the process drastically transforming themselves, the commodity and the market for their product even as they retained their social and kin networks.

Suraj Beri's chapter in the volume, on the other hand, indicates the trajectory of a hitherto socially and politically dominant peasant community in North India that failed to generate surplus from their agrarian dealings and could not enter the urban working milieu due to lack of education, resulting in widespread protests seeking quotas in government services on grounds of social backwardness.

## Institutions and social movements: the glocal dynamic

The community and capital dynamic is one dimension of social difference in the emergence of industrial capital in the Indian scenario. In South America, by contrast, economic integration into the global market is brought about by the export of mineral ores and natural resources through a massive process of re-primarisation of the economy. The economy based on extractivism developed in the recent decades has created a new regime in which multiple stakeholders – the state, private capital, civil society and indigenous communities – are negotiating rights over natural resources and use of the commons from different social vantage points. In Svampa's words,

> traditionally in Latin America, a large part of the Left and progressive populism sustains a vision of development focused on production, offering a reading that privileges the conflict between labour and capital and tends to neglect the new social struggle around the defence of the territory and the commons. In this political and ideological framework, blinded by its focus on production and staunchly opposed to the principles of the environmental paradigm, the current dispossession dynamic becomes a blind spot, impossible to conceptualise. As a consequence, socio-environmental conflicts are considered a secondary problem or

> one that could simply be sacrificed, in light of the grave problems of poverty and exclusion in Latin American societies.
>
> (Svampa 2015: 50–51)

In Latin America, the assertion of their environmental values by indigenous communities, the new social movements, civil society organisations and some church-based initiatives have brought in important social forces in environmental negotiations that the state and the market have to reckon with. 'New forms of mobilisation and citizen participation, centred on the defence of natural goods, biodiversity and the environment' have led to what Svampa refers to as 'socio-environmental conflicts linked to the access and control of natural goods and territory which presuppose diverging values and interests, in a context of power asymmetry. These conflicts bring to the forefront different conceptualisations of territory, nature and the environment and at the same time foster disputes about the understanding of development and, at a more general level, of democracy' (2015: 52–53). In their chapter in this volume, Pelfini, Fulquet, Marchegiani and Christel present several case studies from among the Latin American nations to show how different patterns of governance have emerged around mining and water management, bringing about new alignments and old social values around the conventional triad of the state, market and civil society, even as global linkages are forged through re-primarisation rather than through production and manufacturing. Thus, their chapter shows how substitution of institutional functions by new social arrangements leads to a complicated glocal dynamic in the management of environmental resources.

Institutional adaptation and the recasting of functions are not restricted to any domain. They are found in other domains of life undergoing transformation, as in the case of family and gender relations producing new dynamics every decade. This dynamic reflects the way in which the social and existential factors and sociopolitical forces in the immediate vicinity or a given site play a key role in recasting, ignoring or selectively assimilating global discourses. Devika's chapter in this volume proposes an approach in which the centrality of the given social fabric is emphasised without it being incorporated into a one-way relation from the global to the local. Adopting multiple levels of analysis of the individual, family, community, class and nation, she presents a social history of both changing gender relations and feminist discourses in the southwestern Indian state of Kerala. Shifts in women's labour participation in twentieth-century Kerala society made new demands on the organisation of familial roles, values and property rights. The subsequent decades of massive migration to Gulf countries was followed by compounding of the affective labour required of women left behind and by the reinstatement of the social practice of *dowry*[1] even as women's education was improving, leading to new forms of gender asymmetry within the Malayalee family. Through this social historical narrative, Devika points out how the brand of feminism promoted by state agencies, global feminist discourses and the assertion of the different classes among the women in Kerala blurred the binary between indigenous and foreign, producing a mosaic of many contesting hybrid feminisms.

## Nation-state, citizenship and the global connection

Another line of thinking that challenges the linear theory of globalisation as the onward progression of the global market erasing traces of primordial identities through modern ideas of association is the controversy about the modern idea of citizenship and the vexing nature of the issues in granting of citizenship in the global era. Drawing on the works of Mignolo and Quijano, Manuela Boatcă and Judith Roth, in their chapter in this volume, talk about the coloniality of citizenship and foreground how the institution of citizenship emerged with colonial capitalism and how glaring social inequalities continue to be produced by citizenship. The authors show how the recent trend in acquiring citizenship by monetary deposits and payments only widens the inequality and puts the poor from colonised countries at a double disadvantage. In this situation, women, especially racialised women, tend to migrate largely as nannies, sex workers and mothers and are in a precarious situation as far as labour provisions are concerned. Romance tourism, women's trafficking and housework are the most common options open to the poorer women from racialised and non-white groups. Tracing the issues around citizenship and social inequality in the global era, Boatcă and Roth raise critical questions about how the institution of citizenship systematises unequal allocation of life chances through ascriptive criteria, and opening it up through the market mechanism only promotes further racial and gender profiling of people seeking upward social mobility through migration to richer countries.

There are other social aspects to the notion of citizenship, and a totally different vantage point to consider the pressures of the nation-state is through the idea of space. Sudha Vasan's chapter in this volume engages with the manner in which social differences in the high-altitude region around the Himalayas in India deflect and accommodate the pulls of global tourism and Hindu nationalism. Ladakh is a sensitive geopolitical region sharing its borders with Pakistan and China and also has a unique cultural fabric adapted to the ecological and social conditions. Starting with the social history of Ladakh, Vasan offers an account of how the Ladakhi elites deal with the conflicting demands of being an international tourist destination known for its Buddhism and its growing importance as the site of Hindu cultural revivalism promoted by the Indian government. The global image of Ladakh as the home of Tibetan Buddhism created by international tourists imposes Tibetan characteristics on Ladakhi Buddhism, which has its own history, Buddhist denominations and symbols. On the other hand, the nationalist Indian state tries to fashion Ladakh as a Hindu sacred destination and organises a festival on the banks of the river Sindhu every year in which Buddhist dignitaries are also invited to participate. The festival has increased the volume of domestic tourists in Ladakh in the recent decades. Taking us through the details of the festival and the way in which the Ladakhi elite transformed it, Vasan points to the agency of the local Ladakhi leadership and monks in absorbing the global and the national and recasting them according to the Ladakhi social setting, even as the Indian state and tourist markets retain their hold on the local economy and polity.

## Media, borders and emergent subjects

Internet technology and media constitute a critical component of the globalisation process and have as such been cardinally associated with the drastic changes in the way in which time and space have been experienced. Not just compression of time and space, the social role of the internet in creating new and agentive forms of subjectivity is of great interest. It is intriguing that while the internet has created a realm beyond the conventional physical boundaries of place, it also sets up new regulations and definitions which could be virtual boundaries. Patricia Ferrante's chapter in this volume examines the issues around digital piracy in the world of audio and video productions. Digital technologies have created a peculiar situation in which copies are identical to originals for the first time in history. This has ushered new media affordances in which users can 'access, copy, share, reuse and modify any content from a connected device' (Ferrante, this collection). This has blurred the distinctions between producers and audience/users, giving rise to categories like 'produsers' and 'prosumers'. Platforms for audiovisual content such as YouTube have drastically altered the landscape of films and TV series distribution, bridging community and commerce. While a lot of open sources have enhanced the possibilities of creativity, the booming shadow economy for digital audiovisual content has propelled media corporations to criminalise some forms of copying. Interrogating the definitions of digital piracy, Ferrante takes us through the debates on reproduction of films and TV series by fans and art lovers, showing how piracy is not just about legality but about the socio-technical structure of the agency of audience produsers/prosumers.

Kumar's chapter on sonic texts in this volume takes the kinds of listening cultures produced by audio texts as its core theme, highlighting, as it were, the emergence of new listening subjects. Starting with the days of the All India Radio (AIR) in the India of the seventies, when the social background of the artiste and the clear identification of the genre of music were strictly monitored, he shows how in those days, binaries such as Western and Indian music, classical and film music ran rife in the field of music. The digital reconfiguration of audio productions has radically altered the position of the listener, giving rise to the listening subject. Numerous versions of a Malayalam film song in several genres across the world – rap, Carnatic, rock and pop – could be seen to proliferate on YouTube, leading to endless modification and remixing. Citing Castells and Freeman on the mutual interplay of technology, culture and social structure, Kumar argues that new formats and communication technologies generate distinct forms of socialities even as they are shaped by them. For instance, the audiovisual experience of YouTube, the container technologies of MP3 and the most recent mobile phone–mediated audio experiences cater to different classes of people, though musical genres seem to cut across rural–urban, rich–poor and other social binaries. These create fertile ground for the study of sonic texts in terms of the new subjectivities they give rise to in various locations.

The chapters in this volume dwell upon divergent themes but together point to a more broad-based approach to understanding the dynamic interaction between economy, society, polity and culture. The chapters in several ways foreground how social differences challenge linear narratives of contemporary globalisation based on singular criteria and how proximate and distant social factors could be considered in a non-hierarchical manner in contrast to the global–local framework. The chapters also supply an alternative framework to understand the significance of social difference in the ongoing processes of integration through the market by drawing attention to the centrality of provincial capital in socioeconomic transformation, highlighting the role of traditional artisanal skills and community networks in the generation of provincial capital and the social power of peasants and community leaders in state formation and policy. By describing new societal roles, institutional forms and new social movements that deflect, recast or selectively absorb global models and discourses and by discussing how digital and internet technologies thrive on the social fabric, bridging community and commerce even as they break the barriers between audiovisual genres giving rise to new subjectivities and participative agency to users erasing the thin line between legality and illegality in reproduction of digital content, the chapters here seek to offer fresh perspectives on the issues at hand.

## Note

1 Dowry refers to durable goods, cash and movable and immovable property given by the bride's family to that of the bridegroom at the time of marriage and is said to be fallout of inheritance laws in India now tilted against the woman. From the customary practice of a few elite communities, dowry in contemporary India has come to be a widely found social menace, leading to the harassment of the bride and her parents for money and wealth.

## Bibliography

Ake, Claude. 1996. *Democracy and Development in Africa*. Washington, DC: The Brookings Institution.

Akokpari, John. 2000. 'Globalisation and Migration in Africa', *African Sociological Review*, 4 (2): 72–92.

Appadurai, Arjun. 1990. 'Disjuncture and Difference in the Global Cultural Economy', *Theory, Culture and Society*, 7 (295): 295–310.

Boatcă, Manuela. 2015. *Global Inequalities beyond Occidentalism*. London and New York: Routledge.

Brubaker, Rogers. 1992. *Citizenship and Nationhood in France and Germany*. Cambridge, MA: Harvard University Press.

Csordas, Thomas (ed.) 2009. *Transnational Transcendence. Essays on Religion and Globalisation*. Berkeley, CA: University of California Press.

Dhanagare, D.N. 2003. 'Globalisation: Towards an Alternative View', *Sociological Bulletin*, 52 (1): 4–31.

Giddens, A. 1990. *The Consequences of Modernity*. Stanford: Stanford University Press.

Granovetter, Mark. 1985. 'Economic Action and Social Structure: The Problem of Embeddedness', *American Journal of Sociology*, 91 (3): 481–510.

Harvey, David. 1989. 'From Managerialism to Entrepreneurialism: The Transformation in Urban Governance in Late Capitalism', *Geografiska Annaler. Series B, Human Geography*, 71 (1): 3–17, The Roots of Geographical Change: 1973 to the Present.

Held, David et al. 1999. *Global Transformations: Politics, Economics and Culture*. Cambridge: Polity Press.

Inda, Jonathan X. and Renato Rosaldo. 2002. *The Anthropology of Globalization: A Reader*. Cambridge, MA: Blackwell Publishers.

Kaur, Ravinder and A. Wahlberg (eds.). 2014. *Identity, Inequity and Inequality in India and China: Governing Difference*. London and New York: Routledge.

Lash, Scott and John Urry. 1987. *The End of Organised Capitalism*. Cambridge: Polity Press.

Mayaram, Shail (ed.). 2013. *The Other Global City*. New Delhi: Yoda Press.

Nandy, Ashis. 1995. 'History's Forgotten Doubles', *History and Theory*, 34 (2): 44–66.

Nayar, Baldev Raj. 2007. *Globalisation and Politics in India*. New Delhi: Oxford University Press.

Nayyar, Deepak. 2006. 'Globalisation, History and Development: A Tale of Two Centuries', *Cambridge Journal of Economics*, 30 (1): 137–159.

Obeyesekere, Gananath. 2003. 'Buddhism', in Mark Juergensmeyer (ed.) *Global Religions*, pp. 63–77. Oxford: Oxford University Press.

Parthasarathy, D. 2015. 'The Poverty of (Marxist) Theory: Peasant Classes, Provincial Capital, and the Critique of Globalization in India', *Journal of Social History*, 48 (4): 816–841.

Patnaik, Prabhat and C.P. Chandrasekhar. 2007. 'India: *Dirigisme*, Structural Adjustment and the Radical Alternative', in Baldev Raj Nayar (ed.) *Globalisation and Politics in India*, pp. 218–24. New Delhi: Oxford University Press.

Robertson, R. 1992. *Globalisation: Social Theory and Global Culture*. London: Sage Publications.

Sanyal, Kalyan and Rajesh Bhattacharya. 2009. 'Beyond the Factory: Globalisation, Informalisation of Production and the New Locations of Labour', *Economic and Political Weekly*, XLIV (22): 35–44.

Sassen, Saskia. 2007. *A Sociology of Globalization*. New York: W.W. Norton & Company.

Shachar, Ayelet. 2009. *The Birthright Lottery: Citizenship and Global Inequality*. Cambridge, MA: Harvard University Press.

Sujatha, V. 2020. 'Globalisation of South Asian Medicines: Knowledge, Power, Structure and Sustainability', *Society and Culture in South Asia*, 6 (1): 1–24.

Svampa, Maristella. 2015. 'The Commodities Consensus and Valuation Languages in South America', *Alternataus*, 2 (1): 45–51.

Uberoi, J.P.S. 2012. 'Marxism of Labour or Property?', *Economic and Political Weekly*, XLVII (32): 73–80.

# Part 1

# Social change and temporality

## Interrogating linear time and sequentiality in the social sciences

# 1 Capital, time and difference

## Modernity and the European episteme

*Aditya Nigam*

In this chapter, I look at the twin categories of 'capitalism' and 'modernity' and how they construe 'economic difference'. Modern, that is, 'capitalist', economies see themselves as homogeneous entities where difference is essentially seen as survivals of 'past' forms. On the other hand, proclaiming such living forms too as 'modern' is not of much help either, as it simply leaves the category of modernity uninterrogated while at the same time expanding it so much as to render it meaningless. In engaging with this key question, this chapter attempts to disaggregate both 'capitalism' and 'modernity'. In doing so, it also references a body of recent work that seeks to bring the debate on 'capitalism' and 'modernity' out of its very narrow, European history, thus providing a global background to their emergence. However, this body of scholarship too, this chapter argues, suffers from the same problem – of laying claim to a modernity and a capitalism whose theoretical contours, erected on the European episteme,[1] are never interrogated. The term 'European episteme' in this essay refers to something very specific: a mode of thinking which installs the 'economic' – not in the sense of livelihoods and well-being of people at large but as a reified instance that has nothing to do with the well-being of the population – as the foundational level of social being. This is a large and complicated issue, and some scholars like Timothy Mitchell (2002) have been persuasively arguing, in recent years, that the idea of 'the economy' is a much later, early twentieth-century product. What I refer to here is not the object of macroeconomics that Mitchell talks about but rather the idea that the modern, rational and civilised mode of being entails the creation of new wealth by harnessing all the forces of nature, bringing all its land into productive use. This notion is closely tied to the idea that lives lived close to the natural state are indicative of savage existence. Closely allied to this is the emergence of the notion of the modern, self-maximising individual who thus becomes the exalted figure driving the machine of human progress. Indeed, this notion of the economy or the economic undergirds all notions of progress, which drives much of the violence of modernity.

## 'Globalisation' and economic difference

The onset of the 1990s saw the rapid rise of the term 'globalisation' – not just as a way of describing but rather of *ordering* the new politico-economic configuration emerging in the wake of the collapse of 'actually existing socialisms' and the global victory of neoliberalism. Labelled a trifle too hastily as the 'end of history' by Francis Fukuyama (2006), the word 'globalisation' did not just name that conjuncture; it soon became an *imperative* that arose from a heightened sense of an inexorable movement of destiny that demanded specific ways of thinking and acting – both of political elites and ordinary citizens. Finally, that long-deferred destiny was here and prognostications about the 'bourgeoisie building the world in its own image' made by Marx and Engels in the *Communist Manifesto* were proving to be right. Curiously, it was not just neoliberals and the corporations who were celebrating but radicals of various hues, too. Celebratory anticipations of the world rapidly being transformed into a 'global village' became the order of the day. The era of the nation-state was supposedly over. Talk of global institutions of government and global civil society and even global 'governance' was in evidence everywhere. Theorists like Habermas (2001) announced the emergence of the new 'postnational constellation' – where 'postnational' meant little more than 'global'. Scholars like David Harvey (1990) talked of the phenomenon in terms of an unprecedented 'space-time compression', while still others like Zygmunt Bauman (1998) even went so far as to announce that globalisation amounted to a virtual 'liberation from space' for capital. More radical versions of this imagination of the new global order brought Deleuzian categories like 'nomads' and 'flows' into play in order to gesture to what they saw as the new emancipatory possibilities immanent in a world without nation-states and borders. This radical imagination reached its apogee in the figure of the multitude – the supposed new revolutionary subjectivity produced by Antonio Negri and Michael Hardt in their trilogy [*Empire* (2000), *Multitude* (2004) and *Commonwealth* (2009)].

It is not my intention, in this chapter, to go into an examination of the various 'theoretical' flights of fancy that that moment of celebration, emanating mainly from the West, produced. Nor do I want to suggest that all prognostications were necessarily wrong – even if sometimes highly exaggerated. Now that the euphoria has long passed and we have had results of Brexit polls on the one hand and the rise of Donald Trump in the United States of America on the other, alongside rampant xenophobia in our own society, it is time perhaps to look back critically.[2] There is indeed a close connection between economic transformations like the integration of global production chains and the 'liberation' of markets from the constricting 'protectionist barriers' imposed on them in the heyday of the nation-state, on the one hand, and the fearful rise of xenophobia that we witness today, on the other. I am not suggesting a causal connection here but one that calls into question the separateness of 'the economic' domain from other questions like culture, habits and traditions, for all these tumultuous changes in the economic realm cannot be considered purely economic – unlike goods and commodities, when human beings and cultures cross borders as migrants or when jobs move to more lucrative parts of the world, they aren't apprehended through the sanitised language of social sciences; they create fears and anxieties and open up the political field for all kinds of xenophobic mobilisation. It might be easier to understand the way migration of people affects people in host countries, but equally important has been the effect of relocation of industries and jobs from the first to the third world, where both labour and environmental regulations are lax: It is the losers of this process, the white working class in many parts of the United States and Europe, who often rally behind xenophobic political mobilisations.

In this chapter, I focus my attention on one key element of what came to define 'globalisation', namely 'capital', and in particular, one aspect of it – one that relates to the problem of difference and, more specifically, *economic difference*, and try to suggest that no reconsideration of the economic question is possible today without a re-opening of the larger story of modernity itself.

From the point of view of the 'three continents' of Asia, Africa and Latin America, globalisation was that moment when the anxieties of economists in general, as well as of Marxists, regarding the inability of capitalism to develop 'properly' on a world scale, gave way to the celebratory rhetoric of its global triumph. Even Marxists who opposed globalisation and saw it as a manifestation of 'imperialist threat to national sovereignty' (Aijaz Ahmed 1983; Prabhat Patnaik 1995, among others) could not resist the temptation to invoke the well-known formulation from the *Communist Manifesto* that 'the bourgeoisie cannot live without constantly revolutionising the means of production and transforming the whole world in its own image'. What this meant for Marxists in the postcolonial world and in countries like India, in particular, was that they would now, finally, be able to liberate themselves from the 'curse' of 'arrested' or 'retarded' development. The heterogeneity of Time would now come to an end, as it were, as 'backward' societies like India too would now be able to step into the 'common' global present.[3]

The desire to see a clean break from 'past' economic and life forms was equally shared by economists whose discipline and profession themselves are predicated on the need to eliminate problems posed by the existence of 'dual economies' by devising ways of expanding the modern/capitalist sector such that it eventually eliminates what is seen as the 'traditional' sector. As is well known, the existence of precapitalist agriculture and the preponderance of an urban informal sector have always constituted serious problems for them, as they represented both an 'irrational' lack of enterprise and a 'sub-optimal' level of existence that was and is said to be inimical to the theology of growth. Many economists, including radical ones, have long believed, after Joan Robinson, that the one worse thing than being exploited by capital is *not being exploited* by it.[4]

## Are we always already modern?

This coexistence of 'past' forms alongside modern/capitalist ones has often been theorised in the received categories of social and political theory in two extremely problematic ways. On the one hand, there is the view that recognises them as *past* forms and therefore views them as *survivals* of earlier social formations that either need to be eliminated or are historically destined to be eliminated. A variation of this view would hold that though these forms belong to the past, it is important to ensure that no violence is done to them, and though they need to be incorporated into modern development, they should be gradually transformed and incorporated into it. This is the path that many postcolonial states adopted via the strategy of what is often referred to, after Gramsci, as the 'passive revolution' – import-substituting industrialisation accompanied by some form of land reforms being one predominant form. However, as can be seen from the case of Nehruvian India, it was not as if violence was totally avoided. After all, it is well known that Jawaharlal Nehru, while proclaiming big dams to be the 'temples of modern India', actually appealed to the displaced adivasis and peasants to 'suffer for the nation'. Nonetheless, it is equally true that the violence of the postcolonial Indian state, for instance, was quite marginal compared to the violence of industrialisation in Britain, which, for some strange reason, came to stand in for the 'standard' or 'classic form'.[5]

On the other hand, there are those who see such forms as *already* 'modern' or 'capitalist' – in the sense that they are no longer untouched by the modern or by the 'logic of the capitalist world-market'. Modernity and capitalism, in such theorisations, are understood as all-encompassing global totalities that are the conditions of our 'being' in the world today. As such, this view holds, we cannot talk of 'tradition' or a 'non-modern' or 'non-capitalist' way of being any longer in any meaningful sense. We therefore have had theories that talk of the 'invention of tradition' or even the 'modernity of tradition' on the one hand (by theorists of modernity) and of the 'formal subsumption of labour under capital' on the other (by theorists of capitalism).

Take for instance, the following passage from Dipesh Chakrabarty's *Provincializing Europe*, where he elaborates on Ranajit Guha's (1983) discussion on peasant insurgencies in his spirited refutation of Hobsbawm's claim that peasant insurgencies were 'pre-political':

> His [Guha's] point is that *what seemed 'traditional'* in this modernity were 'traditional *only in so far as* their roots could be traced back to precolonial times, but [they were] by no means archaic in the sense of being outmoded.' *This was a political modernity* that would eventually

> give rise to a thriving electoral democracy, even when 'vast areas of life and consciousness of the people' escaped any kind of 'bourgeois' hegemony.'
>
> (Chakrabarty 2000: 15, all emphasis added)

I want to underline here the expression, 'this was a political modernity that would eventually give rise to a thriving electoral democracy'. A few pages earlier, Chakrabarty presents us with the category of 'peasant-as-citizen' and claims that 'Guha's statement recognized this subject as modern' and hence 'refused to call the peasants' *political behavior or consciousness "prepolitical"*'. (ibid.: 13, emphasis added). Why must we suppose that this peasant-as-citizen was modern? Because, says Chakrabarty, 'The political sphere in which the peasant and his masters participated was modern' (ibid.: 12).

This, I submit, is the standard mode of the argument: Once we are 'in modernity', we can no longer be anything but modern. This may be a comforting thought insofar as we can now claim that 'we' are all each others' contemporaries, while little may have actually changed in the ways in which, say, the ordinary peasant or adivasi relates to his/her world – and, by extension, we could say the same about the majority of people who have not yet been put through the pedagogical machine of the modern state. Can we say with any confidence that once the peasant/adivasi has become incorporated into the political domain as citizen, there is an automatic change in consciousness and ways of thinking? Is there not another kind of reductionism at work here that seeks to do away with the more complicated questions of subjectivity – by simply claiming that everything is modern, though in a *different* way? I would argue that by simply existing 'in modernity' and being governed by its practices and institutions, one does not become 'modern'. Of course, one is not untouched by the modern, for it indeed structures lives of ordinary people, say the adivasis, but by proclaiming them modern, we end up obliterating their own agency and subjectivity. Are they being modern, really? Do they claim they are and want to be counted as modern? And is there no redemption for them unless they can prove that they too are modern? They may or may not have a take on the modern itself, but they do have a conception of what they are doing. What precisely is this 'difference' if not a continuation, in other forms and perhaps in slightly transformed ways, of modes of thinking (which are always also, at once, modes of being) that we recognise as 'tradition'? It would be interesting to see, for instance, how many peasants/adivasis would find it possible to identify themselves as modern in the same way they would see a babu in Kolkata or a metropolitan intellectual in Chicago. I mean this seriously to underline that the difference might be very differently perceived when seen from the peasant's end.

Hobsbawm (Hobsbawm and Ranger 1983) makes an important argument about the 'invention' of tradition, especially under the aegis of modern state and nationalist elites, which he distinguishes from 'custom' which 'dominates so-called "traditional" societies' (p. 2), which he likens more to lived practices and conventions at the popular level. The distinction is not so neatly drawn as I have schematically put here, but notice here too his reference to *so-called 'traditional' societies* – and the double distancing involved here in using the term 'so-called', while at the same time putting the word traditional in quotation marks. This is characteristic, in a sense, of the enlightened modern's embarrassment at having to say there are societies that may not be 'modern' because, as in Chakrabarty, once in the modern world, they cannot be anything but modern.

Lloyd and Susanne Rudolph (1967) too, in their important study, had used the term 'modernity of tradition' to emphasise that 'tradition' as such no longer existed in any pure form, for it itself becomes the modality through which societies arrive at the modern. Undoubtedly, these are important insights that allow us to see the complex web of relations through which the modern exists in often highly unstable articulation with the traditional. However, it does not follow from this that there is, therefore, no such thing as 'tradition' – in the sense in which large swathes of populations continue to *live* it and to make sense of their rapidly changing world *through* it. For my part, I continue to use the term 'tradition' to distinguish it from the 'modern' – as ways of being, precisely in the way the terms '*parampara*' or '*ravayat*' (or other parallel terms in other Indian languages) might be used even today to mark a distance from what are considered 'modern' ways.

Likewise, the idea of 'formal subsumption of labour under capital' that goes back to Marx himself underlines the fact that with the onset of 'capitalism' and its global spread, the capitalist world market becomes an inescapable background condition of existence, and even social forms that continue to exist with 'archaic' production relations are significantly 'determined' by the laws of the capitalist market. Here, too, it can be very misleading to take this useful insight to mean that therefore, all across the world, capitalist relations have taken over and colonised every 'economic' relation – indeed, the very term 'economic relation' could appear to be highly problematic in such contexts.

If the first perspective is predicated on the idea of an irreconcilable difference between the traditional and modern forms where the older forms must be annihilated in some fashion, in the second way of understanding 'past' or 'traditional' forms, the tendency is to see them as *transitional* – on the way to becoming fully modern or fully capitalist. One set of scholars within this tendency tends to see this transition, in the long run, as a transition to a 'full-blown modernity' – either of the Western type or something of that order achieved via socialism. Much of the theorisation of the 1960s and 1970s, whether coming from modernisation theory position or from the 'dependent development' perspective, would fall under this category. Scholars like Andre Gunder Frank or Samir Amin, for instance, could characterise what they called the 'periphery' as 'capitalist' by first positing a world capitalist system where 'metropolitan' societies were structurally tied to such 'peripheral' ones into a *single* whole, where 'development' at one pole led to 'underdevelopment' at the other pole. 'Underdevelopment' could thus be seen as an effect of capitalist development of the metropolis rather than a remnant of a feudal or precapitalist past. Another set of scholars sees such reconstituted traditions as hybrid forms where 'modernity' ceases to necessarily conform to a single normative model. It is then argued that these forms constitute the modality through which different societies become modern in their own way – leading thus to the idea of 'multiple modernities', which opens the way for eventually recognising difference in some fashion (Eisenstadt 2000; Kaviraj 2005). Eisenstadt's important intervention on the question of multiple modernities, of course, not only brought together some experiences from the non-Western world but also the experiences of fascism, Nazism and socialism as manifestations of different pathways to multiple modernities.[6] His concern was more with the forms 'modernity' could take in different societies, given different cultures and antecedent conditions, and not so much with tradition and whether it is at all legitimate to refer to something by that name.

## *Co-existence of different times*

In the debate on capitalism in 'peripheral' societies that took place in the 1960s and 1970s, there was another perspective that emerged from within Marxism, which basically saw these formations as instantiations of the 'co-existence of different modes of production' – the capitalist and the feudal/precapitalist. Scholars and theorists functioning with this framework therefore argued that the concept of a 'mode of production' could at best be seen as an ideal type which seldom exists in its pure form anywhere; that at the real-historical level, all one could get were different 'articulations' of more than one mode of production. The idea of a 'social formation' was thus put forward to refer to such real-historical societies (Amin 1976: 16–17). Of course, given the Marxist provenance of such theories, the articulation of different modes of production could not simply be understood as mere co-existence, for this formulation posed a serious theoretical problem. After all, the idea of a mode of production made sense only as long as it was understood as an enclosed totality or structure with its own internal logic, its 'laws of motion', so to speak. An articulation of the capitalist mode with precapitalist modes (say, the feudal) would mean that either the totality or the structure of capitalism would also be subject to laws other than its own and one would have a situation of indeterminacy, or it would be necessary to posit the capitalist mode as the dominant mode, within which the pre-capitalist mode would have to exist in a way such that eventually it would have to yield to the dynamic forces of capitalism. Thus, for instance:

> Capitalist formations are all marked by the dominance of the capitalist mode of production. . . . Moreover, whereas the precapitalist formations were marked by a stable coexistence of different modes, linked together

> and arranged hierarchically, the capitalist mode tends to become exclusive, destroying all the others.
>
> (ibid.: 22)

The idea of a social formation, too, then, turned out to be a transitional one, a kind of temporary formation where one mode – the capitalist – would ultimately supersede the other. One of the assumptions implicit in all these theorisations and quite explicitly stated in some of them is the claim that both modernity and capitalism are Western products. Thus, in the end, if we have no escape from either or both of them, we have, in a manner of speaking, no escape from the West's dominance, either.

The claim, however, that modernity, like capitalism, is a Western invention has been contested in a variety of ways – many of them challenging the inherent Eurocentricity of such a claim. On the one hand, there has been a longer tradition of historical thinking that sought to do this by drawing attention to specific features in different societies like India or China that display features akin to some modern tendencies. These have led to propositions regarding the existence of something called 'early modernity' in these societies (Perlin 1983; Subrahmanyam 1997; Wong 1997; Pomeranz 2000; Leiberman 2008). Much of this scholarship has tended to move towards a more global explanation of modernity, showing its roots in larger global networks of what have often been called 'connected histories' (Subrahmanyam 1997). As Sanjay Subrahmanyam put it while elaborating his idea of early modernity,

> At the same time it is of some importance . . . to delink the notion of 'modernity' from a particular European trajectory (Greece, classical Rome, the Middle Ages, the Renaissance and thus 'modernity' . . .), and to argue that it represents a more-or-less global shift with many different sources and roots, and – inevitably – many different forms and meanings depending upon which society we look at it from.
>
> (Subrahmanyam 1997: 737)

It is interesting that Subrahmanyam should recognise, despite the purported globality of the shift, that things might look very different 'depending upon where we look at it from'. In the sections that follow, I want to (a) *analytically disentangle* the two *terms*, 'capitalism' and 'modernity', as they have come to be used and (b) consider some of the more recent counternarratives to Eurocentric accounts of the development of modernity and capitalism and point out that often such accounts do not really break with Eurocentrism because they fail to ask *what* modernity or capitalism really might be.

## Disentangling 'capitalism' and 'modernity'

While I think it is important to emphasise that what we know as 'modernity' today was assembled by drawing resources from different parts of the world, modernity itself was not a collaborative project – nor even a project that emerged from global synergies between equal players in the manner implied in some notions of connected histories or in Bayly (2004). These resources were intellectual, scientific and technological and were drawn from China, India, the Arab world and so on, but there was something distinctively European about the final product. Europe added something to it that no one else could. The great puzzlement of economic historians and social theorists alike as to why, despite having equally high levels of scientific, technological and even industrial development, China did not become 'modern' before Europe has something to do with this key contribution made by Europe, namely 'capitalism'. I should add that by 'capitalism', I do not mean a 'mode of production' or a 'social system' but rather a *whole new relationship* to the world that was enabled by the rise of individualism, individual bourgeois property rights, secularisation ('all that is Holy is profaned') and a moral philosophy that C.B. MacPherson had long ago called the 'political theory of possessive individualism'. Like the terms 'secularism' or 'individualism', 'capitalism', too, in the way I use it, refers to a mode of being where 'capital' is the name of a certain fascination with endless 'production of new wealth' and of exponential growth. This new mode of being arises directly out of a series of prior historical changes in thinking about the world that first emerged in Europe. The distinction between savagery and civilisation, for instance, was predicated upon the urge in 'civilised man' to move away from the savage's 'natural' mode of being, which was no different from animal existence. It was by taking hold of all the land and resources that nature had provided and using it to produce new wealth that civilised man would begin to distinguish himself from savage existence. Considering that land, in most cultures, was sacred, it had to be desacralised before it could be turned into a commodity.

If being modern defines a specific relationship to the world, a particular comportment, then it cannot be simply reduced to any particular feature. In a sense, this is precisely why I believe it is wrong to simply say 'we are all modern' à la Chakrabarty and others, even though 'we' may all be inhabiting the same time of modernity and capital. Being modern, in other words, cannot simply be understood as passively existing in modernity – it must involve a changed attitude to the world, central to which is the bourgeois individual, to put it in a shorthand expression. I will return to some of these issues towards the end of the chapter.

Sudipta Kaviraj opens his important essay, 'Outline of a Revisionist Theory of Modernity' with a question: How should a theory of modernity cope with historical difference? (2005:497). While this particular essay concerns itself with the general question of modernity, it is useful to keep in mind that Kaviraj made his initial moves in this direction in two earlier essays written in the mid-1990s (Kaviraj 2011a, 2011b). These essays directly addressed the question of capitalist development and its relationship to democracy against the backdrop of 'globalisation', although he traces its larger intellectual-historical lineage going back to the early Nehruvian years.

Kaviraj's concern in this essay is not with capitalism or the question of 'mode of production' but rather with the peculiar formation of Indian modernity (and, by extension, postcolonial modernity at large) – of which the question of capitalism forms one part. He aims to provide an account of modernity that could enable us to 'recognize the unfamiliar behavior of Indian democracy, the unfamiliar evolutions of the Indian state [and] the un-Western urbanity of our cities' (Kaviraj 2005: 501).

The key innovation introduced by Kaviraj here is his claim that modernity is not a single process but *a constellation of many different processes* like capitalist industrialisation, secularisation, sociological individuation, the increasing centrality of the state in the social order, radical changes in the structures of family and intimacy and so on, which do not always come in the same symmetrical package (ibid.: 508). That is to say, these different processes and developments are not necessarily functionally related to each other and differ radically from context to context, depending on the specific historical sequence in which they arise. Depending upon which of these elements come into being earlier, the specific formation of modernity would differ in each context, as it would significantly affect the way in which all the other elements took shape.[7]

By the end of the nineteenth century, Kaviraj argues, the dominant theorisations about modernity, drawing on Marx and Weber, came to acquire, over and above an explanatory part which gave insights into the emergence and future of modernity in Europe, an additional normative and prescriptive part as well, regarding its desirability in the rest of the world (ibid.: 504). He suggests accepting the first part while rejecting the second. Instead, he argues, we should work towards 'a theory which holds that there is a *logic of self-differentiation in modernity*', for, '(T)he more modernity expands and spreads to different parts of the world, the more it becomes differentiated and plural' (ibid.: 504, emphasis added).

It is clear from these statements that, for Kaviraj, there is no question of any doubt that modernity is entirely a European affair, and, what is more, differentiation is something that is internal to modernity – *self-differentiation*. In one stroke, he attributes a singular character to modernity which is incompatible with the idea of modernity as a constellation of many different processes, where not all of them can work together in tandem.

At this point, it is worth asking why Kaviraj should choose to cast the contingent historical relationship between capitalism and democracy in terms of the linear idea of sequentiality. It is no doubt important that we see democracy and capitalism as *non-contemporaneous*, as not arising at the same time, but to read this non-contemporaneousness in terms of sequentiality and linear time thus fixes each of these to a single, self-evident origin. It also suggests that we *know*, already, once and for all, what democracy and capitalism really are. In fact, the more radical implications of Kaviraj's unpacking of modernity as a constellation of different processes *need to be further extended to both* democracy as well as capitalism. It is, after all, possible to argue that, like modernity, capitalism, too, is an entity that was produced as an assemblage of many different elements and that we do not really know, for all time to come, whether the histories of technology, commodity production, trade, industrialisation, wage labour, money, finance and banking, book-keeping, statistics and numbers all have their single origin in Europe alone. On the contrary, what we do know – and what is becoming clearer by the day with the new scholarship that has emerged, especially over the last two decades – is that this is precisely not the case.

However, long before this new scholarship began posing questions about the precise lineage/s of capitalism and modernity, there was already a body of scholarship that had been seriously questioning the received story. Eric Williams (1944) and Cederic Robinson (2000, first published in 1983) had rewritten the story of British industrialisation and modern capitalism by bringing the centrality of slave labour and the Atlantic slave trade into the picture. Where Europhile Marxist theory continued to debate 'modes of production' in terms of features like 'free wage labour' (as opposed to, say, serfdom), already scholars like Williams were telling us how integral slavery was to industrialisation, even in that ideal-typical 'classical case', namely Britain. And slavery, both Williams and Robinson are at pains to underline, was *not* primarily a race issue but an economic one, documenting also the large-scale existence of white slavery long before black slaves from Africa and the Caribbean began being transported into Europe and the Americas. But once the story of Atlantic slave trade and colonialism are brought into the story, the neat narrative of 'feudalism' being supplanted by 'capitalism', endlessly debated by the so-called 'transition debate', begins to sound a trifle out of place.

Thus says Robinson,

> (T)he Atlantic slave trade and the slavery of the New World were integral to the modern world economy. Their relationship to capitalism was historical and organic rather than adventitious or synthetic. . . . Certainly, slave labour was one of the bases for what Marx termed 'primitive accumulation.' But it would be an error to arrest the relationship there, assigning slave labour to some 'pre-capitalist' stage of history. For more than 300 years slave labour persisted beyond the beginnings of modern capitalism, complementing wage labour, peonage, serfdom, and other methods of labour coercion. Ultimately, this meant that the interpretation of history in terms of the dialectic of capitalist class struggles would prove inadequate, a mistake ordained by the preoccupation of Marxism with the industrial and manufacturing centers of capitalism; *a mistake founded on the presumptions that Europe itself had produced, that the motive and material forces that generated the capitalist system were to be wholly located in what was a fictive historical entity. From*

> *its foundations, capitalism had never been – any more than Europe – a 'closed system.'*
>
> (Robinson 2000: 4)

In this passage, Robinson makes two methodologically significant observations. First, having complicated Marx's narrative of 'primitive accumulation' as the largely internal process of dispossession of agricultural communities by bringing in slavery, he underlines that this is not a phenomenon one should consign to the pre-history of capitalism. That the Atlantic slave trade and slavery in the New World continued for another 300 years alongside other forms of labour must not be dismissed lightly, simply because it disturbs the happy narrative of the internal evolution of feudalism into capitalism. The relationship between capitalism and this slavery was, he underlines, *historical and organic*. In other words, Robinson is not interested here in producing before us another supposedly 'theoretical' model but wants us to recognise that the relationship was *organic*, even if historical and contingent. Second, he emphasises the fact that neither Europe nor capitalism was ever 'a closed system' – that there was always an 'outside' that remained invisible as long as theory remained fixated on an idea of the 'internal dialectic' of transformation.

It is also interesting that one of the participants in the 'mode of production' debate in India in the 1970s and 1980s, Jairus Banaji (2003), dissatisfied with the very provincial English transition debate, moved on to an exploration of the 'global history' of capitalism. Exploring trade networks in the Mediterranean and its relationship to Islam, Banaji asks us to recognise this complex early history of networks, ideas and mechanisms linked to what he calls 'commercial capitalism', too, as the antecedent of modern industrial capitalism. Whether we agree with Banaji's proposal also to append the history of global trade and commerce to the history of capitalism, it is nevertheless undeniable that capitalism in Europe drew on many of the practices of finance and commerce that were in existence in the Mediterranean from the ninth century onwards. Interesting in this context is also Banaji's reading of Ibn Khaldun's very astute and sometimes prescient analyses of economic processes – including Ibn Khaldun's very own 'labour theory of value'. Banaji cites Ibn Khaldun's text *Muqaddimah* at length in order to demonstrate that notions like 'accumulation of capital' and the idea that labour is the source of all value are already present in his understanding of contemporary economic developments.

There was another debate among historians of India in particular, in the 1980s and 1990s, which partly morphs into the 'early modernity' debate referred to previously – and this had to do with the whole question of 'proto-industrialisation' and supposed autonomous capitalist development in India. Though there were ideological stakes among some participants in proving that colonial rule, as a matter of fact, this did not introduce any rupture in Indian society but simply built upon processes and practices that were already in existence; nevertheless, a lot of evidence *was* produced that showed different degrees of development of some kind of 'proto-capitalism'. As Frank Perlin put it, '*events within India need to be recast as an inseparable part of an international forum of activities*, in which rural industrialisation in Prussia, Bohemia and Bengal are best treated as aspects of a single set of both comparative and historical problems' (Perlin 1983: 34, emphasis added). The proto-industrialisation thesis, initially put forth in 1972, proclaiming it to be a 'first and necessary phase of a transition to industrial capitalism' (ibid.: 34) led to a wide range of historical research and even to its being read as 'a new phase in the debate over the transition from feudalism to capitalism' (ibid.: 35). This was therefore, another way in which the story of capitalism was sought to be taken out of the narrow confines of the Dobb-Sweezy transition debate.[8]

However, the reason I refer to this debate here is different. One of the key questions raised by a lot of revisionist historiography of recent decades, especially from the vantage point of economic history, is this – why, despite having been at comparable levels of technological and economic development, it was in Europe rather than in China that the Industrial Revolution took place. Two key works that have dealt with these issues in different ways are Wong (1997) and Pomeranz (2000). Wong is more dismissive of this question when he argues that 'During the last century, expectations about historical change, over the past millennium of Chinese history, have been based on European history'. There are, he says, two basic views of China which see it either as 'social change gone wrong' or as 'stagnation', both of which come straight out of Western traditions of social theory that trace their lineage to Karl Marx and Max Weber. These traditions identify 'a distinctive cluster of traits that set Europe off from other parts of the world. . . . These account for Western successes and the failure of others' (Wong 1997: 4)

Pomeranz, on the other hand, in undertaking an examination of 'why Europe and not China', references the South Asian debate on proto-industrialisation at length. He cites some of the evidence thus:

> While Perlin and Andre Wink concentrated on north and central India, Sanjay Subrahmanyam found even stronger evidence of the interpenetration of capital-accumulating families and commercialised public finance in south India. Subrahmanyam traces the careers of what he calls 'portfolio capitalists': men who combined an ever shifting mix of interests in long distance trade (mostly high-profit luxury goods); loans, bill forwarding and other financial activities; the purchase or leasing of tax rights and government monopolies (e.g. diamond mines); capital-intensive land reclamation . . . service as local purchasing agents to the British and Dutch; and service as a courtier or general and military supply officer. And here too, rights to future income streams won strong customary and sometimes formal protection; eventually they became

> tradable, heritable and mortgageable, *much like equivalent interests in most of Europe.*
>
> (Pomeranz 2000: 175)

All these bits of evidence undoubtedly complicate the picture of a passive and unchanging Asia, as there were clearly very significant developments taking place at the economic and other levels. Whether they qualify to be called 'capitalist' in any fashion – proto or otherwise – is a question that remains.

## Unpacking 'Capitalism'

Consider some of the more recent attempts at providing alternative theoretical accounts of modernity that seek to go beyond the Eurocentrism of existing hegemonic discourses, such as John Hobson's *Eastern Origins of Western Civilization* (2004) and Jack Goody's *Theft of History* (2006) – both of which argue that much of what Europe had by way of resources for its modernity were drawn in large measure from the East. Goody, as the title of his book itself suggests, simply calls it 'theft' – a theft of 'history', of 'capitalism' and indeed of many ideas and institutions that the West supposedly drew from the Orient.

One of the most dramatic claims put forward by Hobson, in the context of 'globalisation', is, contrary to Eurocentric claims, that the world before 1500 CE was an insular world and that only with the rise of capitalist modernity 'was the European age of discovery launched', leading to the 'battering down of the walls that had kept apart major civilisations' (Hobson 2004: 29). Among his six counter-propositions challenging dominant Eurocentric narratives, one of the key claims is that from 500 CE on, Persians, Arabs, Africans, Javanese, Jews, Indians and Chinese created and maintained a global economy, which he calls 'Oriental globalisation', down to about 1800 CE, in which the major civilisations of the world were interlinked (ibid.: 32). His third 'counter-proposition', in his own words: 'Third, a whole series of sufficiently *rational capitalist* institutions were created and put in place after 500 to support global trade' (ibid.: 32, emphasis added). Hobson develops this proposition at length in one entire chapter, where he claims that 'virtually all the major innovations that lay behind the development of Italian capitalism were derived from the more advanced East, especially the Middle East and China, and diffused across the Islamic Bridge of the World through Oriental globalisation' (ibid.: 117). Hobson also cites evidence to show that many of the financial institutions ranging from the bill of exchange, credit institutions, insurance and banking that Italy was wrongly credited with having pioneered had longer histories going back to the Islamic and even pre-Islamic 'Middle East' (ibid.: 120). Apart from recording the well-known important developments in science and philosophy in the Islamic world that went into the making of the modern

West – including Indian mathematics – Hobson also devotes an entire chapter to the 'Chinese origins of British Industrialisation', where he argues at length that many of the technological and other resources that the latter drew upon had had a much longer history of existence in China – whether it was the case of coal and blast furnaces, iron and steel production or cotton manufacturing (ibid.: 190–218).

In Goody's account, too, everything from 'antiquity' and 'feudalism' to 'capitalism' represents a 'theft' of the East's history. The general premises of his narrative, too, are similar to Hobson's, except that this focus is less on actual evidence (partly because it builds on his own earlier work) and more on the writings of key Western thinkers. The empirical background of history is of course present throughout the text, but it is really the Eurocentric narrative that he is interested in dismantling. Both Hobson and Goody, it seems to me, assume the superiority of 'modernity' and 'capitalism' in some way, so that to restore to the Orient its 'due' place, it is necessary to make the claim either that they too are no strangers to modernity and capitalism, or, at the very least, they too had produced all the necessary ingredients for capitalism and modernity to come into being. While it is right to trace these longer and more global histories of modernity and capitalism so that Eurocentric prejudices are effectively questioned, the problem nevertheless remains as to what precisely it is that we understand by 'capitalism' and 'modernity'.

Thus, for example, when Hobson claims that 'a whole series of sufficiently *rational capitalist* institutions were created and put in place after 500 CE to support global trade', what exactly do we make of such a statement? This statement, in fact, seems to point to one of the key difficulties with the proponents of the 'early modernities' or 'proto-industrialisation' theses as well: modernity and capitalism (or industrialisation) here are sought to be identified by locating certain specific features in the various Asian, African and Latin American societies in a period prior to the rise of modern Europe.

Clearly, the implication of these and similar positions referred to previously is that one can only step outside the frame of Eurocentrism if one denies Europe its unique contribution in the making of modernity and capitalism. It is as if to challenge Eurocentrism, one has to simply show that there are longer global histories of the very processes that Europe values that Eurocentric discourse occludes.

In conclusion, then, I want to draw our attention to a passage from the Peruvian scholar Anibal Quijano in order to pose my question a bit more sharply.

> If the concept of modernity only, or fundamentally, refers to the idea of newness, the advanced, the rational-scientific, the secular (which are the ideas normally associated with it), then there is no doubt that one must admit that it is a phenomenon possible *in all cultures and historical epochs*. With all their respective particularities and differences, all

> the so-called high cultures (China, India, Egypt, Greece, Maya-Aztec, Tawantin-suyo) prior to the present world-system, unequivocally exhibit signs of that modernity, including rational-science and the secularization of thought.
>
> (Anibal Quijano 2000: 543, emphasis added)

Quijano's point is that if we want to identify modernity only, or fundamentally, with reference to the idea of newness or to ideas of the rational-scientific and the 'secular', then modernity could be found possibly *in all cultures and all historical epochs*. We can extend the point Quijano makes about 'modernity' to 'capitalism' as well. We can ask if pointing to certain kinds of material developments in technology and the economy is enough to show that capitalism too existed across societies and historical epochs. If that is the case, what kind of a concept of modernity or capitalism would we be left with?

To quickly recapitulate the main lines of my argument, then, I have tried to look at the problem of economic difference not directly in relation to the phenomenon of globalisation but by going behind this term and trying to unpack the two key concepts that lie embedded in globalisation discourse, namely capitalism and modernity. More specifically, my focus has been on one kind of 'difference' in relation to both capitalism and modernity, and that is what one might call 'temporal difference' – the continued existence of past forms within capitalism and the modern. How do we understand this difference – rather heterogeneity, where we had been given to understand that these past forms were simply destined to exit the stage and enter the pages of history? In order to understand this, I look at two relatively benign ways in which the problems of past forms of life have been dealt with in social and political theory – one that claims they belong to the past but must be eliminated gently, rather than decimated violently, and the other that already bestows on them the tag of being modern in order to rescue them from indignity. The problem, I argue, has to do with the determination of the complex that we call 'modern' and disentangling it not only from 'capitalism' but also simultaneously unpacking these two terms to show that most of the constituent elements of modernity and capitalism have longer and varied histories that go back to different parts of the world. We cannot locate a single point of origin, say, post-Enlightenment Europe, as the space-time of the birth of capitalism or of modernity.

The point that I want to underline here is that a whole range of ideas and practices have developed in different societies and at different points of time – scientific and philosophical ideas as well as material practices of exchange, credit and production – but which do not add up to anything like modernity or capitalism until they are clubbed together once these organising categories are put in place. Just as globalisation was never a descriptive term but also always a way of ordering practices – be they in relation to the economy or in the domain of thought – 'modernity' and 'capitalism', too, were never purely descriptive categories. Once enunciated, they brought into being an entirely new discursive configuration that clubbed together disparate practices and ideas that marked what Kaviraj calls a 'new kind of newness' that pitted itself in opposition to what it, in that very moment, produced as the 'past'. Our description of many such life forms and practices that we call 'past', but which continue to coexist in our present, are thus totally misleading.

Thus, to reiterate, it is entirely possible to have many of the elements that go into the making of modernity (the idea of newness, the scientific-rational, the secular), just as it is possible to have many of the elements that go into the making of capitalism (the market, commodity production, credit and finance, wage labour) without having either modernity or capitalism. For it is the European episteme that lies behind the new discursive configuration that puts these entities in place, reorganising social life in a way that makes these entities material factors in our lives.

## Notes

1 I am told that the term 'European episteme' was used by Achille Mbembe at a conference in University of Virginia recently, though I could not find any written reference to this term anywhere. The specific sense in which I use this term here is of course my own.

2 It is now obvious that one of the key factors behind both these outcomes was the fear, in the popular mind, of the unrestrained global order, whose consequences were understood to affect the 'losers' of this process in very different ways. The fear could as easily take the form of a xenophobic fear of the immigrant as it could fuel investment in demagogues promising the reversal of capital flight from metropolitan countries. The latter was precisely what became so evident in the support extended by the destitute white working class for Trump. The same fear of the immigrant 'other' that underlies some of these developments has, of course, earlier been in evidence, as witnessed, for example, in the run-up to the formation of the European Union.

3 The Marxist response is actually shot through with a profound ambivalence. Politically, Marxists of all hues in India continued to be vigorous opponents of 'globalization' as a form of renewed attempt at colonisation, though, when it came to the economy, they recognised that certain changes were historically 'unavoidable'. In government, in states like West Bengal and Kerala, therefore, they eventually espoused policies that were hardly distinguishable from neoliberal ones. Hence the Marxist chief minister of West Bengal, Buddhadeb Bhattacharya, could say that unless agriculture gave way to industry, it would mean the 'end of history'. (See Menon and Nigam 2014.)

4 To be fair to Joan Robinson, her exact quote that appears in *Economic Philosophy* (1962) was made in the context of unemployment and goes thus: 'The misery of being exploited by capitalists is nothing compared to the misery of not being exploited at all'. It needs to be borne in mind that when it was written, the idea that capitalism was the most advanced, modern form of economy was pretty much an unchallenged idea. It was only possible to think of transcending capitalism by going beyond it toward socialism, but to argue that other ('precapitalist') forms too could have a continued reason for existence would have been blasphemous. In that context, this statement can also be read as arguing that since there is

no 'outside' to capital, one could either be exploited by it or remain unemployed. This is also an idea that this chapter seeks to interrogate.

5 This production of the English experience of 'enclosure of the commons' and mass dispossession of agricultural populations as the 'classic form', alongside the attendant idea of 'primitive accumulation', was in no small measure due to Marx himself, who gave it that status in *Capital, Volume I*.

6 The essays are brought together in the special number of *Daedalus* (Eisenstadt 2000 Winter), in which Eisenstadt's own essay was published.

7 Interestingly, Kaviraj draws this distinction between what he calls the 'symmetrical' theory of modernity and the 'sequential', primarily from within the European experience itself, where the question of the expansion of democracy as a results of struggles came to be understood in terms that rejected any functional relationship between it and capitalism.

8 The debate took place in the 1950s in the pages of the journal *Science and Society* and was published by Verso with an introduction by Rodney Hilton in 1978. I refer here to a more recent Indian imprint. See bibliography (Hilton 2006).

## Bibliography

Ahmed, Aijaz. 1983. 'Imperialism and Progress', in Ronal H. Chilcote and Dale L. Johnson (eds.) *Theories of Development: Mode of Production or Dependency?* pp. 33–73. Beverly Hills, CA: Sage Publications.

Althusser, Louis. 1979. *For Marx*. London: Verso.

Althusser, Louis. 2003. *The Humanist Controversy and Other Writings*. London and New York: Verso.

Althusser, Louis. 2006. *Philosophy of the Encounter: Later Writings, 1978–87*. London and New York: Verso.

Althusser, Louis and Etienne Balibar. 1977. *Reading Capital*. London: NLB.

Amin, Samir. 1976. *Unequal Development: An Essay on the Social Formations of Peripheral Capitalism*. London and New York: Monthly Review Press.

Banaji, Jairus. 2003. 'Islam, Mediterranean and the Rise of Capitalism', *Historical Materialism*, 15: 47–74.

Bauman, Zygmunt. 1998. *Globalization: The Human Consequences*. New York: Columbia University Press.

Bayly, C.A. 2004. *The Birth of the Modern World 1780–1914*. Oxford: Blackwell Publishing.

Birla, Ritu. 2011. *Stages of Capital: Law, Culture and Market Governance in Late Colonial India*. New Delhi: Orient Blackswan.

Chakrabarty, Dipesh. 2000. *Provincializing Europe: Postcolonial Thought and Historical Difference*. Princeton: Princeton University Press.

Chatterjee, Partha. 1986. *Nationalist Thought in the Colonial World – A Derivative Discourse?* Tokyo and London: Zed Books and United Nations University.

Chatterjee, Partha. 1994. *The Nation and Its Fragments: Colonial and Postcolonial Histories*. Delhi: Oxford University Press.

Chilcote, Ronald H. and Dale L. Johnson. 1983. *Theories of Development: Mode of Production or Dependency?* Beverly Hills, CA: Sage Publications.

Dussel, Enrique. 1993. 'Eurocentrism and Modernity (Introduction to the Frankfurt Lectures)', *Boundary 2*, 20 (3): 65–76.

Dussel, Enrique. 2002. 'World-System and "Trans-Modernity"', *Nepantla: Views from the South*, 3 (2): 221–44.

Eisenstadt, S.N. 2000. 'Multiple Modernities', *Daedalus*, Special Number on 'Multiple Modernities', 129 (1): 1–29.
Foucault, Michel. (Colin Gordon ed.). 1980. *Power/Knowledge: Selected Interviews and Other Writings 1972–77*. New York: Pantheon Books.
Foucault, Michel. 1998. *Aesthetics, Method and Epistemology. Essential Works of Foucault*, Vol. 2. London: Allen Lane The Penguin Press.
Frank, Andre Gunder. 1969. *Capitalism and Underdevelopment in Latin America: Historical Studies of Chile and Brazil*. London and New York: Monthly Review Press.
Gibson-Graham, J.K. 2006. *The End of Capitalism (As We Knew It): A Feminist Critique of Political Economy*. Minneapolis: University of Minnesota Press.
Goody, Jack. 2006. *The Theft of History*. Cambridge, UK: Cambridge University Press.
Guha, Ranajit. 1983. *Elementary Aspects of Peasant Insurgency in Colonial India*. Delhi: Oxford University Press.
Habermas, Jurgen. 2001. *The Postnational Condition: Political Essays*. Cambridge, MA: The MIT Press.
Hardt, Michael and Antonio Negri. 2000. *Empire*. Cambridge, MA and London, England: Harvard University Press.
Hardt, Michael and Antonio Negri. 2004. *Multitude: War and Democracy in the Age of Empire*. New York: Penguin Books.
Hardt, Michael and Antonio Negri. 2009. *Commonwealth*. Cambridge, MA: The Belknap Press of the Harvard University Press.
Harvey, David. 1990. *The Condition of Postmodernity: An Inquiry into the Origins of Cultural Change*. Oxford, England and Cambridge, MA: Blackwell.
Hilton, Rodney. Compilation. 2006. *The Transition from Feudalism to Capitalism*, Introduced by Rodney Hilton. New Delhi: Aakar Books.
Hobsbawm, Eric and Terence Ranger. 1983. *The Invention of Tradition*. Cambridge, UK: Cambridge University Press.
Hobson, John M. 2004. *The Eastern Origins of Western Civilization*. Cambridge, UK: Cambridge University Press.
Hui, Wang. 2011. *The Politics of Imagining Asia*. Cambridge, MA: Harvard University Press.
Kaviraj, Sudipta. 2005. 'An Outline of a Revisionist Theory of Modernity', *European Journal of Sociology*, XLVI (3): 497–526.
Kaviraj, Sudipta. 2010. 'The Passive Revolution and India: A Critique', in *Trajectories of the Indian State – Politics and Ideas*, pp. 100–43. Ranikhet: Permanent Black.
Kaviraj, Sudipta. 2011a. 'Dilemmas of Democratic Development in India', in Sudipta Kaviraj (ed.) *The Enchantment of Democracy and India: Politics and Ideas*, pp. 85–115. Ranikhet: Permanent Black.
Kaviraj, Sudipta. 2011b. 'Democracy and Development in India', in Sudipta Kaviraj (ed.) *The Enchantment of Democracy and India: Politics and Ideas*, pp. 116–60. Ranikhet: Permanent Black.
Leiberman, Victor. 2008. 'The Qing Dynasty and Its Neighbours: Early Modern China in World History', *Social Science History*, 32(2): 281–304.
Ludden, David. 2002. 'Modern Inequality and Early Modernity: A Comment for the AHR on the Articles by R. Bin Wong and Kenneth Pomeranz', *American History Review*, 107(2): 470–80.

Lyons, Jonathan. 2010. *The House of Wisdom: How the Arabs Transformed Western Civilization*. New York: Bloomsbury.
Menon, Nivedita and Aditya Nigam. 2014. *Power and Contestation: India Since 1989* (with a new epilogue). New Delhi: Orient Blackswan.
Mignolo, Walter. 2011. *The Darker Side of Western Modernity: Global Futures, Decolonial Options*. Durham and London: Duke University Press.
Mignolo, Walter. 2012. *Local Histories/Global Designs: Coloniality, Subaltern Knowledges and Border Thinking*. Princeton: Princeton University Press.
Mitchell, Timothy. 2002. *Rule of Experts: Egypt, Techno-Politics, Modernity*. Berkley: University of California Press.
Nesbitt, Nick. 2017. *The Concept in Crisis: Reading Capital Today*. Durham and London: Duke University Press.
Nigam, Aditya. 2016. 'Afro-Asian Solidarity and the "Capital" Question: Looking Beyond the Last Frontier', *Inter-Asia Cultural Studies*, 17(1): 33–51.
Patnaik, Prabhat. 1995. *Whatever Happened to Imperialism and Other Essays*. New Delhi: Tulika.
Perlin, Frank. 1983. 'Proto-Industrialization and Pre-Colonial South Asia', *Past and Present*, 98: 30–95.
Pomeranz, Kenneth. 2000. *The Great Divergence: China, Europe, and the Making of the Modern World Economy*. Princeton and Oxford: Princeton University Press.
Quijano, Anibal. 1983. 'Imperialism, Social Classes and the State in Peru, 1890–1930', in Ronald H. Chilcote and Dale L. Johnson (eds.) *Theories of Development: Mode of Production or Dependency?* pp. 107–38. Beverly Hills, CA: Sage Publications.
Quijano, Anibal. 2000. 'Coloniality of Power, Eurocentrism and Latin America', *Nepantla: Views from the South*, 533–80.
Quijano, Anibal. 2007. 'Coloniality and Modernity/Rationality', *Cultural Studies* 21 (2–3): 168–78.
Robinson, Cedric J. 2000. *Black Marxism*. Chapel Hill: The University of North Carolina Press.
Rudolph, Lloyd I. and Susanne Hoeber Rudolph. 1967. *The Modernity of Tradition: Political Development in India*. Chicago and London: University of Chicago Press.
Sanyal, Kalyan. 2007. *Rethinking Capitalist Development: Primitive Accumulation, Governmentality and Post-Colonial Capitalism*. New Delhi: Routledge.
Subrahmanyam, Sanjay. 1997. 'Connected Histories: Notes Towards a Reconfiguration of Early Modern Eurasia', *Modern Asian Studies*, 31 (3): 735–62.
Williams, Eric. 1944. *Capitalism and Slavery*. Chapel Hill: The University of North Carolina Press.
Wong, R. Bin. 1997. *China Transformed: Historical Change and the Limits of European Experience*. Ithaca and London: Cornell University Press.

# 2 Capital (in)difference in Africa

## The examples of Nigeria and South Africa[1]

*Faisal Garba*

Beginning from the late 1950s, independent African states embarked on publicly funded social provisioning in order to mitigate the systematic deprivation that defined colonialism and to meet what Zeleza (2014) called the triple promise of independence – decolonisation, democracy and development. With varying degrees of success, the immediate post-colonial states in Africa provided education, healthcare and public transportation (Ake 1981). Employment was created through the establishment of import substitution industries (ISIs). Many ISIs were established or supported with loans from international financial institutions (IFIs) – the World Bank and the International Monetary Fund (IMF), in particular. A combination of structural inequalities ranging from persistent unequal terms of trade at the international level to local political arrangements and considerations meant that many of the ISIs were in crisis by the middle of the 1970s (Adesina et al. 2006).

The crisis of the ISIs was connected to and affected the capacity of states to continue providing publicly funded social services. Having incurred large amounts of debt (with significant debt servicing costs) to set up the ISIs and meet other developmental initiatives, states across Africa turned to the IFIs for further loans. Some of the preconditions for further loans included reduction of public spending on education and healthcare, privatisation of state-owned enterprises and parastatals and retrenchment of public sector workers. The result of the policy package that came as structural adjustment programmes (SAPs) was the reversal of gains made against preventable diseases like cholera, decrease in literacy rates, mass impoverishment and unemployment. Many of the retrenched workers moved into the informal sector as petty traders and service providers of various kinds (Soludo and Mkandawire 1998). In the midst of declining public provision of services and unemployment, greater numbers of people migrated to neighbouring and distant countries within and outside Africa.

While SAPs are manifestly an economic intervention, their latent impact went beyond the economy; it affected inter-group relations and provided the breeding ground for the politicisation of ethnic identities. British colonialism in Nigeria functioned through indirect rule, as it did in other colonies. The elevation of chiefs, emirs and native/tribal authorities served what Mamdani (2012) terms 'define and rule'. Ethnic groups were categorised into natives and non-natives to a given place. The designation of nativity was closely tied up with a characterisation of ethnic identities that had been contingent and changing as fixed and natural. The naturalised ethnic identities provided the basis for the creation of administrative and geopolitical units. They also served colonial labour needs and capital accumulation. Due to regional and ethnic discrepancies in access to education and training, certain occupations came to be linked to particular ethnic groups.

Faced with an ethnically ruled but socially heterogeneous population, the nationalist anti-colonial movement, National Congress of Nigeria and Cameroons (NCNC), and its allies promoted the identity of Nigerian as opposed to the naturalised ethnic identities that colonialism had cultivated (Usman 2006). The nationalist anti-colonial movement was rivalled by regional and ethnic-based parties that mobilised on the basis of ethnic identities. While the nationalist movement won power upon independence in an alliance with a regionally based party, the Northern People's Congress (NPC), the struggle between a nationalist outlook that prioritised nation-building and regionally based parties and interest groups was precarious. In their quest to gain advantage over each other, different segments of the elite instrumentalised their ethnicity and often present themselves as ethnic or regional representatives with the implication that what was in their interest was in the interest of their ethnic group or region (Usman 1979).

With the advent of economic crisis, the instrumentalisation identity for inter-elite economic competition was heightened (Osoba 1978; Usman 1979). Ethnicity was combined with religion as tools for mobilising popular support behind the individual and class interest of businesspersons, some of whom doubled as politicians (Usman 1984). While it can be argued that hostile ethnic and religious outlooks are widespread in society, this chapter will attempt to show that the entrenchment of ethnicity and religion as markers of social difference in Nigeria furthers accumulation by competing elites, most of whom are also active politically.

Similar politicisation of difference aids the generation of a consensus that favours capital accumulation by the elites in South Africa. While, in Nigeria, ethnicity and religion serve as instruments in competition over state contracts, ownership of privatised state-owned enterprises and general accumulation, in South Africa, citizenship has become an important tool for generating a hegemony that serves capital accumulation by the established white capitalists and the newly emerging black economic and political elites. The result is that African migrants who find themselves in South Africa are being blamed for 'stealing' jobs, business, trading opportunities and public services like healthcare.

State functionaries in South Africa frequently blame migrants (mostly working-class and poor migrants) for inadequate housing and for crime. This is happening at a time when inequality in South Africa is the highest in the world. Since the end of Apartheid, a black elite affiliated to the governing African National Congress has acquired shares in major corporations through a scheme to create a black capitalist class now known as Broad-Based Black Economic Empowerment (BBBEE) (van der Walt 2018), while the majority of the black population remains poor, with many living in corrugated iron sheets. It is estimated that the share of capital owned by this black elite as measured by shares on the Johannesburg Stock Exchange is around 23%. Anecdotally, this inequality can be seen in the cars driven by the black elite and their relocation to the suburbs that used to be exclusively inhabited by the white elite under Apartheid. By successfully generating a climate of hostility towards poor migrants, the new black-led state and its counterparts in business that has benefitted from social stratification have displaced the source of inadequate social services to a marginal social group – African migrants.

The chapter presents a broad and general account of the role of capital in the making of identity and difference in Africa. The thrust of the chapter is to show how capital, in alliance with the state, creates, harnesses or instrumentalises and, at times, shows no regard to social difference. The chapter is situated at the intersection of the movement of global capital and the ordering of society, polity and culture. The experiences of Nigeria and South Africa will be used to illuminate some of the general points of the chapter. This introduction is followed by a general description of society in pre-colonial Africa; the next section is 'Colonial Accumulation and the Making of Difference', 'The Promise of Independence', 'The Immediate Post-Colonial Moment', 'The Unravelling', 'Nigeria: Ethnic and Religious Difference as Mechanisms of Accumulation', 'South Africa: Xenophobia as Stratification' and 'Conclusion'.

## Aspects of pre-colonial social formations in Africa

The structure of African societies prior to European colonialism vary in degree of socioeconomic and political organisation. While many of the societies were acephalous formations with no centralised political authority, like the Tallensi of present-day Ghana (to date), others were highly centralised and differentiated, such as the Luba of Central Africa, the Hausa states of West Africa and the monarchical dynasty of Ethiopia, ruling over vast territories and agglomerations of peoples of diverse linguistic affiliation and religious convictions in East Africa. Some of the centralised states maintained tributary relationships with smaller units, exacting tributes in the form of labour power, items of trade and luxury goods (Niane 1984).

The social groups and the polities in which they were organised were products of social changes arising out of migration and the exchange of ideas and goods within Africa and parts of Asia[2] (Usman 2006). Production relations were important in the formation of identity. Accordingly, one's occupation and where a person resided were important markers and determinants of their identity (Usman 2006). Thus, occupational categories such as hunter, healer, trader, warrior and intellectual confer social identity and simultaneously represent competing political interests. For example, hunters as a group was composed of people of diverse 'ethnic' origins; however, in the public sphere, they functioned as a corporate group with similar interests, as opposed to, say, farmers (Usman 2006).

## Colonial accumulation and the making of difference

The question of what the character, and therefore the legacy, of colonialism in Africa is has been the subject of a longstanding debate. While there are a number of perspectives, I will restrict myself to two perspectives whose competing arguments I find most compelling. From the late 1960s and 1970s, an explanation of colonialism in Africa emerged out of the works of a collection of Marxist-leaning scholars based at the University of Dar Es Salaam in Tanzania[3] (henceforth the Dar School). In the analysis of the Dar School, colonialism was primarily motivated by economic imperatives. Accordingly, economic motivation led to the conception of a colonial mode of production whose objectives and consequences included the maximisation of profit from the colonies, the subordination of the economies of the colonies to serve the needs of the colonial power and the development of underdevelopment (Rodney 1973).

An understanding of colonialism as market domination explains the economic underdevelopment of Africa as both the objective and consequence of colonial domination. Under this framework, the extroverted structure of African economies is a consequence of the historic disarticulation that orients production towards cash crop or natural resource export to Europe and increasingly China, with little local and regional integration of production or distribution. There is still very little trade among African countries. Instead, many African countries compete with each other for market opportunities in the European Union and the United States.

A similar competition was fostered with regard to labour power and livelihood opportunities (Asamoa 2001). Colonialism created labour reserves in certain parts of a colony – often coinciding with ethnic boundaries – for the supply of unskilled labour. This class of workers are recruited from places with little to no access to formal Western education. A layer of semi-skilled workers performing administrative and bureaucratic functions is usually drawn from the parts of a colony where formal education is available to some. The difference between the workers from the labour reserves and the semi-skilled workers is a function of the location of missionary schools and colonial policy that provides limited education in select places. (Asamoa 2001).

Dissatisfied with what some critique as an economistic understanding of colonialism and its legacy, a counterperspective that centralises statecraft was put forward. Mahmood Mamadani, previously a member of the Dar

School, shifted his focus from the economy to statecraft. In his book, *Citizen and Subject, the Legacy of Late Colonialism in Contemporary Africa*, Mamdani argued that colonialism's lasting effect on Africa is identity engineering (Mamdani 1996). Colonialism, according to Mamdani, created the category of the native and divided society into antagonistic groups, each occupying an ancestral home to which one can only claim right of domicile based on ancestry. As part of the colonial nativist project, political power was made the preserve of certain social groups, while other social groups were systematically denied access to power (Mamdani 2012). The case of Rwanda, where the Tutsi elite were privileged by the French while the Hutus were denied access to political power, is a case in point.

Drawing from aspects of the two competing explanations of colonialism in Africa, it is possible to piece together a picture of how colonialism as a system of accumulation propped up social difference in furthering its ends. Colonial anthropology saw African societies as made up of distinct and exclusive tribes. In its classic rendition, a tribe is a social group whose livelihood, culture and political structures all take place in self-contained geographical and social space with little to no contact with the outside world (Mafeje 1972). For colonial anthropology and the colonial officials whose outlook on Africa it shaped, the African 'tribes' they encountered were a continuation of a long unbroken chain of social organisation.[4] Tribe, to them, was the core of African society. The entirety of social organisation in Africa supposedly revolves within the boundaries of a tribe.

Going by the previous, each tribe must have a natural ancestral home, also called a 'tribal homeland' ruled by a 'tribal chief' or 'traditional leader' guided by 'tribal laws' or customs that have been handed down through generations. This colonial theory of the structure of African societies guided colonial policy. In both Nigeria and South Africa, colonialism and Apartheid viewed any deviation from this model as a contamination of the purity of the traditional African society. In northern Nigeria, an ever-changing social structure where social identity shifts as people change residence and occupation was seen as an anomaly in need of correction. A person had to identify as a member of one ethnic group; multiple affiliation, which is the norm given multiple ancestry, pattern of residency and occupation activities, was discouraged. Difference was imposed by fiat (Usman 2006). The success of this model in northern Nigeria encouraged the British colonial authorities to impose chiefs among groups in eastern Nigeria that had historically had no chiefs or centralised political authority (Amadiume 1987). Apartheid South Africa also ruled its subjects through imposed chiefs. Apartheid assigned every black South African to an ancestral homeland ruled by a chief. A person could only leave their homeland if they obtained permission to do so (Mamdani 1996).

The implementation of the colonial theory of the structure of African societies that led to the division of societies into tribal homelands with tribal chiefs facilitated the control and supply of labour to colonial plantations, farms, mines and infrastructural projects linked to the export of resources that undergirded the colonial economy. Having a critical mass of concentrated populace whose movement was largely delimited within the homelands, it became possible to force them to sell their labour in the emerging cash economy in order to pay taxes or to force them to work for no wages (Asamoa 2001). The profit imperative therefore went hand in hand with colonial statecraft's creation and manipulation of identity: Homelands imposed the consciousness of a tribal identity, and the concentration in the homelands made it possible to galvanise labour. Instead of viewing colonial statecraft as separate from market domination, they have to be viewed as integral components of a colonial project whose imperial impulse was as economic as it was politicocultural. Colonialism indeed defined and ruled. In defining and ruling, it also exploited in order to accumulate.

## The promise of independence

The anti-colonial struggle across Africa was waged in order to do away with colonial rule and its socioeconomic impacts. The authoritarian character of colonial institutions denied people basic rights such as the rights to representation, association and human dignity. Decolonisation was conceived to be the opposite of what colonialism and its institutions represented. Decolonisation was supposed to come with the right to self-determination but also the affirmation of the humanity that colonialism denied to the colonised. In northern Nigeria, poll tax, or *Haraji*,[5] was so dehumanising that many people had to run away from their families because they could not afford it. Defaulters were lashed with whips in market squares to inscribe the power of the state on them and others who were present. Given that the African was construed as subhuman and therefore in need of regular tutelage, decolonisation was both a psychological affirmation of the humanity of the dehumanised and a drive to build a different form of social organisation where the humanity of all was a given (Asamoa 2001; Usman 2006).

The end of formal colonialism was supposed to usher in the promises of decolonisation. Within limits, a number of success were recorded by countries across Africa. In the immediate post-colonial period, there came into force a dispensation of respect for the inherent humanity of all and an accompanying obligation to create a condition that negated the legacies of colonialism by meeting the basic human and material needs of the populace. Socioeconomic development was prioritised, and the chosen vehicle in keeping with the global trend of the time was state-led development. Import substituting industries were established across the continent to break the colonial cycle where African countries met the raw material needs of their erstwhile colonisers and served as net importers of their (ex-coloniser's) manufactures. ISIs were established to locally produce goods that were otherwise imported and to generate employment. The ISIs ranged from light to semiheavy industries manufacturing household wares and farm implements. Others specialised in iron smelting, plastic and tyre manufacturing and textiles. The ISIs generated employment and met local needs for consumer goods (Asamoa 2001).

To grow the ISIs and meet the goals set out in development plans that almost every country on the continent drew up for its social transformation, education was made a priority from basic to tertiary levels. While education had been a privilege reserved for the elite under colonialism, it became a right enshrined in the Directive Principles of State Policy section of national constitutions. Teaching and demonstration facilities were provided by the state in addition to free tuition. Mass access to education institutions improved, culminating in increased literacy rates. Skilled persons, some trained locally, and others sent to other southern countries like India and China, but also to the West, provided the skill requirements of the ISIs and other public institutions (Asamoa 2001).

Healthcare, especially preventive and primary care, were seen as necessary to social transformation. The provision of key social determinants of health like access to clean and potable water and the construction and maintenance of drainage systems were prioritised. Improved access to healthcare facilities at no cost at the point of delivery translated into enhanced maternal health and life expectancy and decreased maternal and infant mortality rates on the continent (Adepoju 1993).

As stated earlier, colonialism created and propped up ethnic identities as an instrument of accumulation and rule. In the British colonies, for example, the International Africa Institute and the colonial anthropologists associated with it regularly updated the list of tribes in order to better understand Africa. The definition, classification and definition of identities created antagonistic sectional outlooks that served the interests of colonialism and its accumulations. Groups that were named and administered in their separate ethnic homelands cultivated competitive and antagonistic outlooks towards others whom they came to see as rivals for resources and power. The allocation of differential rights and entitlements to select elite members of certain groups deepened the antagonism between ethnic groups. Accordingly, the anti-colonial movements that defeated colonialism inherited countries that are deeply divided along regional, ethnic or religious fault lines. The task of moulding the hardened separate identities which had hitherto been flexible and changing was one that the post-colonial state had to confront. Nigeria went through bitter warfare whose roots lay in the British colonial policy of strategically placing elites from the northern parts of the country who were favourably disposed to Britain at the helm of the country after the end of British rule over the country (Usman 2006). In South Africa, the transition from Apartheid in 1994 was nearly aborted by the Zulu nationalist claims of a homeland leadership led by Mangosuthu Buthelezi, who insisted on near autonomy for Zululand on account of the distinctiveness of the 'Zulu nation'.

To create coherent countries out of the disparate colonial entities, post-colonial states had to implement a series of social, educational and legal policies. In Tanzania, Julius Nyerere made Swahili, a widely spoken language in East Africa, the national language. This was an attempt to formalise an organic process of nation building given the centrality of Swahili as a language of trade and communication across East Africa. Nyerere also outlawed chieftaincy, given its legacy as a colonial tool of ascribing tribal identities and therefore denying belonging to those who were deemed outsiders (Mamdani 2012). Nkrumah in Ghana diminished the legal standing of chiefs and withdrew their control over land, an important source of their power. Chiefs' control over land enabled them to decide who belonged and who did not belong to a place. Often, they ascribed belonging based on colonial notions of tribal affiliation (Garba 2015).

In other parts of the continent, education was used for nation building. The allocation of schools to learners from one part of the country in another part of the country was meant to cultivate a sense of belonging and oneness. With variations, the attempts at nation building tried to move away from the view of belonging as an essence that does not change to belonging as a social process where people come to belong to a place over time.

## The unravelling

The ISIs were either set up or augmented with loans from international financial institutions. This was indicative of the prevailing political economic doctrine of the time: The state had the responsibility to actively drive development. While production by the ISIs reduced the import of consumer goods by many countries and provided employment, they had a number of weaknesses that led to their eventual collapse. The factors that led to the collapse of the ISIs can be divided into internal and external factors: The internal factors include weak planning in the location of ISIs relative to sources of raw materials, political calculation in the citing of ISIs, appointment of politically connected persons with little competence to strategic roles and corruption. This coupled with external factors, central to which were the unequal economic relations between the developed Western economies and the Third World countries that is at the heart of global capitalism (Amin 1974). In concrete terms, these translated into the inability of the ISIs to compete with Western corporations that enjoyed economies of scale and high cost of capital goods like machineries. The combination of the internal and external factors led to the ISIs either functioning at low capacity or closing down altogether (Soludo and Mkandawire 1998).

This coincided with the African debt crisis that began in the 1970s when African states, having acquired large sums of debt from the IFIs to set up the ISIs and finance social and infrastructural projects, were unable to repay their debts. The high cost of servicing the debts contributed in no small measure. Unable to service or repay their debt, the indebted countries needed further loans to continue providing essential services like healthcare, education and potable water. The IFIs, as the creditors, imposed an onerous set of conditions to continue providing the credit lines that the countries desperately needed. Structural adjustment programmes were sold by the IFIs to the countries as a solution to their indebtedness and a necessary condition for further loans from the IFIs. SAPs required the indebted countries, among other things, to reduce and, in some instances, halt public spending on healthcare, education and potable water. They were also required to retrench workers from the public sector and to privatise the ISIs that had until then been state owned. They had to liberalise trade, devalue their currencies and do away with the tariffs that were then a universal practice of states to protect their industries and economies from the effects of dumping of cheap goods by foreign firms, especially large Western corporations (Adesina et al. 2006).

The implementation of SAPs had a drastic effect on the African population, especially the poor. Mass impoverishment became the norm. In Ghana, where SAPs were first implemented, the effects of SAPS were exacerbated by a drought that left many people hungry and in need of food aid. The desperation reached such an extent that people had to queue for raw corn dough. Kwashiokor, a condition of protein deficiency, became widespread in children (Adesina et al. 2006).

With few exceptions, the gains against illiteracy were rolled back by the introduction of tuition fees as part of the SAP package. While education was made a right in the immediate post-colonial period, the introduction of tuition fees again made education the privilege it had been under colonialism. Girl child education in particular suffered under the weight of a patriarchal arrangement which saw the education of boys as more important. Where a family could only afford to educate one out of, say, two children, they chose to educate the male child instead of the female. Decreasing state subvention led to the educational systems of many countries collapsing, with teachers and academics going for months without pay. Learners had to learn without desks and chairs (Soludo and Mkandawire 1998).

The healthcare system on the continent experienced strain due to the proliferation of primary diseases and a surge in infant and maternal mortality. The poor could no longer access proper healthcare with the introduction of user fees. Hospital beds were limited, and harrowing experiences of women giving birth on the floor of hospitals due to lack of beds or accident victims dying outside hospitals because they were unable to pay upfront for treatment became commonplace. In the absence of employment, the informal sector experienced an upsurge, with attendant precarity. Medical practitioners left Africa in large numbers to go to Europe and the United States in particular (Adepoju 1993; Chipeta 1993; Mwega and Kabubo 1993). That Africa is yet to recover from this crisis is evinced by very high doctor-to-patient ratio and a staggering statistic showing that there are more

Malawian doctors practising in the state of New York in the United States than in the whole of Malawi.

SAPs unleashed a generalised crisis of social reproduction on the African continent. A combination of strategies was devised by groups, families and individuals to cope with the crisis. Just like the medical practitioners who left Africa, ordinary people also resorted to migration within and outside of Africa. Africa post-SAPs has become very unequal, with numbers of the rich growing while those of the poor have increased. An important aspect of social and political organisation in Africa after SAPs is the question of belonging and a rising social difference. Capital sharply differentiates people socially and economically and obfuscates stratification by focusing on ethnic difference as the key question in society (Garba 2012).

## Nigeria: ethnic and religious difference as mechanisms of accumulation

British colonialism systematically limited the opportunities for the formation of local capital to avoid competition for the colonial economic interest. Economic policy under British colonialism in Nigeria was a typical 'dependent colonial economy where economic opportunities were severely constricted – where capital was scarce, indigenous entrepreneurial experience slight, private enterprise foreign dominated, and poverty pervasive and extreme' (Diamond 1983: 462).

The colonial state maximised capital accumulation through the export of cash crops produced by peasants, taxes imposed on individuals and the profits of marketing boards that paid local producers less than the market price for their produce (Usman 1979). The exclusion of local capital that Diamond refers to previously made it impossible for significant local capital to evolve under colonialism.

The tables subsequently show how much the colonial state generated from peasants and on taxes between the years 1954 and 1961.

*Table 2.1* Colonial accumulation in the form of taxes levied on farmers in Nigeria between 1954 and 1961.

| | *£ million* |
|---|---|
| Marketing Board Surplus | 118.0 |
| Export Duties | 110.0 |
| Import Duties | 327.2 |
| Income Tax | 100.9 |
| Company Tax | 34.57 |
| Total | 6090.67 |

Source: Usman 1979.

*Table 2.2* Some exported agricultural goods from Nigeria between 1954 and 1961.

| *Year* | *Qty. Exported (in tonnes)* | *Value per tonne in £* | *Gross earnings in £ m* |
|---|---|---|---|
| Cocoa | | | |
| 1954 | 98,000 | 401.00 | 39.3 |
| 1961 | 184,000 | 183.00 | 33.7 |
| Groundnuts | | | |
| 1954 | 428,000 | 70 | 30.0 |
| 1959 | 497,000 | 55 | 27.5 |
| 1961 | 494,000 | 65 | 32.2 |
| Cotton | | | |
| 1954 | 260,000 | 283 | 7.4 |
| 1961 | 46,000 | 240 | 11.1 |

Source: Usman 1979.

With the end of colonialism and the opening up of opportunities for local capital formation, accumulation took a decisive turn, culminating in the crisis years that began in the late 1970s to 1980s. Like other African countries, Nigeria, which has the biggest economy on the African continent, had to embark on SAPs in the 1980s. The country had a protracted debate in the lead-up to its adoption of SAPs. Labour unions, academics' unions, student groups and professional associations were overwhelmingly opposed to SAPs. In spite of the opposition, the state went ahead and implemented SAPS, with the attendant result that civil servants were retrenched, industries closed down and tuition and user fees were introduced to schools and hospitals, respectively. The beneficiaries of SAPS happened to be multinational corporations that benefitted from market liberalisation and their local Nigerian partners, who acquired stakes in privatised formerly state-owned enterprises. The narrowing of employment opportunities and sources of livelihood disproportionately affected the poor, especially the youth. In spite of the size of its economy, the country has gone and continues to go through the collection of crises that accompanied SAPs across Africa: inadequate access to healthcare and increases in preventable disease, collapse of educational facilities and lack of potable drinking water (Usman 2006).

Given that Nigeria has a history of the instrumentalisation of ethnic and religious identities under British colonialism, the legacy of which it continues to reel under, political contestations and mobilisations lend themselves to ethnic and religious interpretations and manipulation. The post-SAPs period gave rise to the intensification of the politicisation of ethnicity and religion by competing political and economic interests casting themselves as defenders of one shared ethnic or religious interest or another. These forms of mobilisation find fertile ground in a setting where the state has proven incapable of delivering on its 'promise of independence' and therefore suffers a crisis of legitimacy. The economic system that the state protects and which is responsible for the social crisis is made opaque by resorting to ethnic and religious 'others' as the problem. Timeless histories of ethnic groups that are in reality recent social phenomena are produced just as corporations and their local collaborators who function as merchants of ethnicity secure new state contracts, buy up more state-owned enterprises or rake in oil well profits while the poor of various ethnic and religious affiliations continue to lack access to the basic necessities that they require to live decent lives. This is brought out vividly by Diamond:

> state power is the engine of class formation; the competition for it and the manipulation of it represent fundamentally class, not ethnic, action. Hence, the failure of Nigeria's first attempt at liberal democracy must be understood in light of the distinctive interaction among ethnicity, in an ethnically plural and modernising society; class action, in a dependent and highly underdeveloped economy; and political competition, in a democratic polity in which elite competition required mass mobilisation. To understand the tragedy of Nigeria in the 1960s, we must understand the emergent class forces that expressed ethnicity in political terms and used it for class ends.
>
> (Diamond 1983: 460)

So pervasive is the hold of the ethnic difference hypothesis that state policy mirrors it. Indigeneity becomes formal state policy such that admission to universities follows something called the catchment area principle. Universities give priority to applicants who are indigenes of the federal state[6] in which the university is located. To be indigenous to a state, one has to prove that their ancestors are natives of the state. A person and their parents may both be born in a state, but they can still not be considered natives if they do not belong to 'tribes' that were categorised from the colonial era as natives. This definition of belonging is drawn out of the colonial theory of African societies as opposed to the living reality, where every state in Nigeria is made up of people from all across the country who are living there and making livelihoods (Usman 2006).

Though the traditional class structures and the processes of class formation differed sharply between north and south in Nigeria, they shared one feature with diffuse implications for social and political development. In both southern and northern Nigeria, class structure and individual class standing came to be determined essentially by political power (Diamond 1983: 462)

## South Africa: xenophobia as stratification

South Africa ranks among the most unequal societies in the world. While there is a great deal of inequality of income between high earners and low earners, wealth inequality in the country is greater than income inequality.

The top 10% of the population owns 71% of household wealth, while the bottom 60% accounts for 7% (World Bank 2018). This 10% now includes a black capitalist class that accounts for 23% of the national stock exchange (Africa Check 2017).

Capital accumulation in South Africa under Apartheid was mediated by race. Race continues to delimit access to resources for the working class and the poor. In addition to race, nationality has become an important determinant of access to resources for the poor and the working class who happen to have no citizenship. If the question under Apartheid was who was an African in order to exploit her, today it still remains relevant in capital labour relations. An additional question has been added: Who is not South African? – in order to discriminate against her and exploit her. Under Apartheid, those designated 'African' occupied the lowest rungs of the Apartheid pyramid of Whites, Indians and Coloureds. The end of formal Apartheid did not bring about the creation of difference for the purpose of exploitation. Black South Africans continue to make up the highly exploited working classes and the teeming unemployed (Sitas and Lorgat 2010).

Apartheid spatial segregation, inequality and labour relations are still present in South Africa. Within the context of an increasingly deracialised capitalist class (Seekings and Nattrass 2015), a line of division between citizens and non-citizens has become central in the creation of difference. An anti-foreigner stance, in particular against working-class and poor migrants from other parts of Africa, facilities capital accumulation by dividing up the working class along national identities. Capital accumulation by the new black capitalist and the established white capitalists is couched as 'national interest' that must be protected by all, including the South African working class and the poor, against the migrant working class and the poor.

As the subsequent table shows, in addition to the black (direct and indirect) ownership of shares and the white ownership is a substantial foreign ownership of the economy by European and North American corporations. That ownership is not frowned upon. It is encouraged. The state actively pursues foreign stakes in the economy through initiatives to attract foreign direct investments (FDIs). Capital is not only encouraged to move, it is persuaded to move. Workers and the poor, on the other hand, are differentiated based on nationality, and the non-nationals are othered and discriminated against.

| *Group* | *2013* |
|---|---|
| Direct black investment | 10% |
| Indirect black investment | 13% |
| White investment | 22% |
| Foreign investment | 39% |
| Unanalysed portion | 16% |

Source: Johannesburg Stock Exchange, quoted in *Africa Check*.

Employers actively use nationality and stereotypes about people based on origins to differentiate among workers. Employers who pay non-South African workers below the minimum wage say, 'foreigners [Africans] are hardworking unlike the lazy ones [Black South Africans] here'. These and similar words are uttered by employers of all races to foreign African workers as a way of winning their loyalty. Some employers acting upon this stereotype make it a point to employ mainly non-South Africans. The result is the generation of another stereotype, this time by local South African workers who feel aggrieved by their exclusion from employment and decry what they see as 'foreigners taking our jobs' (Hlatshwayo and Choudry 2015).

The South African state is active in managing xenophobia's accumulation by making it difficult for working-class Africans to obtain the necessary documents to live and work in the country. The absence of documents renders them vulnerable to super-exploitation by employers. By creating a layer of highly vulnerable workforce, the state exploits a group of workers for capital whose lack of citizenship means they are unable to negotiate better working conditions for their labour power. This was the Apartheid strategy of withdrawing rights in order to guarantee labour supply. By denying economic citizenship to the vast majority of poor working-class Black South Africans and civic citizenship to many working-class migrants from the rest of the African continent, it makes race and nationality instruments of capital accumulation (Garba 2012). The importance of the politicisation of race and nationality by the state lies partly in the fact that for sections of the black elite, the state remains the primary vehicle of accumulation. Akin to Shivji's study on the role of the bureaucratic bourgeoisie in the economic structure of Tanzania under so-called 'African Socialism' – although with local, historical and contemporary specificities – the blacks located in the state bureaucracy or close to it need to constantly legitimise their failings by pointing to the immigrant and other 'outsiders' as the source of social ills.

## Conclusion: the capital's contradictory generation of difference

In both Nigeria and South Africa, the poor and the working classes see their living standards drop while their aspirations dwindle in the face of a generalised precarity that accompanied SAPs and neoliberal economic direction, respectively. Workers in South Africa are having to go on strike alongside workers that they would ordinarily discriminate against based on national difference (Garba 2015). When ordinary people in Nigeria lament the insecurity brought about by state corruption and lack of public amenities like water and electricity, they realise that they share similar predicaments with people of a different ethnicity and religion.

It is not uncommon in South Africa for politicians and ordinary people to explain away the lack of adequate housing by pointing to migrants as the culprits who take away houses that should go to them. In their struggle for housing, they do so with foreign workers on their side. Through struggle, they see that it is not the case that foreign workers have all the houses: The reality is that there is inadequate housing in the country. In the process of struggle, barriers tend to be broken (Garba 2015).

Street vendors and traders in Lagos and in Cape Town are made up of people from all ethnicities and nationalities. On many occasions, they compete with each other, and origins could play a role in such competitions. In other instances, they fix prices, sell wares for each other when the other is not around and struggle against law enforcement agents that are trying to get them off the streets (Garba 2015).

Even on the question of xenophobia, South Africans, workers and ordinary people have organised campaigns against xenophobic attacks in urban townships which see the looting of kiosks owned by foreigners and physical attacks on foreigners. In the Township of Langa in Cape Town, many African migrants speak of having been defended in the past by their South African neighbours. So organised have the defences become that there have been no xenophobic attacks in Langa since 2009. There have been a number of such attacks in other parts of Cape Town over the past couple of years. Do these acts of solidarity point to a contradictory effect that capital's division is having on workers' relations with one another based on nationality?

The idea of difference in Africa has been a political project tied to the penetration of capital and its further accumulation. From the colonial moment, difference was utilised by the state-cum-capital nexus. The definition of who was a native and who belonged to a particular segment of the natives and was therefore entitled to live on a given piece of land was shaped by the colonial demand for labour, resources and markets. Colonial statecraft and accumulation invented and managed social difference where necessary. The idea of tribe as the core of African society was deployed to freeze a social reality of fluid identities where patterns of residency and occupation conferred identity and not fixed and unchanging ideas of who belongs and who does not belong.

With varying degrees of success, the post-colonial state in Africa attempted to overcome the legacy of the colonial manipulation of difference through nation building and the creation of a unitary citizenship. With the crisis of the 1970s and given the lurking legacy of the colonial construction of difference, the politicisation and 'capitalisation' of difference have come back centre stage. Nigeria provides an example of the 'capitalisation' of difference, while South Africa points to the 'capitalisation' of nationality on the continent. There are countermovements that challenge these divisions. These happen in the course of working-class and popular struggles where the boundaries that appear tight and firm are broken down in struggle when people come to see what they have in common as opposed to concentrating on their differences.

## Notes

1 The chapter has benefited from a fellowship at the Merian Institute for Advanced Studies (MIASA), University of Ghana, Legon.
2 Societies in East Africa and West Africa have a long history of human contacts with parts of South East Asia and the Arab world prior to colonialism. Zanzibar in East Africa is a combination of the Afro-Asiatic world from the make-up of its population, the culinary heritage and sociopolitical organisation.
The spread of Islam on the African continent is closely linked to the trans-Saharan trade which connected North Africa and sub-Saharan Africa to Asia.
The presence of groups in India that trace their origins to the African continent is an instance of the Afro-Asiatic connections before colonialism.
3 The explanation put forward by the Dar School had variants to it. However, the broad tenor of the argument was in keeping with the then prevailing dependency theory that emerged out of the Latin American experience.
4 This view is popularised in more sophisticated versions in accounts of neopatrimonialism and the politics of the belly. This view believes that acts of corruption and abuse of public resources for private gains constitute a long unbroken chain in African societies. Under this view, the effect and legacy of colonialism on the structure of the state and the relationship between the state and populace are insignificant. See Bayart J.F. 1993. *The State in Africa: The Politics of the Belly*. London and New York: Longman.
5 The poll tax was a specified amount that every adult had to pay. In northern Nigeria, it was paid by an adult male.
*Haraji* is the Hausa word for poll tax.
6 Nigeria has a federal system of government with 36 states and the federal capital.

## Bibliography

Adepoju, A. 1993. 'Introduction', in A. Adepoju (ed.) *The Impacts of Structural Adjustment on the Population of Africa: Health, Employment, Higher Education*. London: James Currey; New Hampshire: Heinemann.

Adepoju, A. 2008. *Migration in Sub-Saharan Africa*. Uppsala: Nordiska Afrikainstitutet.

Adesina, J., Y. Graham and A. Olukoshi. 2006. *African and Development Challenges in the New Millennium: The NEPAD Debate*. London, New York and Dakar, Pretoria: Zed Books, CODESRIA and UNISA Press.

Africa Check. 2017. 'Guide: Black Ownership of SA Stock Exchange – What We Know', August 29, 2019. Available at: https://africacheck.org/factsheets/guide-much-sas-stock-exchange-black-owned-know/.

Ake, C. 1981. *Political Economy of Africa*. New York: Longman.

Amadiume, I. 1987. *Male Daughters, Female Husbands: Gender and Sex in an African Society*. London: Zed books.

Amin, S. 1974. *Accumulation on a World Scale: A Critique of Underdevelopment Theory*. New York: Monthly Review Press.

Asamoa, A. 2001. *A Guide to the Study of Social Transformation in Sub Saharan Africa*. Accra: Woeli Press.

Bayart, J.F. 1993. *The State in Africa: The Politics of the Belly*. London and New York: Longman.
Chinweizu, I. 1975. *The West and the Rest of Us: White Predator, Black Slavers and the African Elite*. New York: Random House.
Chipeta, C. 1993. 'Malawi', in A. Adepoju (ed.) *The Impacts of Structural Adjustment on the Population of Africa: Health, Employment, Higher Education*. London: James Currey; New Hampshire: Heinemann.
De Haas, Hein. 2010. 'Migration and Development: A Theoretical Perspective', *International Migration Review*, 44 (1): 1–38.
Diamond, L. 1983. 'Class, Ethnicity, and the Democratic State: Nigeria, 1950–66', *Comparative Studies in Society and History*, 23 (3): 457–89.
Frank, A.G. 1966. 'The Development of Underdevelopment', *Monthly Review*, September.
Frank, A.G. 1969. *Capitalism and Underdevelopment in Latin America*. New York: Monthly Review Press.
Fukuyam, F. 2006. *The End of History and the Last Man*. New York: Free Press.
Garba, M.F. 2012. 'Of Livelihoods and Belonging – Burger or Amakwerekwere?: African Diasporas in Germany and South Africa', MA thesis submitted to the Faculty of Philosophy, University of Freiburg.
Garba, M.F. 2015. 'Migration and Inequality: African Diasporas in Germany, South Africa and India', in A. Lenger and F. Schumacher (eds.) *Understanding the Dynamics of Global Inequality: Social Exclusion, Power Shift and Structural Changes*, pp. 67–86. Munich: Springer.
Goldman, M. 2005. *The World Bank and the Struggle for Social Justice in the Age of Globalisation*. New Haven and London: Yale University Press.
Harvey, D. 2007. *A Brief History of Neoliberalism*. Oxford: University Press.
Hlatshwayo, M. 2015. 'Xenophobia, Resilience, and Resistance of Immigrant Workers in South Africa: Collective and Individual Responses', in A. Choudry and M. Hlatshwayo (eds.) *Migrant Workers Struggles Today*, pp. 21–42. London: Pluto Press.
Klein, N. 2008. *The Shock Doctrine: The Rise of Disaster Capitalism*. New York: Picador.
Mafeje, A. 1972. 'The Ideology of Tribalism', *Journal of Modern African Studies*, 9 (2): 253–261.
Mamdani, M. 1996. *Citizen and Subject: Contemporary Africa and the Legacy of Late Colonialism*. New Jersey: Princeton University Press; Cape Town: David Phillip; London: James Currey.
Mamdani, M. 2012. *Define and Rule: Native as Political Identity*. Johannesburg: Wits University Press.
Manuh, T. 2005. 'Introduction', in T. Manuh (ed.) *International Migration and Development in Contemporary Ghana and West Africa*. Accra: University of Ghana Institute of African Studies.
Marfaing, L. 2013. 'Today, I Would Never Go to Europe: Mobility for Resources and Local Development', in Alesandro Triulzi and Robert Lawrence McKenzie (eds.) *Long Journeys, African Migrations on the Road*. Leiden and London: BRILL.
Mazon, P.M. and R. Steingrover. 2005. *Not so Plain as Black and White: Afro-German Culture and History, 1890–2000*. Rochester: University Press.
Mkandawire, T. and C.C. Soludo. 2003. 'Introduction', in T. Mkandawire and C. C Soludo (eds.) *Our Continent, Our Future: African Voices on Structural*

*Adjustments*. Dakar: CODESRIA; Trenton, New Jersey: Africa World Press; Ottawa: International Development Research Centre.

Morawska, E. 1990. 'The Sociology and Historiography of Immigration', in Virginia Yans-McLaughlin (ed.) *Immigration Reconsidered: History, Sociology, and Politics*. New York: Oxford University Press.

Mwanawina, I. 1993. 'Zambia', in A. Adepoju (ed.) *The Impacts of Structural Adjustment on The Population of Africa: Health, Employment, Higher Education*. UNFPA. London: James Currey; New Hampshire: Heinemann.

Mwega, F.M. and J.W. Kabubo. 1993. 'Kenya', in A. Adepoju (ed.) *The Impacts of Structural Adjustment on the Population of Africa: Health, Employment, Higher Education*. UNFPA. London: James Currey; New Hampshire: Heinemann.

Niane, D.T. 1984. 'Relationships and Exchanges Among the Different Regions', in D.T. Niane (ed.) *General History of Africa from the Twelfth to the Sixteenth Century*. Berkeley, CA: University of California Press.

Nyamjoh, F. 2006. *Insiders and Outsiders: Citizenship and Xenophobia in Contemporary Southern Africa*. Dakar and London: CODESRIA and ZED books.

Olukoshi, O.O., Y. Graham and J.O. Adesina. 2006. 'Introduction', in O.O. Olukoshi, Y. Graham and J.O. Adesina (eds.) *Africa and Development Challenges in the New Millennium: The NEPAD Debate*. Dakar: CODESRIA.

Osoba, S. 1978. 'The Deepening Crisis of the Nigerian Bourgeoisie', *Review of African Political Economy*, 13: 63–77.

Oyewumi, O. 1997. *The Invention of Women: Making an African Sense of Western Gender Discourses*. Minneapolis, MN: University of Minnesota Press.

Piore, M.J. 1979. *Birds of Passage: Migrant Labour in Industrial Societies*. Cambridge: Cambridge University Press.

Rodney, W. 1973 *How Europe Underdeveloped Africa*. Dar es Salaam: Tanzania Publishing House.

Sassen, S. 1991. *The Global City*. London, New York and Tokyo, Princeton: Princeton University Press.

Seekings, J and N. Nattrass. 2015. *Policy, Politics and Poverty in South Africa*. New York: Palgrave Macmillan and UNRISg.

Shivji, G.I. 1976. *Class Struggles in Tanzania*. New York: Monthly Review Press.

Sitas, A. and A. Lorgat. 2010. 'The Human and Social Dynamics in the Development Grand Challenge: Mapping the Third African Diaspora', Working Paper series No. 1.

Sjaastad, L.A. 1962. 'The Costs and Returns of Human Migration', *Journal of Political Economy*, 70S: 80–93.

Sowa, N.K. 1993. 'Ghana', in A. Adepoju (ed.) *The Impacts of Structural Adjustment on the Population of Africa: Health, Employment, Higher Education*. London: James Currey; New Hampshire: Heinemann.

Stark, O. 1991. *The Migration of Labour*. Blackwell: Cambridge and Oxford.

Usman, Y.B. 1979. *For the Liberation of Nigeria: Essays and Lectures, 1969–1978*. London: New Beacon Books.

Usman, Y.B. 1984. *Debates on the Nigerian Economic Crisis*. Benin City: University of Benin.

Usman, Y.B. 2004. *What Exactly Is Globalisation*. Zaria: Centre for Democratic Development Research and Training.

Usman, Y.B. 2006. *Beyond Fairy Tales: Selected Historical Writings*. Zaria: Abdullahi Smith Centre for Historical Research.

Van der Walt, L. 2018. 'Beyond "White Monopoly Capital": Who Owns South Africa?', *South African Labour Bulletin*, 39 (3): 39–42.

Wallerstein, I. 1974. *The Modern World System: Capitalist Agriculture and the Origins of the European World Economy in the Sixteenth Century*. New York: Academic Press.

World Bank. 2018. *Overcoming Poverty and Inequality in South Africa: An Assessment of Drivers, Constraints and Opportunities*. Washington, DC: World Bank Publications.

Zack-Williams, A. 2018. 'The State and Accumulation in Africa', *Review of African Political Economy*, 45 (158): 515–21.

Zeleza, P.T. 2008. 'Africa's Contemporary Global Migrations: Patterns, Perils, and Possibilities', *Journal of Global Initiatives: Policy, Pedagogy, Perspective*, 3 (1): 33–56.

Zeleza, P.T. 2014. 'Africa's Struggles for Decolonisation: From Achebe to Mandela', *Research in African Literatures*, 45 (4): 121–39.

# Part 2

# Capital, class and community

# 3 Global capitalism, social classes and sociocultures

*Boike Rehbein*

This chapter explores the relation between capitalism and domination. It argues that capitalism is merely one particular institutional form or medium of the reproduction of social hierarchies. The hierarchies are more fundamental than capitalism. However, they are partly transformed by capitalism into a hierarchy of social classes, which is invisible, since all citizens of a capitalist nation state are supposed to compete on a level playing field and all inequality is supposed to result from this competition. In order to understand the relation between capitalism and inequality, we need to distinguish between capitalism and the order of domination as well as between the global and national frameworks. With the capitalistic reorganisation of society, the precapitalist orders of domination do not disappear. They partly persist and partly shape the configuration of social classes. In a capitalist society, the hierarchy of social classes becomes more relevant than other dimensions of inequality, and the dominant classes have to reproduce their position via capitalism. The dominant classes also dominate and utilise the State. They are bound to their respective nation state both in their actions and in their social positions. At the same time, capitalism globalises and the nation states seek to improve their global position. The chapter will enquire more closely into this relation between nation states, global capitalism and dominant classes.

The ideas presented in this chapter are based on a research programme which involves empirical studies on inequality in more than ten countries around the globe (c.f. Jodhka et al. 2017). In terms of theory, it is based on Pierre Bourdieu's (1984) concepts of capital, habitus and practice, as well as Ernst Cassirer's (1997) notion of the symbol and Charles Taylor's (1989) sources of the self. Empirically, we employ a qualitative questionnaire, which has been adapted to the particularities of the different societies and makes comparisons possible at the same time. The questions deal with the life course and symbolic classification. So far, we have conducted and interpreted more than 2,000 interviews and added quantitative surveys in several countries. The material forms the background of the argument but is only briefly mentioned in this chapter with regard to Brazil and Germany to clarify a few points.

The following argument first distinguishes economic from social class and then deals in more detail with the notion of social class. The second section studies the emergence of social classes and their relation to precapitalist hierarchies. In the following section, this relation is illustrated with regard to our empirical findings from different world regions. It summarises a few relevant results concerning Germany and compares them with sociocultures and social classes in Brazil and Laos. The final section links the national class structures and especially the position of the dominant social classes to global capitalism.

## The capitalist class

The prevailing idea of inequality in capitalist societies is that the rich have made it. According to the tradition of economic liberalism, we all start with equal chances in life, and whoever is smart and industrious becomes successful and rich (Friedman 1962). This story is reproduced by mainstream media and research. With regard to inequality, they usually present us diagrams and tables illustrating the distribution of wealth or income (World Inequality Report 2018). There is a giant cake, and everybody gets a share, however small it may be. Billionaires, labourers and unemployed appear in the same category and are compared according to the same criteria.

According to many critical accounts of capitalism, wealth is concentrated in a small group of people, who get a head start in the competition for success. The wealthy do not merely own the lion's share of economic capital, they also pass it on to their children, who can invest it for profit, while the rest of the population has to labour in order to accumulate any wealth at all (Bourdieu 1984). This view of capitalism is more realistic than that of liberalism, but it still misses an important point made by Karl Marx (1953). According to Marx, the rest of the population does not own any economic capital at all. We may own means of consumption, a life insurance, a house we live in, a car and even a boat. But none of this can be invested as capital for profit. Even if we own a few company shares, we have no influence over the company's policies and profits.

It is crucial to understand that economic capital is monopolised by a very small economic class, which we may call, following Marx, the capitalist class. The majority of the world population does not own any means that can be used as *capital*, even if they own goods or money. The overwhelming majority of human beings own very little, and those who do own something consume what they own. A well-to-do household owns a house and a car and uses its disposable income for items such as food, insurance, education and entertainment. Seventy-one percent of the world population owns wealth worth less than USD 10,000, and another 21 percent less than 100,000 (Stierli et al. 2015: 26). In Western countries, USD 100,000 is not even enough to buy a house. Ninety-two percent of the world population does not own enough wealth even to be classified as well-to-do consumers.

If we specify who actually owns economic capital that can be invested for profit, we understand Piketty's (2014) claim of an extreme concentration of capital in the hands of very few. However, Piketty and many critical voices of our times estimate their number at 1 percent of the world population. Actually, the number does not even reach 0.1 percent, as I will try to show subsequently.

The economic class of the capitalists disposes of around half of global wealth, which comprises all financial and non-financial assets (Shorrocks et al. 2016: 12). Of the global wealth, only a fraction can be used as economic capital. Therefore, it is safe to say that the economic class of capitalists owns the entire economic capital in the strict sense. According to the Global Wealth Report, 33 million individuals, or 0.7 percent of the world population, own wealth of more than 1 million USD (Shorrocks et al. 2016: 24). All millionaires taken together do not even reach Piketty's famous 1 percent. Of the millionaires, only 4 million own wealth worth more than 5 million USD and 141,000 more than 50 million (ibid.). Most millionaires in the richest countries are still merely consumers and not owners of capital. They have a nice house, an expensive car and a boat. These objects can be worth a million USD or more in the richest countries. Therefore, we have to exclude the majority of people owning less than about 3 million USD in the global North from the group of potential capitalists. This leaves us with less than 0.1 percent of the world population as actual capitalists, most of whom are citizens of Europe and North America. Up to 2 percent of the US population and 0.5 percent of the German population fall into this category but much less in the global South. These 0.1 percent of the world population own virtually all the economic capital in the strict sense. The rest of the population competes for means of consumption but, in most cases, not for capital. Both groups are playing a different game. To confound them in one single table or diagram of wealth distribution is misleading and fulfils the function of liberalist propaganda (see, e.g. World Inequality Report 2018).

Actually, the capitalist class is likely to be even smaller than 0.1 percent of the world population. A large chunk of invested capital does not yield any substantial economic power unless it is coupled with other forms of capital and a link to global capital. The owner of a medium-size enterprise worth a few million USD does not compete with the major global corporations – and if he is successful, he is bought out and his enterprise is traded at the stock exchange. We should exclude him from the capitalist class as well. An approximate identification of the capitalist class can be reached if we look for the owners of the large corporations. Vitali et al. (2011) have identified 43,000 transnational corporations (TNCs). Of these, 15,491 have mutual ownership ties, and 295 form the core of a network of 'corporate control'. Within the core, three-quarters of the corporations' shares are held by other TNCs of the core. One hundred forty-seven of these hold 40 percent of all TNC shares. The authors conclude that these 147 TNCs control the global economy and themselves. Actually, they control about a quarter of the global GDP. This means that global production for the formal consumer markets is controlled by less than 200 private companies.

However, few of these TNCs are owned by identifiable individuals. Private investors appear less and less as the major shareholders of these large companies. They invest via financial institutions. Some of these institutions require a minimum investment of millions of USD. This restricts the circle of possible investors to a very small group – which is recruited overwhelmingly from the group of capitalists in the sense of the 0.1 percent discussed in the preceding paragraphs.

This group is an economic class because their members are defined by their possession of economic capital. It is important to distinguish this class from people who make a lot of money for a brief period of time, as well as from top managers. Not everybody who accumulates a large amount of wealth automatically becomes a capitalist. The winner of a lottery, a football star or a drug dealer usually lose all of their money within a few years and almost certainly within their lifetime. They invest very little of their wealth as economic capital.

More contentious is the distinction between the capitalists and managers of capitalism. According to Sklair (2002), Harvey (2005) and Lind (2017), the dominant class of capitalism consists of the CEOs of the powerful TNCs mentioned previously. The owners of capital take a backseat. However, the top managers are either members of the capitalist class themselves, such as the board members of the major German carmakers, or they are mere employees who may make a lot of money and exert a lot of influence for a while but can lose their job and their influence almost any time. I claim that only the actual owners of economic capital are members of the capitalist class and that they are economically much more powerful than the group of managers. The remainder of the chapter will try to corroborate this point.

## Social class and sociocultures

The generally accepted accounts of wealth, capitalism and class agree on the foundations of the game, especially that capitalism is a competition for wealth. I concede that this characterises the surface of capitalism and that this surface is the defining characteristic of a capitalist economy. However, I argue that domination is more fundamental than the capitalist economy and that the structures of domination are only transformed but not shattered or reshuffled by capitalism. Domination refers to the capability of a group of people to impose their will on others (Weber 1972). Capitalism is an integral part of the contemporary regime of domination – but only a part and not even a fundamental part.

The basic argument by the proponents of managerial capitalism and an economistic interpretation of capitalism is rooted in historical Marxism and the idea that the entrepreneurs of industrialism in Europe staged a revolution, toppled the nobility and became the new dominant class (Marx and

Engels 1964; c.f. Harvey 2005). I rather claim that the successful entrepreneurs merged with the feudal nobility and formed a new class, which was an alliance of the old nobility and the new money. Many families that can be identified as members of the dominant class in Germany trace their dominant social position back to the nineteenth century, some to the Thirty Years' War and a few even further back (Rehbein et al. 2015). Many of the richest families in Germany are old nobility, such as the Thurn und Taxis (who can be traced back to the thirteenth century), the princely family of Sachsen-Coburg or the descendants of the Prussian kings. Many other made their fortunes in the nineteenth century and then intermarried with the old nobility, such as the Thyssen family. At the same time, the carpenters, blacksmiths and other rural craftsmen became industrial workers in their field of expertise during the industrial revolution (Lange-Vester 2007). This transition is partly described in real time by Marx and Engels (1964). In many countries of the global South, the capitalist transformation is not yet complete, and it is happening mostly without bourgeois revolutions. The next section of the chapter will show that the dominant classes in these countries consist mainly of old elites, leaders of the independence movement and capitalists.

Even in Europe, the bourgeois revolutions were not complete restarts of history, turning all social structures upside down. They only allowed a few capitalists access to the dominant segment of society, generated a class society and established the bourgeoisie as a new social class – below the dominant class. In all the countries we have studied, many of the leading precapitalist family names still appear at the top of society today. This is even true for the socialist nation state of Laos. The structure of this type of society is not intelligible if we apply imprecise and random notions of class, which use economic indicators as the sole criteria to determine class. The purely theoretical and deductive approach to class applied by Marxists and Bourdieusians defining the top class as bourgeoisie does not help either, since it obscures the genealogy and composition of each class. Bourdieu (1984) merely claims that there are three classes in France, but he does not state any criteria for their distinction. Each class is supposed to have a different total amount of capital than the others – but which amount of which types of capital remains unclear. Marx and Engels offer an empirical approach to social class in the *Communist Manifesto* (1964), and we can trace the history of their four classes to the present, but at the end of *The Capital* (1953), only capital and labour are left.

First, we need to distinguish social from economic class. The following argument is based on a theoretical and empirical definition of social class, which aims at explaining hierarchies in capitalist societies. I define social class as a tradition line (following Thompson 1963) with a common culture which reproduces itself from one generation to the next by passing on relevant capital (in Bourdieu's sense) and symbolically distinguishing itself from other classes. The culture of a social class is embodied in the habitus and serves as the marker of distinction between classes. Along with the fundamental traits of the habitus, parents pass on social networks, prestigious objects, the family name and economic capital to their children. While economic capital is only one characteristic of a social class, which is statistically likely to be present, it only suffices to define the economic class. A labourer may get rich through the lottery, and the member of an old business family may lose his money, but both still remain members of their social class because they share most other characteristics with their peers, especially the culture.

This concept can be operationalised by establishing the relative limits of social mobility: Empirically, we can observe that the boundaries of social class are rarely crossed. Individuals can be socially mobile for brief periods of time, but it almost never happens that an entire family changes its social class position for good. Class lines are seemingly impossible to cross. There is plenty of social mobility within and between the generations, but it stops at certain boundaries. These are the limits of a social class, which constitute symbolic and moral dividing lines between groups of people in a capitalist society.

Social class only explains inequality in nation states with a long capitalist past. In other societies, many precapitalist structures of inequality persist that have to be interpreted with reference to history, culture and social configuration. I refer to a structure of inequality, which was developed in an earlier historical period of a particular society, as socioculture. An example from Europe would be guilds; an example from India would be caste. These persist up to this day, even though they are formally alien to capitalism and democracy. While their relevance decreases, the capitalist transformation opens up windows of social mobility when people migrate – socially and physically – from a precapitalist structure into the hierarchy of social classes.

The structures of inequality in a capitalist nation state can be explained as a combination of sociocultures and a hierarchy of social classes. While all precapitalist hierarchies tend to transform into social classes, they persist to a certain degree even after the capitalist transformation. The capitalist classes, however, emerge from precapitalist hierarchies as well. As relational categories, classes cannot be understood merely on the basis of capital but have to be viewed from the perspective of social practice as well. Many social practices are passed on through training from one generation to the next. Training, as demonstrated by Bourdieu (1984), largely takes place within the limits of social class. Thus, class cultures are reproduced from one generation to the next, and they comprise practices and ideas that are rooted in earlier and often precapitalist times.

In order to see the class structure of capitalist societies, it would be misguided to reduce the definition of class to the possession of economic capital. Even though the correlation between membership in the dominant social class and a large amount of economic capital is very strong, it remains statistical. Not every member of the upper class is excessively rich (all through his or her life). But he or she will certainly display most characteristics of his or her peers at any given point in time. Economic capital is only one (albeit important) indicator of social class. There is a large overlap between the economic class of capitalists and the dominant social class, but they are not identical.

In order to study social class, we have to look at a combination of indicators. First, only some combinations of factors occur in reality, while others are rare or even non-existent. For example, it is rare that the daughter of an unskilled labourer would get a PhD. And it is almost impossible that she would also be familiar with highbrow culture, own a large portfolio of stock shares and marry a capitalist. Second, we have to understand the totality of the possible combinations to explain the reproduction of social class. Third, we have to study the entire life-course of an individual and his or her ancestors. It is possible that a top manager could become unemployed and a football player rich – but usually only for a limited period of time. What almost never happens is the reproduction of this exceptional situation in the next generation.

To understand social class as a varying combination of evolving factors, our research team has applied a stochastic methodological approach. There are children of top managers without high school diplomas and children of unskilled labourers with PhDs. But there are no children that share no traits with their parents and their childhood peers. Any one characteristic of the particular social class may be absent, but it is empirically impossible that all or even most characteristics would be absent. Social class cannot be assessed by a fixed list of characteristics but involves a varying combination of changing characteristics. Wittgenstein subsumed this type of varying combinations under the concept of *family resemblance* (Wittgenstein 1984: aphorism 65). He illustrated the varying combination of changing characteristics with regard to a family: all members of a family have some traits in common, such as the nose or the intonation of certain words, but no two members share exactly the same characteristics. It is possible to explain many similarities, but it is not possible to reduce them to general categories. The same is true for the socially relevant characteristics of a social class.

Applying the concept of family resemblance, we can identify social classes in capitalist societies. We need to establish the forms of capital and habitus, as well as social practices that are relevant with regard to social inequality in a particular society. This is exactly what we did in our empirical research (Jodhka et al. 2017). Since the dividing lines between the social classes are limits to social mobility as well, it is not difficult to operationalise our concept of social class. We need to study a family over three or four generations, and we can put most of its members for all or most of their lifetimes into one social class. The 'black sheep' (or 'white sheep') of the family is put into the same class – unless they reproduce their odd position in the next generation. While these dividing lines and limits of social mobility are characteristic for social classes, precapitalist sociocultures do not have these dividing lines and may even be more open to social mobility. Mobility especially appears during the capitalist transformation, which took place in Europe between the sixteenth and nineteenth centuries but is still under way in many countries of the global South.

Our research reveals that not all inequality functions according to the limits between social classes but that social classifications and traditions of social practices are rooted in precapitalist hierarchies. Some of them persist beyond the capitalist transformation as sociocultures. In these cases, inequality is not constituted by capital and habitus but, for example, by family relations, honorary positions, patrimonial ties or caste. For example, membership in a guild is essential for economic possibilities in many segments of the German market, even though this market is supposedly free and equal.

## Social classes and sociocultures in three nation states

The following paragraphs seek to show how sociocultures and the capitalist transformation combine to form structures of inequality in three very different nation states, namely Brazil, Germany and Laos. They also compare these structures in order to find similarities and differences. Societies and nation states have different histories and precapitalist structures and therefore different sociocultures. This also means that they differ in their configurations of inequality, including the exact structure, number, cultures and internal compositions of social classes.

The boundaries between the classes are not only rarely crossed, they also have a symbolic value. Each social class has a different moral value from the perspective of the other classes and of general discourse. Therefore, the boundaries of social mobility are also moral dividing lines (c.f. Taylor 1989). In Germany, we found three cleavages or limits of social mobility between social classes. The most relevant cleavage is that between 'worthy' and 'unworthy' people – those who are classified by society as people who contribute something and those who do not. The 'worthy' people live above an invisible *line of dignity*. They are divided by a second line, the *line of expressivity*, into an upper class of people equipped for the leading functions in society and a lower class of the mere labourers. A tiny class aloof from any classification and competition constitutes the top of the hierarchy. *Aloofness* constitutes the third dividing line. The dividing lines between the classes are incorporated actively and passively. They are used to give or deny access to functions and institutions in society, to assess people, to choose a marriage partner and to guide one's own actions.

These four social classes constitute an ideal type of capitalist society, which is approximated by nation states with a long capitalist past, such as Germany or the United States. With regard to Germany, we can trace the four classes back to the *Communist Manifesto* (Marx and Engels 1964). The late Marx seemed to know only the two economic classes of capital and labour. However, the young Marx analysed Western Europe into four social classes. He argued that capitalist society consists not only of the classes of capitalists and labourers but also produces a 'reserve army' or even a class of 'superfluous' non-labourers. And he added that between capital and labour, an old middle class of shop-keepers, craftspeople, employees and privileged labourers partly persists from feudal times and partly develops with capitalism. Theodor Geiger (1932) found the same four classes in Germany of the 1920s but distinguished between the old middle class (small and medium entrepreneurs) and new middle class (highly qualified employees) below the capitalists. In our study of Germany (Rehbein et al. 2015), we were able to detect the successors of Geiger's five classes, but the old middle class has largely dissolved into the lower middle class.

In other words, contemporary Germany is divided into four social classes. We call them marginalised, fighters, established and aloof (Rehbein et al. 2015). The marginalised remain excluded from many sections of society, especially a stable, socially accepted and decently paid profession. They dispose of a small volume of all types of capital. The fighters basically constitute the labouring population. This class consists of two tradition lines, one rooted in Geiger's new middle class (or the skilled labour force investing in education) and one in Geiger's old (descending) middle class (or the petty bourgeoisie). We call them aspiring and defensive fighters. The established class occupies the leading functions and disposes of a large total amount of capital. The aloof are aloof in the sense that they are invisible to the rest of society and do not have to labour. They form the dominant class.

Wealth obviously differs between the classes. An almost surreal gap separates the aloof from the rest of the population. In order to understand the distinctions between the other classes, we have to classify the type of wealth owned. A lot of Germans own real estate, where they dwell themselves. Only the upper crust uses real estate as an investment. If we look at investment in shares or objects, the dividing lines become even more obvious. Forty-five percent of the established own real estate worth less than 500,000 Euros and 10 percent real estate worth more than that. Almost 90 percent of the marginalised, 73 percent of the defensive fighters and 64 percent of the aspiring fighters own no real estate. Sixty percent of the established, 49 percent of the aspiring fighters, 22 percent of the defensive fighters and 7 percent of the marginalised own stock shares. In contrast, all aloof own wealth worth more than 500,000 Euros in all categories.

Wealth alone cannot define social class, even though there is a strong correlation. In Germany, one's educational title defines social class at least as much as wealth. This correlation cannot be observed in Brazil or Laos. An educational degree increases with social class in Germany. In addition, a higher educational degree strongly correlates with competences and preferences in the field of high culture – Bourdieu's cultural capital. All aloof and most established have learned to play a musical instrument in their parental home. If we focus on the correlation between educational degree and musical instrument, the picture becomes even clearer. None of those who did not finish school have learned to play an instrument, while almost all of those with a PhD acquired this skill in their childhood.

Our survey shows that the foundation of social capital is laid in childhood as well, which means by the parents. While most established were members of organisations in their childhood, 92 percent of the marginalised have not been members. Apart from the formal setting for the formation of social capital in organisations, the informal networks of childhood friends are also highly unequal. This distribution tends to persist in later life. Of course, childhood friends are often members of the same social class. Social capital is as clearly distributed unequally between the classes as wealth and cultural capital.

Our empirical study of Brazil also revealed four social classes. They appear to match the German structure, but a closer look shows that the order of classes, their sizes and especially their sociocultural roots are different. While dominant and marginalised classes of Germany and Brazil can be compared to some degree, the lower middle class in Brazil does not exist in Germany. At the same time, the Brazilian upper middle class comprises both the classes that we call fighters and established in Germany. Whereas the Brazilian marginalised class comprises up to 40 percent of the population, the German marginalised class accounts for merely 20 percent. The Brazilian middle class comprises only around 25 percent of the population, while the two German middle classes reach a total of almost 80 percent.

The Brazilian classes have historical roots, which differ greatly from the German configuration. We can trace the marginalised and the fighters in Brazil to the descendants of the slaves, the middle class to the colonial administrators as well as to the skilled labourers and the dominant class to the colonial rulers and landowners. The history of a slave-owning society informs contemporary Brazil and is absent in Germany. However, both nation states are developing similar dividing lines between the classes, namely the lines of dignity, expressivity and aloofness. But even in Brazil and Germany, they do not entirely explain the class structure, since the Brazilian middle class and the German fighter class both comprise two historical tradition lines.

In Laos, we can see how social classes emerge from precapitalist hierarchies as tradition lines and how colonial, socialist and even precolonial social structures persist as sociocultures underneath the capitalist class structure. Our research discovered three sociocultures: a precolonial social formation (called *baan-muang* in Lao and Thai) as well as socialism and capitalism. The precolonial structure consists of villages (*baan*) that are either remote and independent or have come under the influence of and often become dependent on towns or cities (*muang*). While the social structure of the village is mostly determined by family relations, since most villagers are directly related to each other, the structure of the urban centres resembles Max Weber's (1972) patrimonialism. More than half of the population of Laos has grown up in village structures and continues to live as subsistence peasants. Another

20 percent of the population has developed their habitus under socialism and continues to be associated with the communist party.

The older sociocultures of Laos are slowly transforming into a capitalist socioculture. The precapitalist hierarchies are developing into a capitalist class structure. Subsistence peasants, who do not remain peasants, either become commercial farmers or agricultural labourers, or they migrate into the towns, where they become unskilled labourers. The small precapitalist elite that has remained in Laos after the socialist revolution of 1975 is transforming into the new urban middle class. The leading groups of the precolonial and the socialist sociocultures are beginning to engage in business and become capitalists. Chinese and Vietnamese are reappearing partly in their colonial role as businesspeople and partly as farmers, labourers and petty traders.

The sociocultures of Laos differ greatly from the other countries we studied. But the capitalist structure of social classes also differs from countries with a longer capitalist past, such as Germany and Brazil, because it is rooted in those sociocultures. The new urban middle class in Laos comprises professional groups that would be financially much better off in other countries and that would form an established class. In contrast, a petty bourgeoisie or middle class of the Western type does not exist in Laos. Its place is taken by the commercial farmers and traders, who in turn do not really form significant groups, let alone a class, in other countries. Finally, the other four classes are much smaller in Laos than in Germany.

## Structures of global domination

From the perspective of social class and against the background of our empirical research, it is rather misleading to speak of a global ruling class or a transnational capitalist class. The dominant social classes of the three countries discussed in the preceding section differ enormously in their history and composition. They also have different amounts of power and influence. While in Germany political leaders and top managers are often recruited from the established class or even the fighters, these positions are largely occupied by members of the dominant class in Brazil, just as in the United States. This is the result of class struggles and political compromises in Germany. The dominant class in Laos consists largely of former independence fighters, many of whom had been peasants or labourers. Even today, there is some social mobility into the dominant class through entrepreneurship and the socialist party. However, all top positions in politics and the economy are occupied by members of the dominant class. These national configurations are not easily translated into each other or the global level. The dominant classes do not share the same interests, allies and enemies.

Furthermore, the social position of each dominant class is closely linked to the nation state. In terms of social position, the dominant classes are less transnational than the other classes. An academic or IT professional can use his or her capital in most nation states to a similar degree and occupies a similar social position before and after migration. This is not the case for members of the dominant class. Even a Mittal does not automatically become a member of the British dominant class after migrating to London. And even if a British lord actually became a member of the Indian dominant class after migrating to India, which is unlikely, his global position and influence would suffer. Hartmann (2017) has once again shown empirically that very few top managers have international careers. The same is true for the richest capitalists. They may move their place of residence to a tax haven, but they remain largely rooted in their nation state, since they rely on its support – both domestically and globally.

The dominant classes in all three nation states we have studied have to reproduce their social position by accumulating economic capital, which has to be invested in a profitable way. However, economic capital is not sufficient to gain access to the highest social class. One also has to accumulate social capital. Cultural capital is less relevant but plays an important role in management and family strategy to make the right investment decisions. Symbolic capital seems to be less relevant for the dominant class than for the established class, but this is only true for the relation of this social class to the rest of society. The main characteristic of this social class in a capitalist society is its aloofness. There is almost no direct interaction between this class and the rest. The members of the dominant class do not need to prove themselves and therefore do not need symbolic capital. However, symbolic capital is crucial to maintain membership of the class itself.

While economic capital is largely detached from the nation state, cultural, symbolic and especially social capital are very much tied to the national context. One can invest money anywhere, but one rarely has important friends and family everywhere. All three types of capital are also used to directly influence the nation state. One could talk of political capital. Members of the dominant class invest in corruption, party donations, lobbies, think tanks, media ownership and personal networks in order to influence policies. These are mostly national policies, since the nation state can represent the dominant class's interests both domestically and globally.

The dominant classes consist mainly of capitalists, who act globally and strive for economic and political power on a global scale. Their means of action are multinational corporations, international financial institutions and tax havens. All of these are limited in their scope by nation states and their regulations – even if these states were founded to pursue the interests of the dominant classes and are still very much influenced by them. The interests of the dominant class and its respective nation state are not necessarily identical, but the dominant class can reproduce its social position and secure its interests only by means of the state. Furthermore, the interests of the different national dominant classes may collide. The dominant classes do not pursue one common agenda of global domination, but strategies of individual, family and national class advancement prevail.

Finally, the position of each dominant class partly depends on the place of its nation state in the international hierarchy. The European nation state was closely linked to colonialism. The nation state in Europe developed technology, an efficient division of labour and administration in the interior at the same time as colonial expansion and global reproduction of capital. All of this happened under the leadership of the dominant classes in the European nation states. The rest of the world was either forced to adopt this model or the dominant classes in the newly independent countries of the former colonial world adopted it voluntarily to their own advantage. The contemporary world order is a transformation of the colonial world, whose inequalities partly persist and partly have been transformed into capitalist structures.

The inequalities between nation states and their populations are depicted and legitimised in the same liberal way as wealth inequality within the nation state. International inequalities are rooted in colonialism but are depicted as consequences of uneven development and the more or less successful implementation of capitalism. Modernisation theory, which is the capitalist transformation of colonial evolutionism, pervades all discourses on international relations. It is deeply incorporated in our common sense and in the foundations of the social sciences. We think of economically less developed societies, which need to implement reforms in order to reach such standards of social organisation and institutions, and of developed societies, which have by and large met or even elaborated upon these standards. Closely linked to this idea is the interpretation of 'underdeveloped' societies as corrupt, inefficient, undemocratic and somehow incomplete, while their citizens are regarded as untrustworthy and undisciplined.

The explicit or implicit argument claims that capitalism in the West is decent and more developed, while all other arrangements are classified as corrupt and deficient. This view of the world was convincing under colonialism and US domination. It is less convincing since Singapore has achieved the highest GDP per capita and China the largest volume of trade as well as the second largest GDP. It is quite obvious that these countries have institutional configurations that differ significantly from Europe and the United States and will continue to do so for some time to come. However, the general framework of modernisation theory still prevails. All rankings – from the worthiness of credit to corruption to human development – largely translate the colonial order into an order of development and modernisation.

Modernisation theory argues that the richest nation state is the most developed and that all other states should emulate it. This theory is implemented by international organisations, development agencies and national governments. The states are not only standardised, they also form a hierarchy. This hierarchy is rooted in the colonial order and partly explained by it. It is perpetuated by modernisation theory, symbolic classification and the global distribution of capital. Most millionaires and billionaires are citizens of these world regions. In the United States, 5 percent of the population are dollar millionaires, in Germany 2 percent and in Laos a handful of individuals. Western Europe, North America, Japan and Australia host around 80 percent of the world's millionaires (Shorrocks et al. 2016: 27). These are also the world regions that host the richest nation states and the largest TNCs. The economic class of US capitalists is in a position of unique global economic power. It is in an even better political position than other dominant classes, since its interests converge with that of the US nation state. Both strive for global domination. Interests of dominant classes and states tend to diverge in the smaller countries, since the global action of the dominant class is counteracted by a nationalist agenda of the state.

In principle, the dominant social classes have no interest in promoting transnational capitalism, since it threatens their social position and the foundations of the very order that confers this position on them (Hartmann 2017). Instead, the economic class of capitalists promotes transnational capitalism, assisted by the holders of leading functions in society and the classes of consumers. However, the capitalist class mainly consists of members of the dominant social class, who work against their own interests by spurring competition, instability, the rise of newly rich capitalists and the necessity to reproduce the social position via economic capital.

It is likely that the members of the dominant class are no more aware of these correlations than the other classes. They merely see that it is necessary to invest economic capital profitably in order to remain rich and thereby influential. They may deplore all the negative implications this has for them as individuals and a social class as well as for the world at large. While some of their ancestors contributed to the emergence of this destructive organisation of society, others fiercely resisted it. But today, all of them have to comply or perish.

## Conclusion

The relation between globalism and nationalism within the dominant class in the contemporary world is one of the most important issues concerning global capitalism. In this framework, the key question for the coming years is the actual globalisation of the dominant classes. As capitalists, they are already entirely globalised. But their domination is largely limited to their respective nation states, especially in the former colonies and the marginal states of the global North. The families and alliances within the dominant classes are global competitors. As such, their interests partly converge with those of the nation state and partly contradict them. And while they need to reproduce their social position via economic capital and capitalism obscures the mechanism of this reproduction, economic competition also creates instability and competition from below.

Capitalism is an order of global domination, which is based on a combination of dominant classes and nation states. The institution of the nation state was key in the expansion of Western capitalism and in the attempts of dominant classes to achieve global domination. At the same time, the institution of the nation state limits the power of dominant classes, especially in the less powerful states. However, the concentration of economic capital in the United States as well as its political power are being eroded by the rise of China and the return of the multicentric world. This development will increase the contradiction between the nation states and their dominant classes as well as between the national dominant classes. There may be a strong globalising tendency within the dominant classes, but the tendency toward anti-globalisation could be equally strong.

## References

Bourdieu, Pierre. 1984. *Distinction*. Cambridge, MA: Harvard University Press.

Cassirer, Ernst. 1997. *Philosophie der symbolischen Formen*. Darmstadt: Wissenschaftliche Buchgesellschaft.

Friedman, Milton. 1962. *Capitalism and Freedom*. Chicago: University of Chicago Press.

Geiger, Theodor. 1932. *Die soziale Schichtung des deutschen Volkes*. Stuttgart: Ferdinand Enke Verlag.

Hartmann, Michael. 2017. 'Elites', in Gilberto Antonelli and Boike Rehbein (eds.) *Inequality in Economics and Sociology*, pp. 98–108. London and New York: Routledge.

Harvey, David. 2005. *A Brief History of Neoliberalism*. Oxford: Oxford University Press.

Jodhka, S.S., Boike Rehbein and Jessé Souza. 2017. *Inequality in Capitalist Societies*. Singapore and London: Routledge.

Lange-Vester, Andrea. 2007. *Der Habitus der Volksklassen*. Muenster: LIT.

Lind, Michael. 2017. 'The New Class War', *American Affairs*, 1 (2). Available at: americanaffairs.journal.org

Marx, Karl. 1953. 'Das Kapital', in Karl Marx and Friedrich Engels (eds.) *Werke*, Vol. 23–25. Berlin: Dietz.

Marx, Karl and Friedrich Engels. 1964. 'Das Kommunistische Manifest', in Karl Marx and Friedrich Engels (eds.) *Werke*, Vol. 4, pp. 459–93. Berlin: Dietz.

Piketty, Thomas. 2014. *Capital in the Twenty-First Century*. Cambridge, MA: Harvard University Press.

Rehbein, Boike et al. 2015. *Reproduktion sozialer Ungleichheit in Deutschland*. Constance: UVK.

Shorrocks, Anthony, Jim Davies, Rodrigo Lluberas and Antonios Koutsoukis. 2016. *Global Wealth Report*. Zurich: Crédit Suisse.

Sklair, Leslie. 2002. *Globalization*, Third edition. Oxford: Oxford University Press.

Soludo, Charles C. and Mkandawire, Thandika. 1998. *Our Continent; Our Future: African Perspectives on Structural Adjustment*. Dakar: CODESRIA; Ottawa: IDRC; New Jersey and Asmara: Africa World Press.

Stierli, Markus, Anthony Shorrocks, Jim Davies, Rodrigo Lluberas and Antonios Koutsoukis. 2015. *Global Wealth Report*. Zürich: Crédit Suisse.

Taylor, Charles. 1989. *Sources of the Self: The Making of Modern Identity*. Cambridge, MA: Harvard University Press.
Thompson, Edward P. 1963. *The Making of the English Working Class*. Harmondsworth: Penguin Books.
Vitali, Stefania, James B. Glattfelder and Stefano Battiston. 2011. *The Network of Global Corporate Control*. Zurich. Available at: arxiv.org.
Weber, Max. 1972. *Wirtschaft und Gesellschaft*, Fifth edition. Tübingen: J.C.B. Mohr.
Wittgenstein, Ludwig. 1984. *Philosophische Untersuchungen* (Werke 1). Frankfurt: Suhrkamp.
World Inequality Report. 2018. Available at: https://wir2018.wid.world

# 4 Capital, as if community matters

## Silk handloom sari production and the defence of hereditary privilege in South India[1]

*Aarti Kawlra*

> Our thread is different from the thread of the Brahmin. They have the Vedas, we have weaving.
>
> *In conversation with Mr. Sumati Ayyah, leader of the Padma Saliyar caste association at Kanchipuram, 2015*

The Marxian insistence on a singular history of capital, labour and value has tended to disassociate subjectivities of community-based work practices from objective conditions of production. Capital's emphasis on private property has equally disavowed strategies of culture in fostering forms of community that sanction and inculcate the production and reproduction of public good. In a lesser-known but prescient piece written two decades ago, Partha Chatterjee pointed to the inadequacy of capital in explicating cases of value creation as a collective pursuit: 'In the received history of Western political theory, capital and community have been antithetical. When the new history of Eastern modernity gets written in the 21st century, perhaps capital will at last find a resting place in community' (Chatterjee 1998: 277–82). Capital's emphasis on private property has equally disavowed collective histories of sustenance and imagining what JPS Uberoi refers to as 'the brighter side of human work, labour and usage' (2012: 73–80).

Revisionist economic historiography, concerned with recuperating the agency and dynamism of provincial capital in the growth of small towns in south India, has highlighted its caste-based origins in the wake of late 19th-century globalisation.[2] Tirthankar Roy's study on 'Capitalism and community: A study of the Sourashtras', for instance, discusses the rise of artisan-capitalists in Madurai town to show how 'community or collectives matter' and that for a long time, even after the introduction of mineral-based dyes, cloth dyeing remained a Sourashtra enterprise in colonial Madras, well into the post-independence period. According to Roy, 'In 1921, half the Madras Presidency's import of synthetic dyes went to just one town' (1997: 450). Sharad Chari's historical ethnography of capital in the Coimbatore region of Tamil Nadu reiterates the role of caste in reworking social and spatial difference under global production. In the book titled

*Fraternal Capital*, Chari (2004) shows how self-made men of the Goundar community drew upon memories of a shared agrarian past to legitimise 'capital as toil' in the first half of the 20th century and to ultimately control dispersed Goundar capital in Tiruppur's knitwear industry in the industrial present. Delving into the entrepreneurial interventions of caste-based agrarian and handloom capital, Mahadevan and Vijayabaskar maintain, has uncovered sources of 'non-corporate capital' that contributed to the expansion of Coimbatore's organised textile mill industry in the 20th century. 'The Pullicar Mills established in 1935 by Viapuri Mudaliyar, a Kaikkoolar or Senguntha Mudaliar is an instance of this kind. This spinning mill eventually passed into the hands of one of the members of a family of Devanga Chetty . . . Similar is the case with Dhanalakshmi Mills (1932) and the Ramalinga Choodambikai Mills (1933). Established in Tiruppur both these were controlled by prosperous families of Devanga Chettys, a handloom weaving caste' (Mahadevan and Vijayabaskar 2014: 16–17).

The historiography of handloom weaving during the colonial period illuminates collective agency among weavers with numerous references to caste groupings as a vital source of weaver consciousness and solidarity in south India (Ludden 1996; Parthasarathi 2001). Predicated upon kin and supralocal affinal links forged via endogamy, shared identities were articulated through collective donations and rights at important regional temples starting in the medieval period (Mines 1984; Ramaswamy 1985). Caste was reinforced in the natural enlistment of specific weaving castes into textile mills and weaving factories as legitimate heirs to weaving in modern India (Haynes and Roy 1999). Some castes were labelled 'innovative' on account of the techno-entrepreneurial spirit demonstrated by leaders among them and were special targets of reformist initiatives undertaken by the Madras government (Roy 2002: 527–28). The scholarship suggests that weavers' responses to market fluctuations and technological marginalisation under globalisation were enacted collectively through caste associations that mitigated sharp internal differences among groups experiencing precarity. Roy uses the term 'community' to refer to 'a group that communicates internally with relative ease' but wherein 'inequality and hierarchy were often built into collective activity, and individual agency and collective agency were indistinct' (Roy 2002: 527–28).

This chapter contributes to the growing body of scholarship on community as a site of capital, militating against the march of undifferentiated global capitalist development. Tracing the vicissitudes of handloom capital in Tamil Nadu as it unfolds through the biography of the Padma Saliyars engaged in the production of Kanchipuram silk and gold saris allows one to gain a worm's-eye view of capital in the substratum of community. Focusing on codes of conduct and internal differentiation within the community in the context of production organisation of silk saris offers insights into subjectivities of capital and labour in its regional expression. Exploring the entanglement of caste with the pursuit of explicitly economic and mundane goals helps us see the role of artisan capital in socioeconomic constituency building and group mobility. Indeed, as Dirks has argued, caste in its modern avatar is 'a reminder that all claims about community are claims about privilege, participation, and exclusion' in wider society (Dirks 2001: 17). We will see in this chapter that the consciousness of caste in handloom production confronts the discourse of capitalist production as an alternative, indeed subaltern, form of productive organisation jostling for space in modernity.

## Social geography of community-based handloom production

When I began research in the early 90s, members of the Padma Saliyar community were at the helm of regional and national trade in the popularly known 'South silks', 'wedding saris' or 'Kanchipuram saris'.[3] This period coincided with the formal registration of the Tamil Nadu chapter of their caste association as well as the official entry of their caste title, 'Padma Saliyar', into the central list of Other Backward Classes (OBC), a national-level caste-based classification for state-led affirmative action.[4] I chose to explore Padma Saliyar assertions of occupational specialisation and hereditary privilege because their narrative of difference set them apart from the many other castes competing for a share in the rapidly growing silk handloom sari industry in the towns of Kanchipuram and Kumbakonam.[5]

Investigating caste consciousness of a numerically minor, Telugu-speaking group, with virtually no representation in politics dominating the silk sari industry in Tamil Nadu, has meant tracing the intersections between the expansion (and decline) of silk handloom production and the community's biography in the region (Kawlra 2018). Focusing on distributive capital investments in silk sari production along spatially distinct levels led me to supra-local caste and kin-based networks, linking weaving households in small villages to wholesale silk sari producers in Kanchipuram and Kumbakonam, who in turn supply stock to major silk retailers in Chennai. The weaving towns are not only hubs of micro capital, financing the purchase, preparation and distribution of dyed silk yarn, but also collection points of saris woven in hundreds of weaving households in their vicinity.

Research conducted by the Madras Institute of Development Studies in the 1980s revealed that the silk-weaving industry in Kanchipuram had been witnessing rapid growth since the post-independence period. 'The number of silk looms in the district increased by 67 per cent from 1961 to 1983, from 7,200 looms to 12,006' (Bharathan 1985: 94). It is interesting that similar growth has been recorded for the neighbouring Arani and north Arcot region since the 1970s and 80s. What is noteworthy is that the expansion of silk handloom weaving during this period was associated with the rising demand for a certain variety of silk sari, one that employs the three-shuttle or *korvai* technique for solid bordered weaving. More research in the early 1990s attested to a dramatic shift in Arani from simple varieties to more complex weaves along the lines of those woven at Kanchipuram (Nagaraj et al. 1996).

By the 1990s, small producers or wholesale silk handloom capitalists in Kanchipuram and Kumbakonam were in their heyday and Padma Saliyars individuals among them were recognised for their ability to raise capital and expanding the number of looms under their contract. There were many hereditary weavers who had reaped the silk boom and had begun employing weavers and apprentices from non-weaving backgrounds to ply the looms in their homes so that they could be freed to organise credit for the yarn and secure orders from buyers in Chennai. Tracing the genealogies of Padma Saliyar leaders linked to the three spatial levels of production reveals a dynamic network of caste, kin and neighbourhood ties for mobilising capital and labour. The micro level corresponding to relations pertaining to numerous weaving households in Padma Saliyar dominated streets in villages; the middle level in the towns of Kumbakonam and Kanchipuram, where a few leaders have the capacity to raise funds to organise production in villages forming a cluster around a 30 km radius; and the macro level of the city of Chennai where still fewer prominent Padma Saliyar silk business houses, with access to national and international markets retail sari stocks, sourced from these producers. Exchange between the levels takes place across designated relations of contract so that a weaver nearly always deals with producers in nearby towns and never directly with macro-level retailers in cities.

The codes of conduct that underlie unequal relations of capital and labour in handloom weaving are agile to external and internal contingencies, as opposed to the fixity of relations obtained in factory-based production. The stability and survival of this dynamic production matrix involve 'cooperative conflicts', to use Sen's phrase, referring to the bargaining power and respective positions of the different actors involved, both inside and outside the weaving household. Here, getting a fair deal means choosing a mutually beneficial configuration until a more feasible arrangement for all concerned is found. It is in the best interests of the parties seeking productive outcomes to endure the uneven productive relationships in periods of expansion as well as in times of distress and attrition. In households with more than one adult weaver, the looms are often dedicated to different producers and at least one among them is a loom dedicated to a local cooperative society. This is to offset the risks involved with a single source of income and in leveraging subsistence support during lean periods.

Unequal gender-based role entitlements are also governed by the code of cooperative conflicts. Sen has argued that in the case of gender asymmetries in household arrangements, both parties gain a lot more by acting in a framework of pervasive cooperation, even in instances of direct conflict. He suggests that the 'togetherness' fostered by jointly held household responsibilities in the case of men and women living under the same roof renders conflicts 'aberrations or deviant behaviour' within an overall format of cooperation (Sen 1987: 42). The resilience of the differentially valued labouring and non-labouring activities in the household depends on acts of cooperation, of both men and women, old and young, to sustain the productive arrangement even during overt situations of conflict.

The practice of strategic marriage partnerships is at the core of building and expanding a supra-local network of distributive production. Marriage among the Padma Saliyars is not only a means of social reproduction but also an instrument for the expansion of one's influence in the weaving profession. It is even more strategic to establish affinal ties with a family of weaving repute even if it means searching for a suitable alliance among distantly located caste members. Padma Saliyars spend more at weddings and are increasingly finding matches further afield for greater social mobility and presence in big cities. Padma Saliyars engaged in handloom production regularly make such considered matches through advertisements in their caste association's monthly magazine, the *Padma Saliyar Kural*. Indeed, marrying outside of one's caste-group is not a personal matter but a social violation requiring the consent of caste elders. The professional status of a daughter-in-law's natal family, especially the number of looms they control and her own prowess in weaving and related matters, often mark her relative position and bargaining power in her affinal family.

Marriage creates a fiduciary relationship between weaving families. Weavers from the network of villages under a producer can be asked to weave for an affine if desired, making the output of additional looms (rather than the actual looms themselves) transferable. The strategic union of two weaving families not only has material rewards in terms of an expanded production base but also symbolic gains in the form of future credit and social honour in a widening circle of community ties. N. Kuppuswami of the Nallis group and P.C. Jayaraman of Kumaran Silks transformed their generation-long business rivalry into an enduring business partnership through a marriage alliance. Evidence of such marriage exchanges between competing families belonging to the same level is also common at the middle and micro levels of silk sari production and occurs within a code of conduct and ethics that sees conflict and competition as being within the community rather than outside of it.

The fissioning of households occurs along the male line and involves partitioning of the family's loom base at the time of marriage and a consequent loss of resources until another opportune alliance is made. The dynamism undergirding expansion *and* contraction in the social geography of handloom production challenges the rigid structural antagonisms of gender, class and caste associated with other forms of productive organisation. Supporting an expansive production network of caste kin is the mark of a Padma Saliyar leader. Caste enters here as a shared hereditary privilege, vindicating material fulfilment and social eminence through the weaving profession, for those who choose to participate in it.

## Leadership as organising principle

According to a caste official in Kanchipuram, 'there was a time when no one in Kanchipuram consented to forge marriage alliances as far as Kumbakonam but since Nalli Kuppuswamy Chettiar, this practice has become a norm'. The trans-local affinal partnership forged in the 1970s strengthened the caste association in rallying caste-fellows from across Tamil Nadu and set the stage for garnering support of Padma Saliyars from other states. The initial groundwork for Kuppuswami's leadership role in the community had already begun in 1952 when his father Narayanaswami Chetti, along with other community leaders, invited Padma Saliyar handloom activist and MLA Pragada Kotaiah to Madras to discuss the condition of the handloom industry and to raise political awareness among them. In 1982, Nalli Kuppuswami, his father-in-law S.R.G. Ranganathan Chettiar from Kumbakonam and some other silk leaders, including Chengalvaraya Chettiar of Kumaran Silks from Kanchipuram, were invited to attend the All India Padma Saliyar Association meeting held at Hyderabad. Here nationalist Pragada Kotaiah and other caste leaders from Andhra Pradesh encouraged the delegation to expand the activities of the Tamil Nadu chapter of the caste association. Subsequently, Kuppusami re-activated the association and went on to organise the *Akhil Bharath Padmashali Mahasabha* at T Nagar in the compound of his home in Panagal Park, which is also the location of the business house's main showroom.

In Tamil Nadu, the different district-level associations are linked with prominent Padma Saliyar individuals whose leadership roles are recorded in various publications brought out by the caste association. Discussions at the weekly meetings at the Chennai office of the Tamil Nadu Padma Saliyar Sangam (or 'association') revealed that local-level caste associations survived if their respective leaders were able to muster financial support from wealthy members of the caste which, in turn, was dependent upon the latitude and weight of their kin and affinal network. Padma Saliyar caste associations in the smallest ward or municipality indicate the presence of locally elected office-bearers and serve as platforms for their demonstrated ability to organise production and sustain several weaving households in the locality. Padma Saliyar caste leadership at the local level is also evident in the upkeep of the shrine of their mythical ancestor and in the words of a sangam official, 'wherever there is a Bhavanarishi shrine – you will find members of our community residing in the vicinity' (Kawlra 2018: 10). The endurance of local caste associations, indeed their vitality, is mirrored in the ebb and flow of the fortunes of its leaders.

For the Padma Saliyars, a leader is one who is acknowledged as such by an expansive constituency of caste members in handloom publics and who can sustain patronage of the caste association. The term 'handloom publics' draws from Nancy Fraser's formulation of subaltern counterpublics 'where members of subordinated social groups invent and circulate counterdiscourses, which in turn permit them to formulate oppositional interpretations of their identities, interests, and needs' (Fraser 1990: 67). It also draws from Reddy and Zavos' (2009) concept of 'temple publics' and refers to a complex network of public spheres associated with silk handloom production in Tamil Nadu. It refers to the shared spaces in the public life of weavers, producers, retailers, diverse handloom intermediaries, caste association members and handloom consumers, including cultural and political elite. Such caste-based mobilisation is not the same as the culture of political constituency building around the enduring figure of a charismatic individual in Tamil Nadu studied by Pandian (1992) and Dickey (1993). Leadership among the Padma Saliyars also differs from that of the person-centred 'institutional big-man' defined by Mines and Gourishankar (1990) whose authority is enacted through a variety of institutions that he creates and controls and whose charismatic style is sanctioned by a specific cultural model of galactic polity. Gorringe has shown how caste-based mobilisations among groups that have not benefited from Dravidian reform in Tamil Nadu have leadership patterns 'analogous to caste headmen' (Gorringe 2010: 121). While both material and symbolic capital is gained through the development of a supra-local network of production, the voluntary acceptance of fiduciary duties towards the larger community via the caste association is the mark of a Padma Saliyar leader.

The practice of leadership among the Padma Saliyars is not merely a matter of political brokerage but a form of patron-like sociality that permeates and sustains everyday work and community life. It involves presiding at naming ceremonies, marriages, religious functions, temple donations and renovations; providing scholarships and distributing books and stationery to students; setting up facilities for daily feeding of the elderly and poor; arbitrating between disputants; petitioning the government of Tamil Nadu on matters pertaining to the silk handloom industry; staging protests or fasts and so on. Leadership within a network of supra-local production and distribution guarantees benefits (and obligations) within a hierarchical arrangement, but the rigidity and severity of these relations are mitigated through the caste association that facilitates inter-local and supra-local relations within a communal framework comprising caste-based kin and affines. Accumulating capital, engaging contract weavers and keeping a pulse on market trends are skills and capabilities that can be acquired and honed by anyone with a demonstrated ability for taking on leadership roles in the community.

The periodic affirmation and renewal of leaders at each level is evident in the bestowal of honours at public events and ceremonies that leaders and functionaries from other levels also attend. My first such event was in August 1995 in Kumbakonam where I was witness to the 60th birthday celebrations of KG Ramaswamy Chettiar (KGR), the then president of the Tamil Nadu Padma Saliyar Sangam, or caste association, and wholesale supplier of silk saris to big Padma Saliyar concerns like Nalli and Kumaran in Chennai. It was attended by more than five thousand Padma Saliyar representatives from across the state, including some caste leaders from Andhra Pradesh and Karnataka. The fact that prominent Padma Saliyar silk businessmen from Chennai were also present at the occasion was a collective recognition of KGR's role in raising capital, organising production and developing a viable network of more than 500, mostly Padma Saliyar weaving households in and around Kumbakonam. Over the years, KGR's fulfilment of a fiduciary duty towards members of his caste as a handloom capitalist, activist and philanthropist has made him eligible for the honour of upholding a hereditary privilege and shaped his leadership status within the caste group.

The legitimacy of the pyramidal leadership structure and three-tiered spatial organisation of silk sari production – the few retail business houses in Chennai, the large number of wholesale producers in towns like Kanchipuram and Kumbakonam and the numerous weaving households with one or more looms – derives from the public acceptance of hereditary knowledge as innate competence in, and commitment to, the weaving profession. In Kanchipuram, Arterburn noted, for instance, the 'use of the attribute of caste weaving skill as an explanation of rank. . . . Claims to superior skill were openly stated in front of individuals of other castes and their claims were contested with counter claims' (Arterburn 1982: 61–62). According to an official of a silk cooperative society, hereditary silk sari weavers cannot be persuaded into doing simpler designs, as weaving a wedding sari for them is a 'status issue', even a 'birth-right' (Kawlra 2018: 63). Similarly, at the middle level of wholesale production, Padma Saliyar leaders are recognised for their ability not only to harness caste relations in raising handloom capital but also for withstanding market fluctuations and shielding weavers from adversity. The transition from being a weaver of silk saris to being responsible for their production and sale is a prospect open to not just a privileged few. The Tamil referential term *Chetti* or *Chettiar* used as a suffix for silk leaders at all levels of production defends rights to mobility within the group as well as within the wider caste hierarchy.

The relations of exchange between the three levels of silk sari production and sale in Tamil Nadu – the procurement of bulk goods by retailers in cities from middle-level producers in towns, the collection of saris by middle-level organisers from weavers, the disbursement of a dyed silk warp for a fresh batch of saris by the producer to the weaver – are characterised by a system of rotating credit. Here, the promise of payment is tied to the promise of a fresh order. Such a system of credit is possible only if production occurs within a context that ensures continuity of ties beyond those based on impersonal temporary contracts. 'Being of the same community, people are interested in doing business with us'; 'We prefer to do business with those whom we already know'; 'They need us, we need them, but there must also be trust' are comments frequently made in this regard (Kawlra 2018: 78).

Leadership, or achieved mastery in one's work – whether it is to weave, organise production or retail silk handloom saris – is recognised and honoured as a caste ideal. Referring to both the 'thread' of life and livelihood of a weaver and the 'body of knowledge' to ethical living, the poem *Nulum Nulum* draws attention to leader Nalli Kuppuswami as embodying *nul*, which is not only material success but also a moral force in the everyday life of the community. It is intended as a double entendre by the author and was published in the caste association periodical, *Padma Saliyar Kural* in Tamil.[6]

*Nulum Nulum*

Twisting *kora* [raw silk], straightening the warp,
fashioning a life from the loom,
balancing the movements of the heald to and fro
the daily struggle
between that which does not come and that which does not go
[*referring to the ironies of life*].
Without leaving work half-done,
concentrating to make sure threads do not snap;
with precision and feeling
imparting beauty to his work through the skill of his hands,
the creativity of his mind
thereby revealing the excellence of his service.
What he wears is a simple cloth,
what he weaves and offers is a silk sari
in brilliant gold thread in crores of designs that arrest the gaze of
women.
As he wields the thread *[nulum]*,
on the day his son reaches out for it *[nulum]*,
that day the first rays of the sun [dawn] are immanent
Everyone will celebrate his blossoming
with fragrance gathered from eight directions.
Several of our fellow community men,
including Nalli Kuppuswami have risen
by wielding the thread *(nulum)*
you too should take to it *(nulum)*
and become accomplished.
Step ahead with principles to achieve your goals,
enhance the glory of the Padma Saliyars.

(Gopalasami 1995: 15)

Hereditary knowledge of weaving is upheld in this poetic articulation as a cultural right and shared norm for the valuation of skill and the application of justice. Even the product of their work, the silk and gold handloom sari, as will be seen in the following section, is inflected with shared notions of value. Here patrons of silk saris, unlike consumers of mass-produced goods, are not dissociated from the conditions of production, and producers are specialists in the accrual of material and symbolic value, both for themselves as well as for their customers.

## The pursuit of value, symbolic and material

Padma Saliyars believe that to conduct one's life in accordance with certain 'good practices' *(nalla morraighal)* is also a heightening of the auspiciousness of the products of their work. Weavers of silk saris are known for their strict adherence to certain prescriptions during the preparatory and weaving processes. It is believed that well-being will accrue if the *natchaththiram* or 'stellar constellation at the time of birth' and *lagna* or 'planetary conjunctions at the time of birth' of the weaver 'match' that of the merchants on the day weaving is begun. Even Lord Vishnu, the Padma Saliyars believe, is said to have given out lotus stem yarn only after having selected an appropriate time to commence weaving. Failure to follow these prescriptions in the greed for more income may prove inauspicious and even harmful to the cloth, the weaver, the merchant and even to the wearer (Kawlra 2018: 153–54).

Padma Saliyar weavers say that it is their *thozhil dharma* or 'work ethic' to adhere to appropriate procedures, from laying out the warp on the loom to the final weaving and selling of the cloth. J. Nathamuni Chettiar, the caste's subdivisional head at Swamimalai town, in the mid-1990s was a well-reputed silk weaver, not only for his expertise in executing new and complex designs but also for his reliability in satisfactorily completing sari orders in the stipulated time period. In Kanchipuram, Arterburn's field research revealed that members of traditional weaving castes consistently placed non-weaving castes at a lower level of weaving competence. Caste membership often legitimises claims of superior skill. Yet it is a lifetime commitment to weaving and ethical work practice that distinguish leadership and occupational autonomy. In terms of relation to the everyday work of weaving, it means, in Nathamuni's words, 'maintaining the integrity of the warp received by ensuring that the designated loom, the yarn and the design specification is neither shared nor re-used for other clients'.

Even at the level of retail, Padma Saliyar sari showrooms in Chennai are known for the quality of silk and gold used in their saris and have longstanding relations with customers of wedding saris. It is not enough that a wedding sari be woven in accordance with favourable placements of persons and events in time and space, it must also be purchased at an opportune time. Padma Saliyars are known for their ethical practices in sari retail, and their customers trust them for not selling soiled or 'used' saris that may have imbued unknown or harmful influences over time. When customers insist on returning or exchanging saris they have purchased, the latter are kept aside together with saris that have been on the shelf for longer than 60 to 90 days and considered unsuitable as auspicious wear. In the Tamil month of *aadi* (mid-July to mid-August), otherwise an inauspicious period for marriages and other life-affirming ceremonies, Sundari Silks, a Padma Saliyar silk sari showroom in Chennai, holds its largest discount sale, known as the *aadi thallapadi*. Saris bought and sold during this period are done so with complete transparency. Both the buyers and the sellers are aware that the lowered price of the sari indicates the presence of a technical defect or design imperfection.

The *muhuratham*, or bridal sari, is usually bought from the silk sari showroom believed to have proved fortunate for the family in the past. Padma Saliyar–owned sari stores in Chennai have acquired the reputation of being *raasiyaana* or 'auspicious' for their respective clientele, who believe that buying the first sari from them will prove to be *raasi* for the newlyweds. 'Nallis is *raasi*', that is, 'Nallis brings good fortune' is a common phrase among long-term patrons. In fact, Radha Silk Emporium in Mylapore is popularly referred to as Rasi, from the letters *Ra* and *Si* in their name but pronounces the word *raasi*, to stand for 'auspicious'. Nalli Kuppuswami is proud to claim that 'an auspicious time. . . (can) be ascertained . . . from the crowd found at the entrance to our emporium' (Kuppuswami 1983: 54). So inextricable is the Padma Saliyars' identity with auspicious occasions that in the past, a Padma Saliyar groom was made to weave his own bride's wedding sari or the *kurai pudavai* which, apart from being a symbol of a fruitful marriage, constituted the auspicious act of marriage itself.

The pursuit of auspiciousness, as a collective goal uniting the producer with consumers, establishes the efficacy of handloom weaving as a legitimate profession and galvanises silk sari exchange in a competitive marketplace. As a practice of meaning-making in the domain of work, heightening auspiciousness defends shared cultural values and challenges the axiom of self interest in rational economic action. As a politics of culture, symbolic and monetary value creation validates a shared work identity and recalibrates a group's ranking within the overall caste hierarchy. Value creation in the sense of connecting subjective ideas to objective conditions of production contradicts the experience of alienation in factory production or of distancing producers from consumers in capitalist modernity.

## New regimes of value

Returning to Kumbakonam in early 2015, I found that of the 500 looms that once wove saris for KGR in 1994, only a fractional 10 percent remained. Most weavers had either left the profession or simply abandoned their homes without notice. Swamimalai that once had 250 looms in east Raja Street and close to 100 looms in west Raja Street now is left with just 7 looms. These belong to aging Padma Saliyar weavers who have remained on account of inherited property. Those who have left Swamimalai live in confined spaces working long hours in hotels as security guards or in supermarkets and seek avenues to return. Others have set up their own shops selling tea or cloth (*tea kadai* or *javuli kadai*). The story of Kanchipuram is no different as it morphs from a major centre of production into a retail hub of Kanchipuram silk saris. Weavers who own their homes are abandoning the caste profession as they pursue rental or retail revenue as a means of livelihood.

Kumbakonam was a prosperous weaving town in the 1990s, but by the year 2015, its reserve army was spent. If farmers face debt and destitution through suicides, weavers face the same through desertion or dissolution. KGR's family came to Kumbakonam from T. Pollur in Trichy during the 50s following a demand for Kanchipuram silk saris. Their apprenticeships and neighbourly ties with members of the dominant silk-weaving Saurashtra community in Kumbakonam buttressed their entry into the field of silk sari production in the region. Through strategic relationships of marriage and business with small-time producers belonging to their own community in Swamimalai and other weaving villages around Kumbakonam, KGR was able to establish fiduciary relations with over 500 weaving households by 1994. He was able to compete with local Saurashtra silk producers and even gain their admiration as business equals within a single generation. When I met KGR again in 2014, he had suffered a devastating financial loss. Thousands of weavers under his contract had abandoned work and left without repaying their sari advances. Cooperatives and not private producers were eligible for the compensation provided by the central government to mitigate the wave of adverse contingencies. KGR had been forced to repay the bank loan by selling a large portion of his fixed assets. As of this year, that is, 2019, KGR and his wife have both passed away. His only surviving son has moved to work as production manager for a Padma Saliyar concern in Kanchipuram, and their home on J.P. Kovil street, which was once the hub of distributive silk sari production, is shut down.

The silk handloom industry in south India has been battling economic churning since the beginning of the liberalisation era. The opening decades of this century have seen handloom capital being overridden by finance capital, mitigating risk through revenues from new businesses like tourism and real estate. Many retail silk business houses like Nalli and Kumaran have also diversified their capital investment portfolios towards jewellery, powerloom weaves and readymade garments to cater to the lifestyle of the new middle classes. New entrants into the silk sari retail business like RMKV, Chennai Silks and Pothys have taken a piece of the market share in Chennai. Authenticity is the new regime of value, and individual family biographies rather than hereditary privilege gain the weight of 'tradition' in sari branding. Global standards of quality certification such as the GI, or geographical indications, mark for the Kanchipuram sari spatially fix places of production to unmask conditions of production for customers seeking genuine handmade products. A rhetoric of authenticity exhorts customers to 'distinguish between a horse and a donkey' when choosing a 'pure' Kanchipuram sari to counter the plethora of duplicates in the market (Kawlra 2014). Figurative motifs and panels drawing from India's archive of art and architecture, executed through computer-aided design software, are attracting a new generation of heritage-conscious silk handloom sari wearers (Kawlra 2020).

The rise in demand for silk saris in the second half of the 20th century had spawned factory-like production sheds in Kanchipuram where several loom workers wove under a single roof for low wages. It was rare to see Padma Saliyars weavers in such a situation. 'We are used to working on our own time and in the comfort of our own homes'. In dire circumstances, they were known to leave the weaving profession altogether rather than work in crowded weaving factories. Contemporary globalisation, with its spatial reconfigurations of capitalist activity (Harvey 2001), has rendered handloom weaving unviable as a career option, and many Padma Saliyar weavers are migrating for jobs as semi-skilled or unskilled workers in catering, security, IT and the automobile and mobile industries. The contents of the community magazine suggest that upward social mobility through higher education is underway. The *Kural* retains its readership as a marriage alliance bureau and receives contributions from Padma Saliyar silk producers and retailers in the form of silk sari advertisements. Ironically, there are more prospective brides with educational degrees than grooms, a fact that draws attention to the recent departure of handloom weaving as a viable and respectable livelihood option for Padma Saliyar young men.

The continued representation of community as a timeless sphere of culture and subsistence in development rhetoric has only served to deepen the modernist denial of community as a site of capital mediating social, political and economic constituency building among subordinated, less visible groups. Viewed from this perspective, articulations of caste become a legitimate category, representing social difference with a guaranteed subaltern public in modern democratic politics (Pandian 2002). The placement of the handloom in the private domain of the artisanal household in discourses of national development reinforces the interiority, and inferiority, of community-based distributive production in what Herzfeld (2004) has termed the 'global hierarchy of value'. Viewing work in the narrative of a common identity, both in the past and in the present, lends credence to the defence of shared patrimony, which may yet be another basis for contestations between capital and labour.

## Notes

1 This chapter draws from my long-term study of silk handloom weaving among the Padma Saliyars from the early 1990s and then again in 2014 when I returned to the field.

2 See the work of Arterburn (1982) on silk-weaving cooperatives in Kanchipuram; Geert De Neve (2005) on the Sengunthar Mudaliars in Bhavani and Devangas in

Kumarapalayam; N. A. Arivukkarasi and K. Nagaraj (2009) and E. Basile (2013) on Arani silk handloom weaving.

3 The other community whose caste identity is linked to silk weaving in Tamil Nadu is the Saurashtras. Padma Saliyar migrations are said to have taken place between the 10th and 12th centuries from present-day Andhra Pradesh, whereas the Saurashtras settled in present-day Tamil Nadu sometime in the 17th century (Haynes and Roy 1999).

4 The Padma Saliyars are listed as distinct from the Saliyar, Pattusaliyar, Pattariya and Adhaviyar but are placed together with them in entry No. 131 in the central list of OBCs dated September 10, 1993, of the National Commission for Backward Classes.

5 The expansion, post-independence, of silk-weaving towns in Tamil Nadu, like Benares in U.P. and Surat in Gujarat, has been linked to the emergence of a mass market for handcrafting skills and new patterns of consumption in the first half of the 20th century (Haynes et al. 2010).

6 I am grateful to V. Sujatha and L. Kannan for the translation of the poem, which is not true to the original poetic form and attempts to merely grasp the poem's essence.

## References


Arivukkarasi, N.A. and K. Nagaraj. 2009. 'Some Aspects of Socioeconomic Change in Rural Arani with Special Reference to Silk Weaving Industry', Paper presented at the International Workshop on "Market Town, Market Society, Informal Economy", Contemporary South Asian Studies Programme, Oxford, June 8–9.

Arterburn, Y.J. 1982. *The Loom of Interdependence: Silk Weaving Cooperatives in Kanchipuram.* Delhi: Hindustan Publishing Corporation.

Basile, E. 2013. *Capitalist Development in India's Informal Economy.* London and New York: Routledge.

Bharathan, K. 1985. 'The Living Art of Kancheepuram', *Frontline*, December 29–January 11: 94–102.

Chari, S. 2004. *Fraternal Capital: Peasant-Workers, Self-Made Men, and Globalisation in Provincial India.* New Delhi: Orient Blackswan.

Chatterjee, P. 1998. 'Community in the East', *Economic and Political Weekly*, 33 (6): 277–82.

De Neve, G. 2005. 'Weaving for IKEA in South India: Subcontracting, Labour Markets and Gender Relations in a Global Value Chain', in C.J. Fuller and J. Assayag (eds.) *Globalising India: Perspectives from Below*, pp. 89–118. London: Anthem Press.

Dickey, S. 1993. 'The Politics of Adulation: Cinema and the Production of Politicians in South India', *Journal of Asian Studies*, 52 (2): 340–72.

Dirks, N. 2001. *Castes of Mind. Colonialism and the Making of British India.* Princeton, NJ: Princeton University Press.

Fraser, N. 1990. 'Rethinking the Public Sphere: A Contribution to the Critique of Actually Existing Democracy', *Social Text*, 25/26: 56–80.

Gopalasami, S. 1995. 'Nulum Nulum' (in Tamil), *Padma Saliyar Kural*, 7 (4): 15. Chennai: Tamil Nadu Padma Saliyar Sangam.

Gorringe, H. 2010. 'The New Caste Headmen? Dalit Movement Leadership in Tamil Nadu', in P. Price and A.E. Ruud (eds.) *Power and Influence in India: Bosses, Lords and Captains*, pp. 119–43. London: Routledge.

Harvey, D. 2001. 'Globalisation and the "Spatial Fix"', *Geographische Revue*, 2: 23–30.
Haynes, D., A. McGowan, T. Roy and H. Yanagisawa. 2010. *Towards a History of Consumption in South Asia*. New Delhi: Oxford University Press.
Haynes, D. and T. Roy. 1999. 'Conceiving Mobility: Weavers' Migrations in Pre-Colonial and Colonial India', *Indian Economic & Social History Review*, 36 (1): 35–67.
Herzfeld, M. 2004. *The Body Impolitic: Artisans and Artifice in the Global Hierarchy of Value*. Chicago: University of Chicago Press.
Kawlra, A. 2014. 'Duplicating the Local: GI and the Politics of Place in Kanchipuram, Tamil Nadu', Nehru Memorial Museum and Library Occasional Paper, Perspectives in Indian Development N.S. 29. NMML, New Delhi.
Kawlra, A. 2018. *We Who Wove with Lotus Thread: Summoning Community in South India*. New Delhi: Orient Blackswan.
Kawlra, A. 2020. 'Between Culture and Technology: Theme Saris and the Graphic Representation of Heritage in Tamil Nadu, India', in Ayami Nakatani (ed.) *Fashionable Traditions: Asian Handmade Textiles in Motion*, pp. 99–115. London: Lexington Books.
Kuppuswami, N. 1983. *Work is Worship*. Madras: Arunothaya, New edition, 2004.
Ludden, D. 1996. 'Caste Society and Units of Production in Early Modern South India', in B. Stein and S. Subrahmanyam (eds.) *Institutions and Economic Change in South Asia*, pp. 105–33. Delhi. Oxford University Press and SOAS Studies in South Asia, Understandings and Perspectives Series.
Mahadevan, R. and M. Vijayabaskar. 2014. 'The Making of Non-Corporate Capital: Some Historical & Contemporary Entrepreneurial Narratives from Tiruppur, Tamil Nadu', Nehru Memorial Museum and Library, Occasional Paper, Perspectives in Indian Development N. S. 33. NMML, New Delhi.
Mines, M. 1984. *The Warrior Merchants: Textiles, Trade and Territory in South India*. Cambridge: Cambridge University Press.
Mines, M. and V. Gourishankar. 1990. 'Leadership and Individuality in South Asia: The Case of the South Indian Big-Man', *Journal of Asian Studies*, 49: 761–86.
Nagaraj, K., S. Janakarajan, D. Jayaraj and B. Harriss-White. 1996. 'Sociological Aspects of Silk Seaving in Arni and Its Environs', Unpublished paper, Madras Institute of Development Studies, Chennai.
Pandian, M.S.S. 1992. The Image Trap: MG Ramachandran in Film and Politics. New Delhi: Sage Publications.
Pandian, M.S.S. 2002. 'One Step Outside Modernity: Caste, Identity Politics and Public Sphere', *Economic and Political Weekly*, May 4, pp. 1735–41.
Parthasarathi, P. 2001. *The Transition to a Colonial Economy: Weavers, Merchants and Kings in South India, 1720–1800*. Cambridge: Cambridge University Press.
Ramaswamy, V. 1985. *Textile and Weavers in Medieval South India*. Delhi: Oxford University Press.
Reddy, D. and J. Zavos. 2009. 'Temple Publics: Religious Institutions and the Construction of Contemporary Hindu Communities', *International Journal of Hindu Studies*, 13 (3): 241–60.
Roy, T. 1997. 'Capitalism and Community: A Study of the Madurai Sourashtras', *Indian Economic and Social History Review*, 34 (4): 437–63.
Roy, T. 2002. 'Acceptance of Innovations in Early Twentieth-Century Indian Weaving', *Indian Economic and Social History Review*, 55 (3): 507–533. New Series.

Sen, A. 1987. 'Gender and Cooperative Conflicts', in Irene Tinker (ed.) *Persistent Inequalities, Women and World Development, Economic and Social Commission for Asia and the Pacific*. New York: United Nations.
Uberoi, J.P.S. 2012. 'Marxism of Labour or Property?', *Economic and Political Weekly*, 47 (32): 73–80.

# 5 Dynamics of capital and local contexts

## Understanding Patidar resistance in Gujarat

*Suraj Beri*

### Introduction

Social research on the growing inequalities in contemporary capitalism is especially crucial to understand the dynamics of capital and its functioning as well as ways of reproduction in regional contexts. The hypothesis is that a new 'transnational capitalist class' in the Global North and Global South explains how spatial mobility has allowed capital to reorganise production worldwide (Sklair 2001; Carroll 2010). According to this argument, production units that were once located in a single site have been fragmented and integrated externally into new globalised circuits of accumulation. This worldwide decentralisation and fragmentation of the production process has taken place alongside the centralisation of command and control of the global economy in the transnational capitalist class (ibid). However, the structural change in regional contexts might not support these assumptions. The rise of the 'super rich' in countries such as the United States and Britain, as well as nations like India, China and Russia, indicates a different set of economic and political processes of development. The global ruling classes exercise their control through the machinery of the multinational corporations (MNCs), non-governmental organisations and other national agencies. They accelerate the process of change in national economic policies across countries. Globalisation has contributed to the more or less unification of the world into a single 'mode of production' and brought about the integration of different countries and regions into the larger capitalist economy (Wood 2003). The rise of private capitalists in the Global South suggests that process of accumulation has been continuing, especially after the deregulation of the domestic economy.

The capitalist system is rife with several contradictions (Harvey 2014) – the periodic crises within capitalism, the growing rift between the global capital and ethnic divide within it, power relations between foreign capital and the domestic labour markets (growing unrest of workers in both formal and informal sectors) of countries such as India provide complicated issues to be examined critically and empirically. The phenomena of mass emigration, migration from countryside to urban informal economies, reflects the ongoing larger process and its implications for caste and class inequalities. This raises several questions for understanding the dynamics of capital across the globe as well as local conflicts and contradiction in economy and society. For instance, how does one understand the policies of 'land acquisition' (via law) by multinational corporations in several parts of India and many other countries of global South (via special economic zones [SEZs])? How are land accumulation policies related to the growing political and economic crisis of dominant communities in different states, that is, Haryana, Gujarat and Maharashtra, or whether there are other factors involved in this process? These questions are crucial to understand the national and regional functioning of capitalist market development. Scholars have been engaging with such issues while drawing on the ideas of a Marxist framework, for instance, Harvey would conceptualise it as 'accumulation by dispossession' based on Marx's concept of 'primitive accumulation' (Harvey 2003). Harvey describes four broad processes to analyze *neoliberal capitalism*: privatisation, financialisation, commodification and redistribution of resources upwards (ibid: 139–40). On the other hand, Michael Levien, in his work, highlights the inadequacy of Marx's and Harvey's conceptions and suggests that the drive for land accumulation in India represents a new phase of capitalism and thus forms a new 'regime of dispossession' (Levien 2015). Based on the insights developed from the recent literature on the contradictions of capitalism, as well as the insights provided by Luc Boltanski in his theorisation of two critiques ('artistic critique' and 'social critique'), his work would try to explain the dynamics of capital and the resistance to it. The question this chapter aims to grapple with is this: How do we understand the rising demands for reservation by erstwhile 'dominant agrarian communities' (Jats in Haryana, Patidars in Gujarat, Kapus in Andhra Pradesh and Marathas in Maharastra)? Does this demand for 'inclusion' in the formal sector, that is, government jobs, reflect the larger contradiction of the capitalist market in India? In the Indian context, the resistances (by dominant groups) often acquire the language of caste identities via the demand for reservation. As the contemporary political scenario shows, the acquisition of reservation seems to these communities the only reasonable and achievable option available. These resistances also highlight the contradictions within the capitalist market in the different parts of the world.

## Global capitalist development and rising inequalities

In order to understand what is happening to capitalism, one requires knowledge about how the system operates on the ground. The continual transformation of economic systems in different national contexts further complicates the possibility of a general picture of capitalism. Therefore, the debate on capitalist development and its relation to growing social and economic inequalities shifts between general theoretical logic and concrete historical particularities. While Marx and Engels wrote the classic description of capitalism as being a system which continuously expands beyond a given territory, scholars have engaged in critical debate about the divergences and variations of the forms of capitalist development in Asian contexts. Marx and Engels talked about the bourgeoisie's globalising mission, 'the need of a constantly expanding market for its products chases the bourgeoisie over the entire surface of the globe. It must nestle everywhere, settle everywhere, establish connexions everywhere' (1968 [1848]: 38). Marx was emphatic in arguing that capitalism has its own distinctive social property relations, from which derives its own unique systemic logic, and its own imperatives (Marx 1990). This explains the objective need of the capital for self-expansion, but it does not mean that national affinities and cultural identities fall away in the process.

In recent times, capitalism has not developed without facing opposition by several political actors and groups. In the wake of the US economic meltdown of 2007–8, several commentators revisited the trends of capitalist development: Occupy Wall Street movement (We are 99 percent, who is 1 percent!) and also through rising social movements (particularly in the Global South, i.e. anti-Pohang Steel Company (POSCO), anti-Vedanta etc.). The present model of capitalism has been successful in seizing lucrative public assets far below their market value and earning capacity and wealth accumulation with the sell-off of banks, minerals, energy resources, telecommunications, power plants and the private debt by the state. For instance, according to *Forbes* magazine's 'List of the World's Billionaires', published 8 March 2007, the number of the world's billionaires has increased from 793 in 2006 to 946 in 2007 (Petras 2008: 319). Over half of the current billionaires (523) came from three countries – the United States (415), Germany (55) and Russia (53) (ibid.). Interestingly, India had the highest number of billionaires (36) in Asia, with a total wealth of $US 191 billion (ibid.). In a recent report, India was ranked third in terms of billionaires. India has now a total of 111 billionaires, with a total wealth of $308 billion, according to the Hurun Report[1] released in 2016. With 111 billionaires, 14 more than last year's 97, India featured ahead of Germany, the United Kingdom and even Switzerland. The majority of the billionaires are from the manufacturing sector, followed by pharmacy and technology.

Recent valuable work by Thomas Piketty (2014) shows the increasing wealth inequalities in contemporary capitalism, even though he escapes the question of 'exploitation'. According to him, the return on capital is usually higher than the economic growth rate, and there is therefore an historical default towards returns on accumulated wealth exceeding those on current income. He uses tax data, estate tax data and income data available from 1910 to 2010, that is, around 100 years of data, and provides an understanding of global capital and its formation. Furthermore, he even proposes a 'global wealth tax' to control 'patrimonial capitalism' in the twentieth century (Piketty 2014). His work also challenges the *meritocratic values* and principles of equality and liberty so fundamental to modern-day democracies. He realises the *inherent tendencies* of capitalism towards inequality, and therefore the threat to liberal democracies lies within the dynamics of capitalism. Piketty reaffirms the critique of capitalism when he argues that inequalities would not disappear even if there were a completely free market economy at work. Therefore, Piketty asserts the rise of social (class) inequalities as the systematic feature of the development of capitalism and not its failure.

In addition to unequal returns on production, there is also a growing spatialisation of the capitalist economy. Globalisation theorist Saskia Sassen draws our attention to the production sites of the globalised capitalist economy. She argues that the metropolitan cities such as New York, London and Tokyo play a crucial role as production sites for a globalised corporate economy. Focusing on cities brings forth an argument about the economic structuring of globalisation at that local level, that is, 'whether it's factory workers in export processing zones in Asia, garment sweatshop workers in Los Angeles or janitors in Wall Street' (Sassen 2010: 34). In recent times, the socio-spatial order has undergone a shift in terms of its dispersal of economic activities at the metropolitan, national and global levels that is broadly referred to as globalisation of capital, flows and work. This also allows the centralisation of crucial economic functions for control, ownership and accumulation.

The process of capitalist development has led to the formation of multinational organisations with their nationwide structures of networks and inner circles. Scholars like Leslie Sklair, William Carroll and William Robinson in their respective works have put forward the argument of the emergence of a 'transnational capitalist class' (TCC) out of the process of globalisation. Sklair, for instance, based his thesis on two basic points: 1) the flow of foreign direct investments (FDIs) and 2) diffusion of the ideology of consumerism (Sklair 2001: 20–21). According to him, this class composed of corporate executives and global bureaucrats (located in different countries and cities) has developed advanced systems of communications via the membership in organisations. Similarly, Robinson also advances his idea of the rise of the transnational capitalist class on the basis of statistical evidence of corporate mergers. But he advocates that this process marks the global bloc of capitalists which governs through the logic of global accumulation (Robinson 2004). Through his extensive network analysis, William Carroll maps the formation of the transnational capitalist class in the late twentieth and early twenty-first centuries. He denies that there is no global capitalist class detached from the national structures, although the national corporate community has joined transnational interlocks (Carroll 2010). These studies indicate the scholarship on the character of capital formation and production of inequalities and formation of global ruling classes.

## Capitalist development: alternative explanations

Several scholars have tried to understand the nature of capitalist development in India (Kaviraj 1988; Chatterjee 2008). Their formulations have challenged the traditional Marxist categories of violent uprooting of feudal forces and instead have analyzed the Indian situation as 'passive revolution' (Kaviraj 1988). These debates have also challenged the narrative of the 'universalising nature of capital' for its Eurocentric bias and stagist historical understanding. In the recent works, these critiques problematise theorisations about capitalism in India. For example, scholarly writings inspired by postcolonial theory have argued that capital has failed in achieving its agenda (and that there are 'two histories of capital'), and still the world periphery remains 'out of the logic of capital' (Chakrabarty 2000; Nigam 2007). A similar argument is articulated by Kalyan Sanyal in his work on capitalist development in India. Sanyal argues that even though India is experiencing the process of primitive accumulation, one should reformulate the question of the conventional narrative of transition. In other words, Sanyal challenges the popular explanation by bringing in the issues of welfare measures taken by the Indian state as strategies to reverse the effects of primitive accumulation (Sanyal 2007). Partha Chatterjee also agrees with this formulation of the Indian scene, where though the producers are forcefully separated from the means of production, the state still transfers some of the funds from corporate capital to the masses to reverse the effects of extraction (Chatterjee 2008). These new articulations of the Indian situation further expand the discussion of the nature of capitalist development. Still, Chatterjee avoids any discussion on capitalist development in its present form, that is, neoliberalism, whereby public goods and resources are shifted from the public sector to the private sector and there is deregulation of the domestic economy, incentives for private investment and creation of a huge amount of surplus labour. Yet the Indian experience of capitalism may be different in its methods of capital accumulation and different ways of organising labour markets (due to the significant role of caste and regional structures of power).

## 'New Spirit of Capitalism': the framework

Luc Boltanski and Eve Chiapello (2005) have demonstrated in their excellent work that working conditions of the advanced capitalist economies have changed drastically. They have argued that the role of critique in the revival of capitalism needs to be understood empirically. According to them, capitalism is basically a system for the 'unlimited accumulation of capital by formal means' (Boltanski and Chiapello 2005: 4). This explains the unique characteristics of capitalism to continuously introduce new mechanisms by which new spheres are added into the circuit of capital. To achieve this end, capitalism has to continuously formulate new notions of 'goodness' and 'collective good', new motives to involve people in its logic (ibid: 8). True to their Weberian influence, the authors stress the role of meaningful participation of people in capitalism with its own logic.

Post May-1968, the first response of the capital to the ongoing critique by unions was to negotiate with wage earners and concede benefits in terms of wages and security. That was the lesson learnt after the great strikes of 1936. This response focuses mainly on economic inequalities. This was the first response to social critique, and attempts were made effectively to disarm it. Firms were, then, looking for some solutions, and soon they introduced a series of innovations in the organisation of work as well as new values of work, with the dual objective of meeting another series of demands and bypassing the unions. This also led to rendering the previous labour laws null and void in practice. New mechanisms were devised to bypass the labour laws which protected the rights of wage earners.

According to the authors, there have always been four possible 'sources of indignation' (Boltanski and Chiapello 2005: 37) at the reality of capitalism; first, a demand for liberation; then a rejection of inauthenticity; third, a refusal of egoism and, finally, a response to suffering (ibid.). The first two are called 'artistic critique' by the authors, while the second two represent social critique. To mobilise sufficient human energies for it to survive and expand, the system now needed a third 'spirit'. The specific aim of their research is that the capitalist system has 'incredible flexibility' to accommodate critique and then disarm it. Boltanski and Chiapello undertake a comparative analysis of management texts from the 1960s and 1990s. In other words, Boltanski and Chiapello's framework raises the following arguments: as capitalism continues with its crises and contradictions, it finds its resources for its survival by engaging with systemic critiques of itself, and through this engagement and learning, it invents new mechanisms to disarm the critiques. For instance, it would introduce new management practices to deal with changing institutional culture or bringing automisation into production sites. Drawing on the concepts of Boltanski and Chiapello, this chapter makes an attempt to understand how far 'Patel agitation' presents the 'social critique' of the socioeconomic shifts that have taken place in Gujarat. In this work, social critique refers to inequalities, the crisis of the social world. It refers to the response of social groups to the impacts of factors such as capitalist development, regional transformation, caste competitiveness, growth of private capital investment and the combinations of many such factors.

Working with this framework, this chapter analyses the social conditions of Patels in Gujarat. With the changing regional socioeconomic contexts and rising social status of OBC castes, Patels are trying to change their mode of engagement with power. With the changing economic policies of the state and shrinking space of the government sector, along with changing caste relations, Patels have modified their approach towards government, the labour market and political bargaining. Experiencing class differentiation within the community, Patels rearticulate their identities through notions of backwardness and the discourse of reservation, without directly addressing/attacking capitalist developments happening in Gujarat.

## Indian experiences: the regional contexts

Post-1980s, the Indian economy has experienced a decline in the regulation of trade and an increase in capital flows (Kohli 2006; Mukherji 2014). With the declaration of the neoliberal agenda in 1990, then-Finance Minister Manmohan Singh of Congress initiated the most-discussed economic (liberalisation) reforms. It marked an historical moment for the economy of India as it set free the expansionist tendencies of capital, with a reduction in state interventions (Kohli 2006; Corbridge & Harriss 2003). With the onset of green revolution in some states, Indian agriculture foresaw its capitalisation and the rise of multiple cropping and high-yielding seeds. More importantly, the 'structural adjustment' programme achieved its ideological hegemony only in last decade or so. It is precisely this socioeconomic context of the last decade (from 1998 onwards) within which we see an upsurge for the demand of reservation among the erstwhile agricultural (dominant) communities in India (Harriss-White & Heyer 2015). During the 1970s and 80s, these rural elites tended to negotiate power with the Indian state, as the perception was that it was biased against rural India. The popular farmer movements aimed at the bargaining of power and attracting resources from the Indian state. With the decline of the farmer's movement due to various factors, that is, the exit of dominant castes from agriculture and the growing crisis of agriculture with commercialisation, these agrarian communities are left to assert their claims only through the discourse of caste.

There have been rich scholarly debates on the nature and character of capitalism and capitalist classes in India. Some of the literature focuses on the caste character of the business communities and the transformation with the economic policies of Indian state (Timberg 1978; Kochanek 1974; Oonk 2014), while a few others have paid attention to the growing diversification of capitalist development and entry of traditionally agrarian classes into the field of business and trade (Rutten 1995; Sinha 2005; Damodaran 2008). While Damodaran's work brings forth the interesting phenomenon of how regionally dominant agrarian communities have developed themselves as a business class in the respected social and political contexts, his work doesn't provide any analytical explanation of the nature of capitalism in India.

In recent writing on the emergence of provincial capital, Chari (2004) provides an alternative analysis of Indian capitalism in Tiruppur town. In a study of the Gounder caste, he shows that an agrarian community transformed itself into an industrial class of entrepreneurs. Locating himself within agrarian studies debates on the nature of capital formation, his work shows how accumulation of capital happens in provincial India through the network of caste, class and gender (Chari 2004: 41–44). A similar analysis of capital in the regional context of Gujarat is done by Vinay Gidwani (2008). In his work on rural capital, Gidwani disturbs the dominant narrative of capitalism and argues that it is always an incomplete process mediated by aspects of community life, regional structures of economy, agrarian contexts and so on. Challenging the conventional political economy approach to development, the author suggests bringing in cultural analysis of language and identity distinctions to understand how a certain caste emerges as the dominant player in provincial capitalism. Parthasarathy (2013, 2015) raises empirical questions on agrarian change and the strategies of agrarian elite in shaping the contours of state economic policies. His work questions the discourses of globalisation and tries to explore regional factors for the ongoing agricultural crises in the case of Maharashtra. According to him, more than global capital, it's the provincial capitalists who exploit and dominate the landless workers in various forms of bondage (Parthasarathy 2015: 821). These writings provide regional analysis of the development of a local caste elite and its strategies of upward mobility through various means of self-refashioning, orientation toward trade and market, control over state policies of agriculture and so on.

This chapter focuses mainly on the case of Patidars, in Gujarat, who are demanding OBC reservation for their community. There have been scholarly studies on the communal riots of Godhra and the Patidar movement against OBC reservations (Shah 1987). Patidars have been undertaking massive mobilisation in last two to three years. Interestingly, the existing discourses have centred more on the problems with the existing reservation system and its limitations to include these dominant communities within its ambit as against the lower OBCs, which are mainly traditional service communities (barbers, potters, carpenters etc.). More than the question of the relevance or eligibility of Patidars in Gujarat or, say, Jats in Haryana, for affirmative action, it is pertinent to look at the socioeconomic context of Patidars or any other agrarian (dominant) community who is demanding reservation in present times and their status in the economy and polity at large. Regional transformation due to urbanisation and decline of agrarian prospects have produced class differentiation within these communities. Lower-class factions of this community's search for jobs and thus migration from their villages to try their luck in the city are disappointed by the job market (Jaffrelot 2016; Damodaran 2008). In contrast to the middle class inhabiting urban centres for generations, these rural Patels have not received the kind of English-medium education that gives access to the services and the sector (especially in IT) offering opportunities (Deshpande and Ramachandran 2016). In spite of their attempts to enter into the private sector, they have finally fallen back on unskilled jobs in the growing informal sector in these areas.

## Demand for reservation: caste mobility, class differentiation and changing regional conditions

The recent agitations by Jats in Haryana, Patels in Gujarat, earlier Gujjars in Rajasthan and the ongoing Marathas in Maharashtra for their inclusion in OBC lists in their respective states speak to something deeper about the emerging crises. All of these are, broadly speaking, 'dominant castes' according to M. N. Srinivas's argument. More clearly, their dominance is linked to the regional power structure. According to Srinivas, a dominant caste is 'when it preponderates numerically over other castes, and when it also wields preponderant economic and political power. A large and powerful caste group can be more easily dominant if its position in the local caste hierarchy is not too low' (Srinivas 1959: 1). Now, the question is: Why are these dominant communities furious, and why are they on the street in many states? Let's have a look at their representation in state politics; 10 out of the 16 chief ministers of Maharashtra have been from the Maratha community; similar is the case with Jats (7 chief ministers), who make up around 25 percent of the total population in Haryana. In the case of Gujarat, Patels constitute 20 percent of the total population and have contributed 7 out the total of 15 chief ministers to the state (Jaffrelot 2016). Thus, in spite of their robust presence in the state sector, these communities might have perceived their positions as disempowered due to multiple socioeconomic factors related to regional power structures. For instance, the rise of large private corporations in Gujarat (as evident from the Assocham data), ongoing crises in the agricultural sector, increasing presence of OBC castes in the public sector and government's neoliberal policy of land acquisition further shake the material basis of their dominance.

## Patidars and their social profile

Patidars are the dominant community of Gujarat. Patidar, as the name indicates, refers to the strips of land holders who used to pay revenue for its use in Charotar tracts in settled villages (Rutten 1995). They are divided mainly in two groups – Lewa and Kadwa – and are concentrated in the central and southern parts, respectively. Patidars benefitted a lot from tenancy reforms post-independence (Pocock 1972). By the end of the 1970s, Patidars were the dominant agrarian community, with affluent relations with towns and cities. They moved out of their villages, too, though not leaving the village entirely, and became successful in trade and entrepreneurship at national and global levels. Patidars constitute around 15 percent of the total population, second after Kolis' 24.2 percent, according to the Census of India (1931). Historically speaking, Patidars used to own land – approximately 65 percent of all landholding castes, according to the 1931 census (Gupta 2002: 4617).

Gujarat has an urban population of around 42.6 percent, according to Census of India, 2011, and it was 37.4 percent in Census 2001. Similarly, the rural population declined from 62.6 percent in 2001 to 57.4 percent in 2011. In recent years, Gujarat has also been heavily urbanised. More than 55 percent of the urban population lives in four metropolitan cities: Ahmedabad, Surat, Vadodara and Rajkot (Hirway et al. 2014). In terms of social composition, scheduled tribes (STs) make up 14.75 percent of the population and scheduled castes 6.74 percent. The Muslim population is around 9 percent in Gujarat state, according to the census of 2011.

But post-green revolution, several states like Punjab, Haryana, Gujarat and Western UP have experienced structural changes in terms of the subdivision of landed property, a decline in land-holding ownership, rising educational capital and huge in-migration from states like Rajasthan and Mahrashtra. During the 1970s, their numerical strength brought them positions in legislature and political parties. Patidars used to back the Congress in state politics since colonial times, and they emerged strong during their peasant movement against land revenue (Damodaran 2008). Congress, during the time of CM Madhav Singh Solanki, used to work with the electoral formula called KHAM – Kshatriya, Harijan, Adivasi and Muslim. When Congress introduced reservations for OBCs, Patels fought against this extension (Shah 1987). It was after this experience that Patels started tilting towards Hindutva politics and Gujarat experienced the emergence of Hindu-Muslim riots. Renowned for its dairy and agro-processing cooperatives (mainly in Kheda and Surat), Gujarat has India's largest food company, Gujarat Cooperative Milk Marketing Federation Limited (GCMMF), and a particular popular brand named Amul was dominated by Patels, as Marathas dominated the cooperatives in Maharashtra (Damodaran 2008; Rutten 1995). It provided strong economic imperatives to Patels to thrive in the hinterlands by diversifying themselves into areas beyond agriculture (Rutten 1995). The growing political competition with Marwari Banias and Kolis also fuelled the anxieties of Patidars. With their increased economic status, they tend to move towards the Bharatiya Janta Party (BJP), which was emerging as a powerful force in late 1990s.

The populist labels of 'Gujarat Model', 'Vibrant Gujarat' and 'Gujarat Miracle' are given to celebrate the success in poverty alleviation and job creation (Panagaria 2012). Gujarat has emerged as success story for private investment.[2] During the period of 2012–13, Gujarat was considered the best destination for real estate business opportunities.[3] Several institutions have noted the growth of private capital in Gujarat. The state has accounted for the top position in total cost of private corporate investment[4] for financial year 2016–17, according to a study by the Reserve Bank of India (RBI). RBI data shows that for the past five years, 62 percent of business projects were taken up by states like Gujarat, Odisha, Maharashtra, Andhra Pradesh, Chhattisgarh, Madhya Pradesh and Karnataka. Similarly, in terms of private investment, Gujarat has the third highest share in it. According to an economist, factors that explain the high investment by the state are the sum total of policies of tax concessions, investment subsidy amounts, low-interest credit services, providing land for cheaper prices and an overall pro-business labour policy.[5]

Indira Hirway et al. (2014) have worked through official documents to argue that the earlier policy objectives of promoting small-scale industries and balanced growth have been discarded and the recent trend is to promote larger industrial units and mega-projects, without paying attention to their employment generation capabilities. With all these capitalist-promoting policies, these dominant social groups are experiencing rising class inequalities in the process of capital accumulation, corporate policies of land acquisition via SEZs and so on. Recent studies have shown that with the process of urbanisation, the service sector has expanded, but this has not resulted in the creation of more employment (Hirway et al. 2014) for the large number of the young generation from erstwhile farming communities who want to enter neither agriculture nor the informal sector.

Gujarat, along with Haryana and Punjab, is mentioned as a success story of capitalist development and high rates of economic growth.[6] Data available from the government reports and surveys shows that employment has been stagnant in the state for the last decade, and the economy has experienced a severe process of informalisation of labour. As studies have shown, Gujarat places itself among the top states in attracting corporate investments. The rates of annual growth are cited to explain the success. For instance, it will be said that it has increased from 5.92 from 1993–4 to 1999–2000 to 10.27 between 2001–2 and 2009–10 (Government of Gujarat 2013–14). State policies of welfare schemes aimed at curbing unemployment and promotion of public sector units took a turn towards new industrial policies (2003, 2009) post-1991. Instead the government of Gujarat introduced the Gujarat Special Economic Zones Act (2004), announcement of new mega industrial projects and heavy cuts to the subsidies given to small-scale industries which are labour intensive and can reduce unemployment. According to government reports on fiscal responsibility, total amount of subsidies given for small-scale industries (SSI) for the period of 2001–11 was of Rs. 869.36 crores, which is only 2.27 percent of the total subsidies allotted to the industrial sector (Hirway et al. 2014: 148).

## Regional social transformation and the 'world of work'

In addition to the quantitative aspects of the rural economy, the quality of jobs has also dwindled. It has led the economically well off section to convert its agrarian capital into urban property and the real estate market, while some have sold it for SEZs. This is the process by which these groups have been separated from the land; thus, the next phenomenon is their migration to urban areas. But most of the migrants who left their villages to try their luck in the city are disappointed by the job market. In contrast to the middle class inhabiting urban centres for generations, they have not received the kind of English-medium education that gives access to services or the sectors (especially in IT) offering opportunities ('cultural capital', to use Bourdieu's vocabulary). In spite of their attempts to enter the private sector, they have finally fallen back on unskilled jobs in the growing informal sector in these areas.

Not just is the economy not producing enough jobs,[7] over the years, wages in the private sector have also gone down significantly, at times even lower than the public sector, thanks to the informal sector. The wage rates have also not increased in proportion to the increase in labour productivity. Gujarat has also been facing the problem of in-migration from other states such as Rajasthan, Maharashtra and Madhya Pradesh, and it contributes significantly to the informalisation of labour. State domestic product (SDP) distribution across sectors shows a change, too. The primary sector's contribution to SDP has decreased from 19 percent in 2003–4 to 14 percent in 2010–11, but it still dominates in terms of workforce participation, that is, 54 percent. The share of the primary sector was 17.9 percent, the secondary sector 35.1 percent and the tertiary sector 47 percent during the year 2012–13 (Government of Gujarat 2013–14). While the secondary and tertiary sectors contributed around 85 percent of SDP, they contribute only 45 percent of the workforce (Government of Gujarat 2013–14). Similarly, the share of the informal workforce is growing rapidly, and in the case of Gujarat, it is as high as 88 percent (NCEUS 2007). Another fact which highlights the declining power of labour is the low wage rates for male regular workers – Rs. 187 for rural and Rs. 306 for urban Gujarat. The nature of employment is declining each year for regular male workers in non-metro regions of Gujarat. According to NSSO (2007), only 39 percent of the male workforce has regular employment. During the last decade, employment for the male workforce, self-employment (SE) and regular employment (RE) have decreased, while the share of casual labour (so called 'outside of capital') has increased. It has increased the vulnerability of the workforce in Gujarat after the initiation of neoliberal policies which have led to a shift from small-scale, labour-intensive industries in different districts to mega projects in metropolitan regions. This also explains the swelling informal sector in India in general and Gujarat for the present purposes. It has increased up to 80 percent in urban Gujarat for male workers and 68 percent for female workers (NSSO 2012).

The anxieties of Patels represented by Hardik Patel does not result only from the changing political strategies of BJP and Congress but also from a deteriorating economic position. According to the Indian Human Development Survey (IHDS), a minority section has experienced a rise in annual per capital income from 17,470 in 2004–5 to 51,045 in 2011–12 (Jaffrelot and Kalaiyarasan 2017). Similarly, 40 percent of Patels, according to this survey, till the land, while 8 percent belong to the casual labour category, another 19 percent are doing petty business and 19 percent are included in salaried jobs (ibid.). Thus, these groups have seen their transformation from agrarian land-owning community to rural capitalists (Rutten 1995) and gradually gained political leadership of the state. Occupation-wise, elite Patels are dominant in medium-scale enterprises and big business such as Ajanta clocks, Nirma detergent, pharma groups, engine oil factories, windmill-making companies, diamonds, cement, engineering, manufacturing, real estate, construction, local newspapers and magazines and medicine and surgery in Gujarat. The economic difference among Patels is sharpened by the rural/urban divide as well (NSS 66th round).

Patidars claim that due to increased competition, increasing unemployment among Patidar youth and lack of access to higher and professional education, this agitation has been started. But there is one crucial question on which you see complete silence of Patidars about the market model of Gujarat. In this case, the agitation is not framed in the language of 'exploitation' or 'oppression' but as more of a decline of their dominant status of land-owning community in the larger social structure. Adding to it, these caste-based mobilisations emphasise their 'difference' more than class similarities with other castes. For instance, there is no horizontal solidarity taking place among these castes to raise the problems of the economic model per se. The ideological hegemony of the market has led them in the past to defy and protest against reservations (Deshpande 2015).

## Patidar agitation: response to shrinking public sector, internal class differentiation and capitalist development

This is where the theoretical insights developed by Boltanski and Chiapello in their analysis of the 'new spirit of capitalism' are helpful. If one looks at these movements, it is not difficult to relate these communities' critique of models of development and response to the ongoing decline in their dominant status. The classic response of the state and political parties in these cases has been to speak traditionally. It consists of a false 'promise' for reservation in some category, mostly OBCs, during the elections. It tends to burden even more the status of employment in the public sector which is any way declining in its scale; second, it saves the crises of capitalism by diverting the problem from economic realm to the question of the singularity of 'difference' in political domain. All these instances show how, in doing so, the state and political elites fundamentally transform the whole debate, and now it becomes a question of the corruption of political parties (in implementing affirmative action) and sheer opportunism of vote bank politics, while the (market) business, in the real sense of the term, runs as usual. There are also instances where several welfare provisions, such as Mahatma Gandhi National Rural Employment Guarantee Act (MNREGA), are brought in to 'reverse the effects of primitive accumulation' (Chatterjee 2008: 62). In the context of the absence of occupation diversification, these communities are compelled to find jobs other than agriculture. NSSO data suggests that the percentage of Gujarat rural households is quite high (66.9 percent) in agriculture, and simultaneously the manufacturing sector is primarily concentrated in metro areas. Patidars have been experiencing economic change, and it has separated them from their land, which traditionally used to be their capital. In northern India, 'land relations' are important to understand caste dominance. Their landed authority has decreased over the years with the marginalisation of the land from their control. The decreasing size of land holdings in Gujarat shows the decline of the landed elite. Therefore, the decline of small-scale and heavy labour-intensive industries which absorb the demographic surplus and the systemic blockage of occupational diversification among these agrarian communities have produced economic and sociocultural crises.

The case of Patidars also demonstrates that in most cases, social mobilisation entails economic hardship; the problem of class position, that is, property is declining or destroyed, jobs are lost, the state's biased attitude towards corporate groups, the relative decline in class position and blocking of the class position via social reproduction, are crucial factors, though not the only ones. As we learn from Boltanski and Chiapello, one of the fundamental concerns of capitalism's 'new spirit' is to satiate the one major anxiety – how far the system can assure those who are engaged and involved within capitalism of their economic and social security (Boltanski and Chiapello 2005). Many studies have pointed out the increasing class differentiation within these agrarian communities and overall 'disintegration of village social life' (Gupta 2005; Jodhka 2014). In continuation of the argument discussed in the section previously, changes in the regional political economy of Gujarat require brief analysis as well. The transformation in the 'world of work' for many social groups has produced 'fragmentation in their collective identity'. Therefore, it can be argued that Patidars have mobilised against the socioeconomic crisis which resulted from various factors of regional capitalist development, changing caste equations and increasing class differentiation. This also brings forth another crucial issue relevant in differentiating the demand for reservation by OBCs, SCs and STs (Prakash 2015). While SCs experience social exclusion not just in the economic sphere but also in culture, for these agrarian communities, mobilisation for reservation is based more on class concern and less on identity (Oommen 2014: 99). This point needs to be examined empirically, as the notion of backwardness is constructed in terms of caste/community identity as well as to articulate class position. For instance, Patidar, Jat and Maratha mobilisations are far from being an Ambedkarite movement which poses a critique of the Brahmanical caste system. Thus, the ongoing depoliticisation of economic crises has a substantial connection with the politicisation of differences and identities, which indicates changes occurring in regional power structures.

## Towards conclusion

In the postcolonial world, capitalist development is both conditioned by the local social dynamics of power and in turn shapes issues of cultural identity. In the wake of mobilisations by Jats, Patidars and Marathas, one needs to understand the changing nature of political economy in relation to sociocultures. Turbulence in regional power structures has contributed to increasing social resistances of several communities. With the sharpening of class differentiation within communities and ethnic groups, community identities have weakened, and that disturbs their caste or cultural/political pride. Socioeconomic transformations may exacerbate widespread anxieties which are real, need to be understood and must be addressed.

## Notes

1 'With 111 Billionaires, India 3 on the rich list', *The Tribune*, 25 February 2016.
2 'At 12 percent Gujarat tops private investment list: Assocham'; see www.thehindubusinessline.com/economy/At-12-Gujarat-tops-private-investment-list-Assocham/article20519943.ece (accessed on 15 March 2020).
3 'Gujarat Attracts 41 percent investment in real State: Assocham', https://economictimes.indiatimes.com/realty-trends/gujarat-attracts-41-investment-in-real-estate-assocham/articleshow/19912636.cms (accessed on 15 March 2020).
4 'Gujarat sees highest share of private investment in 2016–17: RBI', www.business-standard.com/article/economy-policy/gujarat-sees-highest-share-of-private-investment-in-2016-17-rbi-117091300058_1.html (accessed on 15 March 2020).
5 Atul Sood & Kalaiyarasan. 2014. 'Gujarat Model: Fiction and Facts', *Frontline*, https://frontline.thehindu.com/cover-story/fiction-and-facts/article5795324.ece (accessed on 15 March 2020).
6 The Official Portal of the Government of Gujarat mentions that 'Gujarat has been the first state to enact the Special Economic Zone i.e. SEZ Act, 2004. Special Economic Zones (SEZs) are growth engines that can boost manufacturing, augment exports and generate employment. SEZ is a specifically delineated duty free enclave and shall be deemed to be foreign territory for the purpose of trade and operations and duty and tariffs. The Gujarat SEZ Act, 2004 has made key provisions with respect to the appointment and termination of labour for units established in SEZs'; see, for instance, www.gujaratindia.com/business/special-economic-zones.htm (accessed on 15 September 2016).
7 According to the Labour Bureau reports, employment creation for eight key areas was at an historic low in 2015 at 1,35,000 jobs. See 'Job Growth falls to 7 year low in 2015: Labour Survey', *Financial Express*, 15 April 2016.

## References

Althusser, Louis. 2014. *On the Reproduction of Capitalism: Ideology and Ideological State Apparatus*. London: Verso.
Boltanski, Luc and Eve Chiapello. 2005. *The New Spirit of Capitalism*. London: Verso.
Carroll, William K. 2010. *The Making of a Transnational Capitalist Class: Corporate Power in the Twenty-First Century*. London: Zed Books.

Chakrabarty, Dipesh. 2000. *Provincializing Europe: Postcolonial Thought and Historical Difference*. Princeton: Princeton University Press.

Chari, Sharad. 2004. *Fraternal Capital: Peasant-Workers, Self-Made Men and Globalization in Provincial India*. New Delhi: Permanent Black.

Chatterjee, Partha. 2008. 'Democracy and Economic Transformation in India', *Economic and Political Weekly*, 43 (16): 53–62.

Corbridge, Stuart and John Harriss. 2003. *Reinventing India: Liberalization, Hindu Nationalism and Popular Democracy*. New Delhi: Oxford University Press.

Damodaran, Harish. 2008. *India's New Capitalists: Caste, Business and Industry in a Modern Nation*. New Delhi: Permanent Black.

Deshpande, Ashwini and Rajesh Ramachandran. 2016. 'Dominant or Backward? Political Economy of the Demand for Quotas by Jats, Patels and Marathas', *Economic and Political Weekly*, 52 (19): 81–92.

Deshpande, Satish. 2015. 'The Patel Idea of Reservation', *The Hindu*.

Gidwani, Vinay. 2008. *Capital Interrupted: Agrarian Development and the Politics of Work in India*. Minneapolis: University of Minnesota Press.

Government of Gujarat. 2013–14. *Socio-Economic Review*. Gandhinagar: Annual Publication of the Directorate of Economics and Statistics.

Gupta, Dipankar. 2002. 'Limits of Tolerance: Prospects of Secularism in India after Gujarat', *Economic and Political Weekly*, 37 (46): 4615–20.

Gupta, Dipankar. 2005. 'Whither the Indian Village: Culture and Agriculture in "Rural" India', *Economic and Political Weekly*, 40 (8): 751–58.

Harriss-White, Barbara and Judith Heyer. 2015. *Indian Capitalism in Development*. New York: Routledge.

Harvey, David. 2003. *The New Imperialism*. New Delhi: Oxford University Press.

Harvey, David. 2014. *Seventeen Contradictions and the End of Capitalism*. London: Profile Books.

Hirway, Indira, Amita Shah and Ghanshyam Shah. 2014. *Growth or Development: Which Way Is Gujarat Going*. New Delhi: Oxford University Press.

Hirway, Indira, Neha Shah and Rajeev Sharma. 2014. 'Political Economy of Subsidies and Incentives to Industried in Gujarat: Some Issues', in Indira Hirway, Amita Shah and Ghanshyam Shah (eds.) *Growth or Development: Which Way is Gujarat Going*, pp. 139–92. New Delhi: Oxford University Press.

Jaffrelot, Christophe. 2016. 'Quota for Patels? The Neomiddle Class Syndrome and the (partial) Return of Caste Politics in Gujarat', *Studies in Indian Politics*, 4 (2): 218–32.

Jaffrelot, Christophe and A. Kalaiyarasan. 2017. 'Alienation of the Patels', *The Indian Express*.

Jodhka, Surinder S. 2014. 'What's Happening to the Rural? Revisiting "Marginalities" and "Dominance" in North-West India', in Nandini Gooptu and Jonathan Parry (eds.) *Persistence of Poverty in India*. New Delhi: Social Science Press.

Kaviraj, Sudipta. 1988. 'A Critique of the Passive Revolution', *Economic and Political Weekly*, 23 (45): 2429–44.

Kochanek, Stanley A. 1974. *Business and Politics in India*. Berkeley: University of California Press.

Kohli, Atul. 2006. 'Politics of Economic Growth in India, 1980–2005: Part II: The 1990s and Beyond', *Economic and Political Weekly*, 41 (14): 1361–70.

Levien, Michael. 2015. 'From Primitive Accumulation to Regimes of Dispossession: Six Theses on India's Land Question', *Economic and Political Weekly*, 22 (50): 146–57.

Marx, Karl. 1990. *Capital Volume I*. London: Penguin Classics.
Marx, Karl. and F. Engels. 1968 (1848). 'Manifesto of the Communist Party', in K. Marx and F. Engels (eds.) *Selected Works*. Moscow: Progress Publishers.
Mukherji, Rahul. 2014. *Political Economy of Reforms in India. Oxford India Short Introductions*. New Delhi: Oxford University Press.
National Sample Survey Office (NSSO). 2012. *Informal Sector and Conditions of Employment in India, 2009–10. NSS 66th Round (July 2009–June 2010)*. Ministry of Statistics and Programme Implementation, Government of India.
NCEUS. 2007. *Report on Conditions of Work and Promotion of Livelihoods in the Unorganised Sector*. New Delhi: National Commission for Enterprises in Unorganised Sector.
Nigam, Aditya. 2007. 'Genealogies of Globalization: Unpacking the "Universal" History of Capital', *Economic and Political Weekly*, 42 (12): 1047–53.
Oommen, T.K. 2014. *Social Inclusion in Independent India*. New Delhi: Orient Blackswan Private Limited.
Oonk, Gijsbert. 2014. 'The Emergence of Indigenous Industrialists in Calcutta, Bombay and Ahmedabad, 1850–1947', *Business History Review*, 88: 43–71.
Panagaria, Arvind. 2012. 'The Gujarat Miracle', *The Times of India*, Available at: https://timesofindia.indiatimes.com/edit-page/The-Gujarat-miracle-There-is-no-denying-the-major-economic-advances-the-state-has-made-under-Narendra-Modi/articleshow/16495127.cms [Last accessed March 11, 2018].
Parthasarathy, D. 2013. 'Rural, Urban, and Regional: Re-Spatialising Capital and Politics in India', in T. Bunnell et al. (eds.) *Cleavage, Connections and Conflict in Rural, Urban and Contemporary Asia*, pp. 15–30. New York: Springer.
Parthasarathy, D. 2015. 'The Poverty of (Marxist) Theory: Peasant Classes, Provincial Capital, and the Critique of Globalisation in India', *Journal of Social History*, 48 (4): 816–41.
Petras, James. 2008. 'Global Ruling Class: Billionaires and How They Make It', *Journal of Contemporary Asia*, 38 (2): 319–329.
Piketty, Thomas. 2014. *Capital in the Twenty First Century*. Translated by Arthur Goldhammer. Cambridge: The Belknap Press of Harvard University Press.
Pocock, David F. 1972. *Kanbi and Patidar. A Study of the Patidar Community of Gujarat*. London: Oxford University Press.
Prakash, Aseem. 2015. *Dalit Capital: State, Markets and Civil Society in Urban India*. New Delhi: Routledge.
Robinson, William I. 2004. *A Theory of Global Capitalism: Production, Class and State in a Transnational World*. Baltimore: John Hopkins University Press.
Rutten, Mario. 1995. *Farms and Factories: Social Profile of Large Farmers and Rural Industrialists in West India*. Delhi: Oxford University Press.
Sanyal, Kalyan. 2007. *Rethinking Capitalist Development: Primitive Accumulation, Governmentality and Post-Colonial Capitalism*. London and New Delhi: Routledge.
Sassen, Saskia. 2010. 'The Global City: Strategic Site, New Frontier', in Swapna Banerjee-Guha (ed.) *Accumulation by Dispossession: Transformative Cities in the New Global Order*. New Delhi: Sage.
Shah, Ghanshyam. 1987. 'Middle Class Politics: Case of Anti-Reservation Agitations in Gujarat', *Economic and Political Weekly*, 22 (19/11): AN155–AN172.
Sinha, Aseema. 2005. *The Regional Roots of Development Politics in India: A Divided Leviathan*. Bloomington: Indiana University Press.

Sklair, L. 2001. *The Transnational Capitalist Class*. Oxford: Blackwell.
Srinivas, M.N. 1959. 'The Dominant Caste in Rampura', *American Anthropologist*, New Series, 61 (1): 1–16.
Timberg, Thomas A. 1978. *The Marwaris: From Traders to Industrialists*. New Delhi: Vikas Publishing House Ltd.
Wood, Ellen Meiksins. 2003. *The Empire of Capital*. New Delhi: Leftword.

# Part 3

# Institutions and movements

## The glocal dynamic

# 6 Neo-extractivism, developmental models and capital formation

## Substitutive natural resource governance in South America

*Alejandro Pelfini, Gaston Fulquet, Pía Marchegiani and Lucas G. Christel*

### Introduction

In South America, but also in other regions of the Global South marked by an export-oriented extractivist development model, finding the right balance across interests for a more responsive natural resource governance is a pending challenge. Increasingly, corporations and investors in our region are becoming so powerful that they have begun to assume functions traditionally related to the role of the State. By maintaining direct relationships with local communities and Civil Society in a broader sense, these corporate actors are even emerging as 'development agents'. Other less expected cases can also be registered when analysing natural resource governance. In the search of exploring the so called 'postdevelopment' paradigm, occasionally the State can also seek to replace corporations in their role as investors and traders, or even Civil Society in the representation of collective interests. Also, Civil Society can occupy vacant roles left by the State when it comes to managing conflicts. That increasingly present evidence makes it necessary to exercise a novel conceptualisation but also to rethink the canons under which the very idea of governance has been defined in the Global North.

Under the discussion of natural resource–based development, in this chapter, we introduce the concept of substitutive governance to portray situations marked by a deliberate replacement of one of the traditional governance agents (State, Market or Civil Society) by another that either ignores or assumes its functions. This scheme leads to bilateral instead of trilateral relationships, directly undermining a core element intrinsic to the notion of governance. After presenting the concept, we will analyse concrete South American cases that highlight the fundamental variations of this concept and their linkages with different developmental models (neoliberalism, neodevelopmentalism and postdevelopment).[1]

## Substitutive governance as a new concept

### *The devaluation of the idea of governance*

The concept of governance, with origins in the Global North, has been extensively used in the international relations and political science literature for a wide array of purposes and applied to a series of processes with different ideological backdrops. In the 1990s, when it was believed that the State sought to lead 'too many' processes, it was instrumentally used to displace the discussion from government to governance. In that direction, it was a useful tool for discussing the State's capacities in articulating and regulating the economic and social spheres. The notion of governance without government was thus introduced (Rosenau and Czempiel 1992), highlighting the idea of networks and collaborative politics in the context of European welfare States (Mayntz 2002). The State did not disappear as a crucial entity; however, its direct control over the other spheres was transformed into a capacity of influence (Peters and Pierre 1998).

In South America, the reception of the idea of governance was mostly sceptical, especially within social sciences and social activist groups. Critical voices still consider that the notion of governance does not express the regional particularities. The assumed symmetry in the balance between State, Market and Civil Society tends to idealise the consensual component of politics, underestimating its agonistic and conflictive elements (Hewitt de Alcántara 1998). In that context, and without dismissing its critics, this chapter proposes to discuss and analyse a more specific form of governance directly associated with the neo-extractivist accumulation model that prevails in our region. For South American societies, historically and still dependent on extractive exports, the governance of its natural resources constitutes a crucial element in its strategies towards autonomous development.

The beginning of this century coincided with a new boom of natural resources due to a peak in commodity prices and an increasing demand for these goods coming from the Chinese and East Asian markets. In a context of some kind of rare macroeconomic and political stability, governments of different political colours in the region took advantage of this situation for introducing social reforms, poverty reduction and redistributive politics (timid or radical depending on the ideological orientation). The so-called 'Commodities Consensus' (Svampa 2015)[2] – in opposition to the neoliberal 'Washington Consensus' – shows the contradictions of this short-term strategy in which progressive and leftist governments were not able to bring into question the foundations of an accumulation model based on the exploitation and the export of natural resources.

Therefore, the term 'neo-extractivism' (Gudynas 2013; Burchardt and Dietz 2014) emerged in the region for characterising the new process of re-primarisation of South American economies in the 21st century under progressive governments promoting distributive politics (universal social policies and tax reform) and a more active role of the State in regulating both Society and the Market. The term posed the paradox of progressive coalitions trying to introduce social reforms but based on the profits obtained from a classical, neocolonial accumulation model (Pelfini 2012); it is classical and neocolonial in the sense of keeping enclave and export-oriented economies: it is new in the sense of its global linkages, its technological sophistication and the role of the State in taking advantage of its utilities for distributive politics. This extractivist dynamic is always located at the core of all different development models proposed for the region (either protectionist, industrialist and oriented to the internal market or open and export oriented), and its resilience explains the difficulty of keeping a sustainable strategy for autonomous development in South American countries.

### *What is substitutive governance? Main features of substitutive governance*

As mentioned, in South America, the notion of governance acquires specific forms and does not necessarily respond to ideal types. In that direction, we observe modes of governance with a tendency to privilege a bilateral bond over a tripartite one (State, Market, Civil Society), excluding the third actor by explicitly ignoring or replacing its specific functions. While the canonical notion of governance refers to mostly symmetric and collaborative linkages between three fundamental realms and agents, our conception of substitutive governance supposes the intentional exclusion of one of them.

In the field of natural resource governance, this type of substitution is increasingly common, marginalising one of the three realms or agents from the process of public policies and from the associated management of resources. What one can observe is quite different and deeper than a mere strengthened or privileged relationship between two agents promoting a by-pass of the third part. This kind of bilateral linkages has many examples in the field of environmental politics, particularly in developing countries: potential conflictive Civil Society actors are often excluded from large-scale projects secretly negotiated between powerful corporations and hungry-for-investment nation-states. Moreover, the substitution takes place not just by eliminating the functions and tasks of one of the agents but by deliberatively assuming the role originally and traditionally associated with the other. Another form of substitution is possible when one of these three realms or agents occupies a vacant space left by the other because of ineffective action or of a lack of capacities and resources. In this sense, the substitution tends to be a 'second-best option': an artificial and failed version in the performance of functions and tasks that are being replaced, according to Adorno's concept of *Ersatz* (substitution, replacement).

That substitution among agents can assume different forms beyond the classical by-pass, and it also develops distinct affinities with different development models that directly impact the governance of natural resources.

- Market + Civil Society replacing the State in neoliberal contexts.
  In these cases, corporations assume the functions of promoting development and mediation, facing or preventing conflict with local communities. This is the most common substitutive relationship in different parts of the world introduced by large investors and wide-ranging projects. For example, in Chile, it is increasingly frequent to observe corporations willing to go beyond corporate social responsibility. These private actors seek to be the real developmental agents by being equipped with more information, resources and territorial embeddedness than the State itself (Pelfini and Mena 2017).
- State + Market replacing Civil Society in neodevelopmentalist contexts.
  In these cases, the State assumes the function of legitimisation and of representation of Civil Society's collective interests. This substitution tends to be found within populist regimes and was typical in Argentina under Kirchner's administration, where the State incorporated part of Civil Society's agenda in its antagonistic dynamic (Godio 2008). Within a populist logic, the State knows 'more' and 'better' than those directly affected. Those that still resist being incorporated under this dynamic are stigmatised as fundamentalist or particularistic with the accusation of hindering the general interest (De Ipola 1982).
- State + Civil Society replacing the Market in contexts exploring 'postdevelopment'.
  In these cases, the State performs the functions and tasks of an investor and a trader, assuming the role of companies normally engaged with that function. For example, in the case of Bolivia's hydrocarbon extraction and lithium exploitation, new State-led companies are created, generating compromises with local communities for the sustainable use of resources while integrating them in the harnessing of profits.

### *Previous and related approaches to substitution*

By all means, it is not the first time that the very term 'substitution' has been used in questions of governance and political regimes. Our approach to 'substitutive governance' recognises previous works and related notions. Probably the most important one is the classical article by Helmke and Levitsky (2004) in which they analyse the possible combinations of informal institutions and political outcomes. The focus does not rely on substitutive forms of governance but on the articulation between the functionality of informal institutions such as patronage linkages or clientelism ('whether following informal rules produces a substantively similar or different result from that expected from a strict and exclusive adherence to formal rules', ibid. p. 728) with the effectiveness of existing formal institutions. The combination of both variables results in four possible alternatives: complementary, accommodating, competitive and substitutive. The last alternative is a less familiar institutional pattern and combines ineffective formal institutions and compatible outcomes: 'Like complementary institutions, substitutive informal institutions are employed by actors who seek outcomes compatible with formal rules and procedures. Like competing institutions, however, they exist in environments where formal rules are not routinely enforced. Hence, substitutive informal institutions achieve what formal institutions were designed, but failed, to achieve' (p. 730). In contexts of weak State institutions, the substitution emerges for replacing this lack of authority trying to generate similar outcomes (i.e. *rondas campesinas de autodefensa*, or communitarian self-defence patrols, as in Mexico).

The only problem with this analysis is related to certain mechanicisms between formal and informal institutions: the substitutive governance of natural resources does not always have to do with replacing formal institutions by informal agreements when the first ones do not function effectively. Substitutive governance is not a matter of a relationship between the formal and informal dimensions of politics. In contrast, it is a question of an intentional replacement when one agent or realm considers that it can better perform the function of the other or because it occupies a vacant space.

More interesting is to understand the notion of substitutive governance by identifying its specific differences with other closer forms as cooptation, bypass or marginalisation and even with the deliberate transfer of sovereignty and competences. Instrumentalisation or cooptation supposes that one realm or agency takes advantage of the resources and competences of the other for its own goals. As mentioned previously, the by-pass implies the intentional overleaping using opaque bilateral agreements, because the bypassed realm or agent has veto power or because it can hide or delay the fulfilment of the goals of the agreement. Finally, the deliberate transfer of sovereignty and competences from one realm or agency into the other could be understood as substitution but in this case as an intentional form by the instance of agency that allows the replacement. On the contrary, substitutive governance takes place mainly when one dominant agency chooses to replace a silent or inactive member.

In order to refine the concept and show its empirical explanatory force, in the following pages, we introduce different forms of substitutive relationships schematising three fundamental cases and combinations between State, Market and Civil Society, considering three main levels of analysis, subnational, cross-national and regional focus.

The first example, at the subnational level in the Catamarca Province in Argentina, Civil society represented by the Catholic Church replaces the State in generating an open dialogue around the mining problems of the province.

Then we show a more complex scheme focusing on three countries and showing at least three types of substitutive governance which are also linked with three developmental models around the governance of lithium in the so-called 'Southern Lithium Triangle' (that includes Argentina, Bolivia and Chile) with the main reserves of the 'white gold' in the world.

Finally, a regional case shows how the Market, represented by a large State-owned binational company (Itaipú Binacional – Brazil/Paraguay) tries to fill the lack of regulation and authority left by regional institutions in the management, conservation and provision of water along the Paraná River and the La Plata Basin. The lack of a more regional overarching approach to water management allows for a quasi-exclusive regulation of water for extractivist use (in this case, mainly power production and intensive agriculture).

## Substitutive governance at the sub-national level: civil society protagonism in mining activity

In the past two decades, the mining industry in Argentina has been at the forefront of conflicts and controversies. Although the activity experienced a significant process of expansion and growth, protests against mining spread across several Argentine provinces. Subsequently, between 2003 and 2009, laws that banned open-pit mining in nine provinces[3] were passed.

The contrasting trajectories – development and prohibition – of mining activity in Argentina illustrate a complex scenario for harmonious relations between the State, Market and Civil Society. Different processes, like high levels of social contention, governments without clear institutional tools to canalise conflicts and companies with a little predisposition to give public information, provided concrete stimuli to move towards substitute governance practices.

In this section, we analyse the case of the Mining Dialogue Board of Catamarca province. This proposal, promoted by the local Catholic Church, sought to open a broad dialogue and discuss the mining problems of the province. The initiative appears as an opportunity to replace the role of a provincial State always reluctant to engage in a broad dialogue and to seek consensus.

Catamarca was the first Argentine province where open-pit mining was exploited. From the early 90s, the State showed mining as a central activity for a new economic development in the region. The State-owned company *Yacimientos Minerales Aguas de Dionisio* (YMAD) associated with transnational companies[4] set up the needed infrastructure to extract gold, copper and molybdenum on a large scale and promised economic development and private jobs. Thus, in 1997, *Bajo La Alumbrera* was inaugurated and most parts of the population granted it 'social license'. However, in the following years appeared the first complaints given the lack of economic development and limited employment opportunities. Towards 2003, heated environmental protests began in the city of Andalgalá and then spread over the province. Despite the increase in social conflict, the emergence of protests in other places such as Tinogasta and strong claims for the prohibition of mining activities, the provincial State never allowed an open dialogue on mining policy.

In a context of a progressive increase of social pressure and limited channels of dialogue between the contenders and provincial government, a key actor in Catamarca society surfaced on the scene: the Catholic Church. Catholicism is the majority religion in Argentina and particularly in the Northwest region, where the percentage of Catholics reaches 91.7%, the highest in the country (CIEL 2008). Historically, the Catholic Church has been a relevant actor in the structuration of social and political life. Even today, the weight of this religious actor exerts a huge influence on educational, sexual and familial issues,[5] especially in the more conservative Argentinean provinces. Even more, today, the Catamarca Provincial Constitution establishes the protection of the Roman Catholic Apostolic cult (article 4 CP) and determines that the governor must profess that cult (section 2, art 131 – CP).

Thus, faced with increasing social unrest and a provincial State closed to a consensual solution, the Catholic Church decided to replace a State task and called for a mining dialogue. At the end of 2006, Monsignor Elmer Miani called to jointly discuss the problems of mining: 'Moments before finishing a Mass I went to the Cathedral, and exclaimed: I want to warn to everyone interested, I invite you to talk about the mining issue in the Bishopric' (Monsignor Miani, San Fernando del Valle de Catamarca, Interview, September 2012).

In December 2006, a novel instance for environmental conflict resolution took place: the first meeting of the Mining Dialogue Board in the Bishopric of Catamarca. Then, during the first months of 2007, four more meetings were organised. The participation was broad and plural, with different sectors interested and several positions and interests. Throughout the five meetings, provincial and national legislators participated, mostly representing parties opposed to the ruling party (Frente Cívico y Social); mayors of the localities closest to the mining site; members of different environmental assemblies; representatives of non-governmental organisations, among others *Bienaventurados Los Pobres*; mining engineers and experts from the *Universidad Nacional de Catamarca*; mining sector representatives (Xtratta Cooper, BHP and YMAD); left-wing political parties and a few representatives of the provincial government.

The provincial executive strategy did not favour the institutionalisation of the dialogue. Provincial officials did not attend the first three meetings of the Dialogue Board, and nobody from the government expressed a position on the issue. This attitude provoked strong criticism from different actors, and church authorities sent a formal invitation to provincial authorities. In the two subsequent meetings, some second-line representatives of the Ministry of Health assisted. Only at the fifth and last meeting was the provincial secretary of mining, José Sinner, present. He strongly defended the activity and expressed that 'mining production in the province is compatible with the preservation of the environment and its sustainable development' and an effective contribution in economic and labour terms (Mining Press 2007).

The Mining Dialogue was abruptly interrupted due to Elmer Miani's health problems. Although he was planning to reopen the dialogue when he was better, ultimately the debate was cancelled and they did not meet again in the Bishopric. A couple of weeks later, the Social Pastoral Team of the Diocese of Catamarca published a document called 'Environmental Issue of Mining'. Those conclusions, other than pointing out the government's low propensity for dialogue, highlighted the deficient role played by the provincial State in mining activity control, recognised the legitimacy of the claim and the environmental concern of citizens and argued that large-scale mining had not fulfilled its promises of development. Finally, the document recommended a popular consultation to decide mining policy:

> It is well known that large-scale mining is a concrete reality in Catamarca since the mid-1990s. The provincial State was not prepared to handle the challenge of evaluating and controlling the environmental impact. Instead, they took a passive attitude and left the environmental issues to the mining companies, omitting their own responsibilities . . . Finally, based on the diversity of opinions and views over the mining environmental problems in Catamarca, properly highlighted in the Mining Dialogue Board, we consider the use of a valid constitutional tool such as that of the Popular Consultation, in order to ratify or rectify the provincial mining environmental policy.
>
> (Diocese of Catamarca 2007)

In line with the lack of willingness to participate in the Dialogue Board, the authorities of the provincial mining secretary discredited the final conclusions and were very harsh with the possibility of public consultation about mining:

> The conclusions of the Dialogue Board were lamentable. There has not been dialogue goodwill. Even one of the bishop collaborators played in favour of the 'antimineros', they are groups that do not want to listen. This initiative was very bad for everyone, nobody could have satisfied with this process, this dialog falls on deaf ears. . . . Social participation usually improves acceptability but participation does not improve the solution by itself. I believe that people have to participate in order to accept what is already done. If twenty people join together to decide something and three are experts and seventeen do not know anything,

> they will arrive to the same conclusions of the three experts. Participation helps the other seventeen to accept the decision.
>
> (Ángel Betelu, Undersecretary of Mining of Catamarca, City of Catamarca, Interview, September 2011)

The results of the Mining Dialogue Board were not positive. The Church sought to play a mediator role in a very specific and conflictive issue: open pit mining. The board was created as an exceptional instance, did not achieve the major objectives and quickly disappeared as a space for dialogue. This case is perfectly useful to show some of the limits and deficiencies usually faced by substitute governance. In this particular experience, an actor from Civil Society replaced the provincial State as guarantor of social peace and promoter of dialogue over controversial issues. However, the lack of an institutional framework for negotiation, the weakness of previous links between different actors and the impossibility of arriving at binding agreements undermined the effectiveness of the initiative. Additionally, the non-proactive attitude of the provincial State limited dialogue efficacy. The experience of Catamarca shows an interesting finding. Substitute governance easily fails if the replaced actor keeps the function to be replaced under its control and decides to boycott the initiative. In other words, the governmental actor, which has the responsibility to build consensus and promote social dialogue, decided to block the substitution process instead of taking a 'let pass' attitude about the initiative. So then, the substituted actor condemns substitute governance to play an artificial and decomposed version of those functions that others have tried to replace.

## Strategies and modes of governance in the lithium triangle (Argentina, Bolivia, Chile)

The discovery of lithium as a key supply for batteries for electronic devices and for hybrid or electric vehicles has placed the politics and policies of this mineral in an important position regarding two current global debates: information technology and climate change. Particularly, its capacity to store energy and its malleability to be converted into different shapes have been of significance. Moreover, lithium's importance for the green economy and the post-development debate, and its scarcity and unequal distribution, turn it into a strategic natural resource (Fornillo 2014b). Its price has significantly increased. Its demand has tripled in the last decade, and experts estimate it will double in the next due to the growth of the Asian market driven by batteries for electronic devices in the short term and batteries for vehicles (electric and hybrid) in the medium and long term. The demand for vehicle batteries is expected to rise from 2% to 25% (Cochilco 2013).

The countries in the so-called 'Southern Lithium Triangle' composed of Argentina, Bolivia and Chile hold around 60% of the world reserves of the mineral in their salt brines, which are today the most profitable to extract. Along their historic, economic, political and cultural differences, the three countries have developed varying strategies aiming to take advantage of the 'white gold'.

In Chile, which has positioned itself as the world's leading exporter of lithium carbonate (the main derivative and input for lithium-ion batteries), lithium extraction is limited by a decree of 1979 declaring the resource strategic due to military and nuclear interests. Thus, production today is in the hands of two companies (Rockwood, SQM) who were granted permission prior to that time. However, since 2014, the country has revised its strategy through the work of the National Lithium Commission, which has recommended more State involvement in the regulatory, control, operational, rent-capturing and innovation functions. The results in terms of policy shifts remain to be seen.

For the Plurinational State of Bolivia, the extractive sector is central for policies that seek to follow alternative paths in the frame of *Buen Vivir* and Postdevelopment. A three-phase strategy seeking to control the entire value chain was developed by the State, giving limited and controlled intervention to foreign capital.[6] Cooperation with foreign companies was sought for the design of the lithium carbonate and potassium salts for industrial plants and for the construction of a pilot phase battery production plant.

Argentina is the only one out of these three countries in which companies fulfilling the administrative procedures can be granted a license. Today there are approximately 42 projects in different phases, involving foreign companies, which generally operate through a local subsidiary and make joint ventures with a provincial entity and an automobile or technological company. Hence, multinationals manage to secure access to the extracted mineral at a beneficial price.

This contribution aims at revising three different types of substitutive governance present in varying negotiation-arrangements and relationships between social actors in the three referred countries.

## *Strategies and negotiations*

The different arrangements between State, Market and Civil Society actors do not only depend on the capacities and resources of each player but also on the cultural, historical and political configurations in each country and sector. While Chile, for example, has followed liberal policies granting stability to investment and economic activities with little State intervention for many decades, Bolivia – one of the poorest countries in the region – has, since the arrival of *Movimiento al Socialismo* (MAS), pursued revising and changing existing inequality patterns both within and with other countries. It has tried to empower indigenous populations, which, although they were the majority, were often excluded from public positions. Also, it has sought to intervene in economic matters to change the existing situation.

Argentina – a Federal State – has alternated between periods with more and less intervention of the State in economic affairs. Depending on the area, it has an active civil society, particularly in urban areas, seeking to advance more rights, while in different rural and isolated areas as the Puna, populations are weak and have less access to rights and services.

In Chile, negotiations occur mainly between the private sector and communities at the sub-national level. The Council of Atacameñan People, which nucleates 18 communities living in the *Salar de Atacama* area, negotiated an agreement with Rockwood Lithium in 2016. The agreement, based on the principles of Convention 169 of the International Labour Organization (ILO), involves sharing the benefits derived from natural resource exploitation. Annually, the company will deliver the equivalent of 3.5% of the sales of lithium carbonate and potassium chloride obtained on the basis of the production of the plant located in the area. Moreover, the company is committed to developing technology for the protection of the salt flat.

As opposed to their competitor (SQM is involved in scandals for financing politics), Rockwood thus manages to position itself as the good pupil who follows the Lithium Commission's recommendations on the governance of the salt flats around constructing shared value. The agreement implies replacing regulatory functions normally provided by the State, who in turn has received recommendations by the Commission responsible for the implementation of the 169 Convention, commenting on the limitations of the government in fulfilling its obligations around consultation, land situation and conflict resolution.[7]

Putting into practice the considerations of the Convention through the private sector, particularly those of benefit sharing which are not contemplated in national legislation, implies advancing in regulatory functions and occupying a vacant space left by the State. The communities, in turn, in some cases, have a vision of resignation and acceptance not only with respect to the State (for example, they do not expect to be consulted prior to the expansion of the projects that are already in operation) but also regarding changing the status quo as to put an end to production. Lithium extraction has been happening for more than two decades and is perceived as hard to stop or modify. In this context, some communities see the approach of the company as an opportunity that can generate greater economic benefits and channel environmental concerns.

The situation in Bolivia has a different setup. First, at the national level, there is a clear intention of the State to move forward in limiting the Market's influence. The government rejected strategic alliances with northern countries at the early stages, a strategy which only started changing due to delays and technical challenges and thus demanded incorporating different companies in specific and controlled tasks in the design and engineering of the plants.

The State decided to focus on alliances with social actors. Actually, the idea to have State-led lithium exploitation emerged from a farmers' union in the Department of Potosí, the FRUTCAS (Single Regional Federation of Rural Workers of the Southern Altiplano). FRUTCAS had already been active in the opposition to FMC ex Lithco exploitation of Uyuni's salt flat (FARN and CEDIB 2013). The national lithium development project continues to be supported by FRUTCAS, also due to the entitlement of millions of hectares for the communities in the area in exchange for allowing the salt flat to be granted the status of a fiscal reserve (Fornillo 2017). Thus, while communities of the salt flat do not participate directly in the extraction of lithium, there are no manifested conflicts or widespread critical voices against the State project. The main critiques emerge from some academics and Civil Society groups in Potosí concerned with the distribution of income or the delays in keeping up to date with the plans. What will happen when the project begins to give higher returns remains to be seen. For Revette (2017), this lack of confrontation at the subnational level is based on an understanding derived from a collective memory of marginalisation and difficulties. Exploitation and impoverished populations were two sides of the same coin with relation to extractive activities. The benefits from extraction were long taken away from Bolivian's miners and workers, generating positive impacts elsewhere. It is believed that the control of natural wealth under State rule will bring benefits. State control is seen as a deviation from the past.

Argentina's case is even more complex and less clear. At the national level, main interactions manifest themselves between State actors (mainly provincial governments granting access and control to projects but also national entities in creating support structures around the agenda of the innovation and research) and the economic actors (transnational mining, automobile or manufacturing companies).

The sub-national scenario varies from case to case. While in *Salinas Grandes*, the indigenous communities have organised themselves and with the support of external organisations carried out a process of resistance to the arrival and settling of lithium companies in the area[8] and struggle to change the power asymmetry, in *Salar de Olaroz*, communities are being integrated into the project in an instrumental way. The State has 'delegated' to the company the required procedure of prior consultation, which breaches international regulation on the matter. Thus, consultation processes have been carried out without adjusting to standards, resulting in a fragmentation between communities for and against the project. Those in favour managed to get working opportunities within the project or contracts to provide indirect services (catering, transport). Also, they are involved in the participatory monitoring led by the company.

Although the relationship between companies and communities happens without State intervention, the nature and conditions of this relationship seem to have emanated from a previous agreement between companies and the government. Did the State or the Market take over functions normally inherent to Civil Society, like those of social control and project contestation?

The substitution in this case seems a way to neutralise a social action that would cause obstacles to own interests, differing from the situation of Chile and Bolivia. Thus, it seems more a case of co-optation than one of replacement or attempted substitution.

## *Types of substitutive governance and development models of natural resources*

These three national cases show different setups around the governance of a mineral of increasing relevance. In all cases, some realms or agents have replaced a function generally inherent to another one.

In Chile, the association between the Market and Civil Society prevails at the subnational level; replacing the State in neoliberal contexts seems a deliberative strategy, particularly in regulatory and mediation functions. There is a sort of implicit understanding that corporate actors can become development agents and provide functions which the State cannot provide or is not interested in providing.

In Bolivia, the association between Civil Society and State is prominent and can be explained in the foundation of the Pluri-national State seeking to define and implement – in the frame of *Buen Vivir* and Postdevelopment – strategies which are less dependent on foreign investment and capital. The private transnational sector is deliberately excluded due to the historical context of unfair interaction between the State and the Market. However, these constructions and balances could be rattled when lithium enters mass production and produces higher revenues. At this point, it is interesting to reflect on the sustainability of the substitution mechanism over time. Those arrangements between State and Society could be dismantled. However, even if this happens, the Market actors would not automatically occupy a third place, as entry is controlled and regulated by the State. This will require a change in existing regulations, as today the lithium is to be extracted only by the State or State actors.

In Argentina, at the national level, the Market–State relationship prevails. At the sub-national level, with the Olaroz case, communities play a secondary role that could be framed as co-optation. What is at stake is the appropriation of the possibility of contesting a project, or some of its dimensions, generally a Civil Society's irreplaceable function. This is not done in the belief that a function could be more efficiently provided by another actor.

While in the three country cases, there is some functional substitution (regulatory in Chile, investors in Bolivia and control or contestation in Argentina), the three situations occur with different level of conflict or opposition between the replaced and replacing actors.

Interestingly, the two cases in which the functions that are replaced could be interpreted as inherent to the actor replaced (regulatory functions from the State in Chile and social control from Civil Society in Argentina) have shown minimal or no opposition by the affected actor. Neither the State in

Chile nor Civil Society in the Olaroz case in Argentina has publicly challenged the situation of replacement; contrarily, they have accepted the situation. Bolivia's case could be seen as the one in which the decision to substitute a function has brought about more discomfort from the replaced actor. Market players have criticised Bolivia's position and sought different approximation strategies to change the given scenario.

## Water governance: a South American strategic resource in a (neo)extractivist context

In this section, we would like to take the concept of substitutive governance to the regional level. South America is the world's region with the greatest availability of water, counting in its territory the largest hydrographic basins in the planet. Despite this blessing, the region finds enormous difficulties in constructing consensus and articulating interests for advancing the environmental management of shared water resources.

The traditional geopolitical view of our States over the La Plata Basin must necessarily open way to a newer hydro-governance vision capable of bringing forward a shared understanding of water resources as a common good. Water is one of South America's most strategic resources, as its abundant availability has allowed the expansion of relevant extractivist economic activities such as agriculture, mining and oil production. Additionally, the successive construction of hydraulic mega-projects, such as hydroelectric dams, has provided the needed power to support that expansion. Nonetheless, this intensive use of water is causing strong impacts on environmental flows and water quality, and because of that, the idea of governance of this resource acquires particular relevance for the La Plata Basin.

### *The La Plata Basin and its traditional governance structure*

The La Plata Basin is the second largest in the world after the Amazon basin, with an approximate area of 3 million $km^2$. A series of key ecosystems (forests, wetlands, etc.) lay along this basin, providing not only habitats for a rich biological diversity but also important environmental goods and services that support the livelihoods of its inhabitants. This explains the strong concentration and orientation of the region's population around the different watercourses associated with this basin. Without going any further, the relevance of these resources for society is confirmed by just observing that the capital cities of Argentina, Uruguay, Paraguay, Bolivia and Brazil are located within the limits of the La Plata basin.

The foundational stone on which the governance structure of the La Plata Basin was based is the Treaty of the La Plata Basin signed by those five countries in 1969. This instrument of international law gave rise to a supranational regional body: The Coordinating Intergovernmental Committee of the La Plata Basin (CIC). This body aims to promote and coordinate the development and integration of the basin among governments. Despite constituting a necessary coordination mechanism, an integrated governance of the resources and ecosystems present throughout the La Plata Basin requires, in present times, a broader framework than mere cooperation among States.

Due to the rapid pace of territorial transformations taking place within the basin, users and Civil Society as a whole (social movements, environmental organisations and the academic community) often hold a solid base of information and evidence that could be transmitted to the world of politics, thus improving decision-making in the resolution of socio-environmentally complex phenomena. The participation of these actors is key, as it guarantees that societal demands permeate the decision-making process. However, the treaty and statute that originated the CIC (as well as other similar international commissions in the 1960s and 1970s) did not foresee instances of participation for this sort of actors, not even within consultative bodies.

The ecosystems and processes that regulate the stability and resilience of the system do not occupy a truly preponderant position in regional water governance. A more productivist approach reigns, indifferent to the guiding principles of sustainable development. As a consequence, the La Plata Basin is nowadays subjected to the overexploitation of its natural resources and to the increasing degradation of its ecosystems. The main productive uses of water are associated with the agricultural, industrial, mining, energy, transport and urban services sectors. On the other hand, it is necessary to emphasise that agriculture is the main economic activity that takes place within the basin, being responsible for the greatest changes in land use and for an alarming increase in the presence of agro-toxics in water. Regarding mining and industrial activities, pollution by heavy metals and persistent organic compounds that accumulate in sediments or in biological membranes, respectively, is an element repeatedly highlighted in the study. The rapid growth of cities and the lack of sanitation facilities and wastewater treatment services has led to pollution with a risk to the health of the human population settled by the courses of water. Thus, episodes of waterborne diseases, such as diarrhoea, cholera, malaria and dengue, are common in certain regions of the basin (CIC 2016).

In line with Sassen (2014), a series of deep socioeconomic dislocations introduced by the very dynamics of the 21st century's global economy begin to become evident. The regional trend that we observe in the La Plata Basin and dialogues with other geographies and histories of socio-environmental deterioration make it evident that our era is the one that registers the greatest impacts of human activity on nature.

### *Substitutive governance in the integrated water resources management of the La Plata Basin*

An integrated water resources management approach promotes a coordinated use and development model around water, land and other associated resources in order to maximise the resulting social and economic wellbeing without compromising the sustainability of ecosystems and their functions. It implies an open and flexible process that links decision-makers from the different sectors (whose activities impact water resources) and brings all relevant actors to the table to establish policies and balance decisions in response to the conflicting uses of water. Nonetheless, the disconnection between the regional governance of water resources in the La Plata Basin and the needs of users and society in the territory has led to a model of water resources management aimed at guaranteeing more productivist uses of water (navigation and transport, irrigation, mining, energy) over its most essential uses (life of the biota, drinking, recreation).

Before this situation, under some sort of 're-loaded' corporate social responsibility, Itaipú Binacional (one of the largest hydroelectric dams of the region) has promoted since 2003 a programme for the management of the Paraná waters with a strong socio-environmental component. The Cultivating Good Water Program (*Cultivando Agua Boa*, or simply CAB in Portuguese) programme involves direct intervention actions in the territory of the municipalities grouped under the so-called 'Paraná Basin 3', an extensive region located in Brazilian territory west of the State of Paraná and south of Mato Grosso do Sul. This area, including almost 8,000 km$^2$ of tributaries of the Paraná river, involves 29 municipalities with an approximate population of 1 million inhabitants just on the Brazilian side. More than 2,000 partners participate in the programme, including government bodies, non-governmental organisations (NGOs), academia, cooperatives and community and business associations. This effort to implement actions for the integrated management of water resources has allowed the CAB programme to earn the 2015 UN-Water Award.

The CAB programme implements actions under the water, sanitation and hygiene (WASH) and integrated water resources management (IWRM) approaches by creating and supporting 29 local management committees that work on the recovery of over 200 micro-basins, protecting riparian forests and biodiversity and disseminating values and knowledge that contribute to the training of human resources, among other relevant actions. Noticeably, in this case study, a productive actor (Itaipú Binacional) whose goal is the production of electric power is the one taking the lead in promoting a better-integrated management of water resources (Friedrich 2015). Over time, and given its relative degree of success at a local level in Brazil, it has managed to drag the State into supporting its implementation through the direct sponsorship of specific State agencies such as the Ministry of Environment and the National Water Agency (among others). Additionally, CAB's successful experience of articulation between companies, local governments and Civil Society for water management is being exported as a governance model to other binational hydroelectric dams such as Salto Grande (Argentina-Uruguay) and Yaciretá (Argentina-Paraguay), which have begun to develop pilot projects for the management of micro-basins in their respective areas of influence.

Undoubtedly, this experience is an interesting way to revisit the links between State, Market and Civil Society in the environmental management of water resources in our region. The primacy of the productive uses of water is reflected in CIC's supranational structure, based on the reproduction of asymmetric relations by excluding other affected actors. However, Itaipú – as a corporate player – has managed to establish itself as a relevant actor in the participatory environmental governance of water in the Paraná 3 sub-basin.

A salient feature of these power corporations is that they were all born as binational State-owned companies. The question that remains open is if that nature is sufficient to justify a certain degree of substitution of an existent regional management committee (CIC) in such fundamental governance functions directly associated with the sustainable developmental path of the La Plata basin. There is a set of strategic elements directly associated with regional transboundary water cooperation whose definition cannot be substituted by corporate actors. In this sense, before a complex map of overlapping and competitive uses among all involved stakeholders, the very conception of water as a regional common (more related to resource and ecosystem use under a shared scheme) is a guiding principle that must still be defined and managed by the State as a central realm and agent.

## Conclusions and research agenda

Although it is evident that substitutive governance is far from the ideal way to manage, preserve and provide natural resources and goods, its repetition and recent emergence are signs that many relevant actors find good reasons and enough incentives to substitute at least one of the governance realms and agencies. In this sense, the reason the substitution takes place in the analysis of case studies is central: are they simply economic reasons, issues of vacancy, lack of authority and effectiveness, or is it a matter of by-passing veto powers and/or reducing risks, conflicts and transaction costs? Other important questions relate to the criteria for selecting cases of substitutive governance: Which cases qualify as substitutive governance? Is it something tacit, or does it require an explicit and intentional purpose of replacement?

In order to guide further research, a series of questions emerge from the analysis of the cases previously. Some refer to the different phases of the interaction processes:

1 In the phase before the substitutive interrelation: which elements trigger situations for substitution?
2 Disputes and negotiations: Who enters and who is excluded or forced out from the bilateral relationships?

3 Sustainability of the substitutive relationship: How durable it is?
4 Evaluation: What elements, functions and tasks can be substituted? Which functions are lost or wasted because of a given substitution?

It is to be recognised that we part from a normative preference for a tripartite relationship between State, Market and Civil Society based on the associated and collaborative management of natural resources without excluding disputes and conflicts. This is at least what the idea of governance emphasises. However, this does not imply ignoring that substitution is not always an anomaly. While a rigidly modern reading tends to consider the differentiation of functions an inescapable fact and heir to the notion of governance of the Global North, a more postmodern reading opens us to the concept of dedifferentiation (Lash 1990) as a trend or cultural climate that should not scare us so much. Rather, within the pluralism and variety of existing experiences in South America, the recommendation is to evaluate substitutive governance case by case so as to calibrate its duration and sustainability and gradually incorporate experiences from other contexts of the Global South.

At the end, this chapter shows how the practice of substitutive governance is related to new transregional forms of capital formation. The idea of substitutive governance compared across countries in South America actually demonstrates that capital formation produces different contemporary models defying the unilinear model of capitalism. Different regions and countries are in interaction and influence, entangled between practices of exploitation and expropriation, corporate responsibility and corporate abuse, state power and illegal violence (Leite Gonçalves and Costa 2019) consolidating an imperial mode of living (Brand and Wissen 2017). Following Lessenich's thesis on externalisation (2016), re-primarisation and extraction in Latin America feed industrialisation in other areas, showing that primarisation has not been a transitory stage of capitalism as the canonical discourses in social sciences postulated. These new regional emergences foreground the state as economic actor but without sufficient power to overcome those structural constraints.

## Notes

1 The latter can be also understood as a development model at the end.
2 'The 'commodities consensus' underscores the incorporation of Latin America into a new economic and political-ideological global order, sustained by the international boom in prices of raw materials and the continually increasing demand for consumer goods in both central and emerging economies. This order is consolidating a neo-extractivist development style that generates new comparative advantages – visible in economic growth – at the same time that it produces new asymmetries and social, economic, environmental and politico-cultural conflicts. These tensions signal the opening of a new cycle of struggles, centred on the defense of the territory and the environment, as well as on

the discussion of development models and the boundaries of democracy itself' (Svampa 2015: 45).

3 In Argentina, the National Constitution guarantees the original domain over natural resources to the provinces (Art. 124). For a detailed analysis of the relationship between social resistances and incidence over provincial mining legislation, see Christel 2016.

4 YMAD property is shared between the Catamarca province (60%), the National University of Tucumán (20%) and the National Interuniversity Council (20%). Different companies were part of Minera La Alumbrera, but at the time of Mining Dialogue Board Table, Xstrata Copper (50%), Goldcorp Inc (37.5%) and Yamana Gold (12.5%) were the owners of the mining company.

5 A sample of this actual influence was the lobby power of the Catholic Church in the debate on legal abortion. In 2018, National Congress discussed a free and legal abortion project. During the legislative process, several legislators denounced pressure from religious sectors. Finally, the upper chamber rejected the free and legal abortion law.

6 Phase I involves the pilot extraction of the salts needed, phase II the industrial production of them and phase III the production and commercialisation of lithium-ion batteries.

7 More information at: www.politicaspublicas.net/panel/chile-oit/1705-oit-ceacr-chile-2014.html (accessed on 4 March 2020).

8 Salinas Grandes' communities filed a lawsuit before the Supreme Court of Justice, and after it was rejected, they continued their complaint before the Inter-American Human Rights Commission. They seek to get recognition for their consultation and participation rights and thus avoid the beginning of lithium extraction, which they believe to pose a threat to their culture and main activities.

## References

Brand, Ulrich and Markus Wissen. 2017. 'The Imperial Mode of Living', in Clive Spash (eds.) *Routledge Handbook of Ecological Economics*, pp. 152–61. London: Routledge.

Burchardt, Hans-Jürgen and Kristina Dietz. 2014. '(Neo-)extractivism: A New Challenge for Development Theory from Latin America', *Third World Quarterly*, 35 (3): 468–86, doi:10.1080/01436597.2014.893488

Christel, Lucas. 2016. 'Resistencias Sociales y Legislaciones Mineras. Los casos de Mendoza, Córdoba, Catamarca y San Juan (2003–9)', PhD thesis, Universidad Nacional de San Martín, Argentina.

CIC. 2016. 'Análisis Diagnóstico Transfronterizo de la Cuenca del Plata-ADT', Comité Intergubernamental Coordinador de los Países de la Cuenca del Plata (CIC). Buenos Aires.

CIEL. 2008. *Primera encuesta sobre creencias y actitudes religiosas en Argentina.* Buenos Aires: CONICET. Available at: www.ceil-conicet.gov.ar/investigacion/sociedad-cultura-y-religion/linea-1-religion-y-estructura-social/primera-encuesta-sobre-creencias-y-actitudes-religiosas-en-argentina/ [Last accessed March 4, 2020].

Cochilco. 2013. Mercado Internacional del Litio, Comisión Chilena del Cobre, Dirección de Estudios, December 2013 (DE/09/2013).

De Ipola, Emilio. 1982. *Ideología y discurso populista.* Mexico City: Folios.

Diócesis de Catamarca. 2007. Tema Ambiental de la Minería, San Fernando del Valle de Catamarca. Catamarca.

Fornillo, Bruno. 2014a. 'A qué llamamos Recursos Minerales Estratégicos? El caso de las baterías de litio en Argentina (2011–14)', *Revista Estado y Políticas Públicas*, 3: 79–89.

Fornillo, Bruno. 2014b. 'Commodities, bienes comunes o recursos estratégicos? La importancia de un nombre', *Nueva Sociedad*, July–August, 252: 101–17. Available at: http://nuso.org/articulo/commodities-bienes-comunes-o-recursos-estrategicos-la-importancia-de-un-nombre/ [Last accessed March 4, 2020].

Fornillo, Bruno. 2017. 'Litio en Argentina. Mistificación, plurisoberanía y posdesarrollo', in en Mariano Feliz (coord.) *El desarrollo en disputa en América Latina*. Buenos Aires: El colectivo.

Friedrich, Nelton. 2015. 'Cultivando Agua Boa', Water and Sustainable Development: From Vision to Action. UN_Water Annual International Zaragosa Conference, Spain, January 15–17. Available at: www.un.org/waterforlifedecade/waterandsustainabledevelopment2015/pdf/friedrich_nelton_casebm.pdf [Last accessed March 4, 2020].

Fundación Ambiente y Recursos Naturales (FARN) y Centro de documentación e investigación Bolivia (CEDIB). 2013. *El litio en la Puna Argentina y Boliviana. Principales implicancias de la explotación de litio en la zona*. Available at: www.farn.org.ar/wp-content/uploads/2014/06/Investigacion-Litio-FARN-CEDIB-Enero-2014.pdf [Last accessed March 4, 2020].

Godio, Julio. 2008. 'The Argentine Anomaly: From Wealth through Collapse to Neo-Developmentalism', *Internationale Politik und Gesellschaft*, 2: 128–46.

Gudynas, Eduardo. 2013. 'Debates on Development and its Alternatives in Latin America: A Brief Heterodox Guide', in *Beyond Development Alternative Visions from Latin America*. Quito/Ecuador: Transnational Institute/Rosa Luxemburg Foundation.

Helmke, Gretchen and Steven Levitsky. 2004. 'Informal Institutions and Comparative Politics: A Research Agenda', *Perspectives on Politics*, 4 (2): 725–40.

Hewitt de Alcántara, Cynthia. 1998. 'Uses and Abuses of the Concept of Governance', *International Social Science Journal*, 155 (50): 105–13.

Lash, Scott. 1990. *Sociology of Postmodernism*. London: Routledge.

Leite Gonçalves, Guillerme and Sérgio Costa. 2019. 'From Primitive Accumulation to Entangled Accumulation: Decentring Marxist Theory of Capitalist Expansion', *European Journal of Social Theory*, January 27. https://doi.org/10.1177/1368431018825064

Lessenich, Stephan. 2016. 'The Externalization Society. Living beyond the Means of Others', in Markus S. Schulz (ed.) *The Futures We Want. Global Sociology and the Struggles for a Better World*. Madrid: International Sociological Association.

Mayntz, Renate. 2002. 'Common Goods and Governance', in Adrienne Heritier (eds.) *Common Goods. Reinventing European and International Governance*, pp. 15–27. Lanham: Rowland and Littlefield Publishers.

Mining Press. 2007. 'Sinner y Barrionuevo en la Mesa Minera de Catamarca', May 4. Available at: www.miningpress.com/nota/21856/sinner-y-barrionuevo-en-la-mesa-minera-de-catamarca [Last accessed March 4, 2020].

Pelfini, Alejandro. 2012. 'Global and National Political Elites in South America: Limited Transnationalization Processes and the Persistence of Inequality', in Boike Rehbein (ed.) *Globalization and Inequality in Emerging Societies*. Basingstoke: Palgrave – MacMillan.

Pelfini, Alejandro and Rodrigo Mena. 2017. 'Oligarquización y extractivismo: Cerrojos a la democratización de la política ambiental en Chile', *Perfiles Latinoamericanos* (FLACSO-México), 49 (25): 251–76.

Peters, Guy and John Pierre. 1998. 'Governance without Government? Rethinking Public Administration', *Journal of Public Administration Research and Theory*, 223.

Revette, Ana. 2017. 'This Time It's Different: Lithium Extraction, Cultural Politics and Development in Bolivia', *Third World Quarterly*, 38:1, 149–68, doi: 10.1080/01436597.2015.1131118.

Rosenau, James and Ernst-Otto Czempiel. 1992. *Governance without Government: Order and Change in World Politics*. Cambridge, UK: Cambridge University Press.

Sassen, Saskia. 2014. *Expulsions: Brutality and Complexity in the Global Economy*. Cambridge, MA: Harvard University Press.

Svampa, Maristella. 2015. 'The "Commodities Consensus" and Valuation Languages in Latin America', *Alternautas*, 2 (1).

# 7 Women's labour, patriarchy, and feminism in twenty-first–century Kerala

## Reflections on the glocal present

*J. Devika*

## Introduction

This chapter[1] attempts to rethink feminist politics in contemporary Kerala, which is now marked by much greater visibility of women in the public and in development and by the arrival of anti-patriarchal discourses that often reject binary gender models (Devika and Thampi 2012; Muraleedharan 2014). My attempt is, first, to reflect on how different global flows and local social dynamics have intersected in Kerala to produce both specific configurations of patriarchy as well as the resistance to it. Post-1970s patriarchy here is shaped by flow of labour from Kerala to the Persian Gulf countries and to the white-dominated and Westernised parts of the world, and not just because it is mainly male (Zachariah and Rajan 2012). I ask whether turning towards the global job market seeking economic and social upward mobility by significant sections of Malayalis may have transformed the nature of women's domestic responsibilities, which may also be a key reason they are less present in the labour market.[2] Nevertheless, this may not be through a confrontation of the 'global' and the 'local' understood as essential categories. For modern notions of gender as they emerged in Kerala were neither exclusively global nor local. The family in 20th-century Malayali society was definitely shaped by colonialism, which not so much destroyed indigenous structures and values as allowed them to mutate (Devika 2007). And besides, events like the Great Depression and transnational concerns such as population control decisively shaped it in the post-independence decades (Devika 2008).[3]

Not just the 20th-century modernised Malayali family but also its critiques have no unambiguously local (or global) roots. If the language of modern gender began to spread in the late 19th–early 20th century Malayali society with claims of universal relevance, the language of feminism appeared here in the late 20th century. By the 1990s, feminism in Kerala was beginning to be irrevocably pluralised. By then, the global discourse of women's empowerment and gender mainstreaming was firmly entrenched in Kerala, and 'governmentalising feminism', which fed on earlier developmentalist feminism, was emergent (Devika 2016a). After the Fourth World

Conference of Women in Beijing in 1995, feminist networking in Kerala proved quite amenable to both governmentalised feminism as well as the radical feminism of global governance feminists. From the early years of the new millennium, however, new feminist subjects who drew upon transnational feminisms made their appearance in sex workers' activism and anti-heteronormative critiques. These emerged as a form of cosmopolitanism which advanced a 'regulative universal' (Connolly 2000) – a contrast, perhaps, to earlier feminism which claimed universal relevance.

Feminist critiques of early macro studies on globalisation have often emphasised the extent to which gender is identified with the local and the ways in which the 'third world woman' 'is defined as either outside globalisation or the back on which its production depends' (Freeman 2001: 1013). Instead, many of these early critiques called for eschewing overly economistic accounts and viewing globalisation as a set of disjuncted processes that are not one-way flows from the global to the local (Marchand and Runyan 2000; Nagar et al. 2002) which may complicate gender binaries without weakening them (Chang and Ling 2000). Also, in contrast to feminist accounts of globalisation which tend to privilege Western ideals and experiences, these interventions move between different levels, seeking to integrate them from the vantagepoint of the local while paying attention to multiple analytical levels – individual, family, class, community, nation, and so on (Freeman 2001: 1014). Further, feminist analyses also highlight the importance of the historical dimension. I am inspired by the feminist methodological insight that in order to understand shifting trends, instead of setting up hierarchies between levels, we must understand 'specific places, with their own particular and changing histories, economies, and cultures vis-à-vis the intensification of global movements' (Freeman 2001: 1012). Related to this, I also draw upon the critiques of global governance feminist solidarity which calls for a more textured understanding of 'glocal' patriarchies and calls for mixed-methodology research that addresses complexities (Kim-Puri 2005; Mohanty 2006).

In the following section, I sketch a 20th-century trajectory of women's labour in Kerala, drawing upon my earlier historical research on the shaping of modern patriarchy there (Devika 2007, 2008) and reflect on its transformation in the post-1970s period. This is followed by reflections on the many strands of globalising feminisms in contemporary Kerala, the possibilities that they offer, and their exclusions. The conclusion collects the main threads of argument and reflects on the shape of feminist politics and policy adequate for these challenging times.

## 'Domesticating' Malayali women

Since the 19th century, missionary discourses and those ignited by the new generation of modern-educated Malayalis close to the colonial apparatus offered the Victorian ideal of monogamous conjugal marriage in Kerala

(Jeffrey 2003). Nevertheless, it may be important to note that the imagination of the modern conjugal family seems to have been also grounded in the ongoing propagation of brahmanical marital and family values through indigenous sources from the latter half of the 18th century (Ganesh 1997). There is evidence of deepening brahmanical elite discourse of feminine duty in the times of the 18th century Travancore monarchy, which excluded women from political power (Devika 2015). It was at the intersection of Victorian ideas about motherhood filtered through colonialism and locally present brahmanical ideologies of feminine chastity and procreative duty that the prototype which would later yield the imagination of the labouring rational housewife was produced.

The ideal modern family was imagined to be the fruit of the adequate development of gendered capacities in male and female bodies through appropriate socialisation and education deemed proper to each sex. The ideal woman was thus imagined to possess both the 'natural' disposition as well as the practical, socially acquired ability to physically care for her family members, especially the young, and also to cultivate their inner selves. Power flowed through two axes within the family, and women's responsibilities were shaped by both. In the husband–wife axis, the wife was expected to provide both care and pleasure and take a greater share of the responsibility to shape moral and affective bonding. On the parent–child axis, she was to provide the affect and perform the supervision necessary to raise children into individuated and industrious subjects of the relevant modern collectivity (say, the nation or the modernised caste-community). This was the period in which such re-imagination of the caste-community and the nation was widespread. This ideal has proved to be highly durable. Even today, the perceived crisis of the family is inevitably regarded as unimpeachable evidence for social breakdown.[4] Not surprising, perhaps, given that the modern family was projected as the very meeting-ground of nature and culture, and its breakdown would signify a crisis of both (Devika 2007).

Also, when parental responsibilities came to be gendered thus, this shift in the understanding of gendered parental responsibilities was also decisive in that it meant that they were now granted agency to which appeals could be made on behalf of modern collectivities (Devika 2008). In other words, the modernising caste-community or the modernising nation could appeal to them to engage in 'responsible parenting' understood in clearly gendered ways. Thus, women were advised to become rational home-makers and overseers of the 'souls'–subjectivities of the young. The new ideal mother was the agent of reproduction and not merely the giver and nurturer of life. Also, non-nurturant care work, when performed by the mother, was often seen to have qualities unique to motherly essence. The mother's non-nurturant care work was seen as essentially a tool of affect – this implied that the labour of the hired help could never match up to it since it would not carry maternal affect. So, both nurturant and non-nurturant caring labour within households associated with mothers were perceived early as crucial to the production of the bodies and minds of worthy industrious citizens of the modern state. This ideological reframing of maternal labour as necessarily infused with affect implies that paid direct care work, in order to qualify as equally good, must contain affect similar to the mothers. This aspect of Victorian family values which arrived here through colonialism has been persistent here and elsewhere, too (Erickson 2011).

However, soon, such arguments were further refined to make a case for income-generating labour by women at home. Such arguments often opened by agreeing to the centrality of women in modern homes and the role they played in ensuring their men's effective performance of modern gendered public roles. They then went on to make the additional plea that women need to engage in income-generating labour from home. Such labouring was seen to be a form of self-disciplining that would enable women to remain industrious and self-controlled subjects. An example of such reasoning that circulated widely in the Malayali reformist circles in the 1920s and 30s may be found in an essay on women's unemployment written by L Meenakshi Amma, clearly a member of the first-generation modern-educated Malayali women, in the late 1920s. She cites six benefits women may receive from home-based income-generating work: the sense of self-respect an earning woman enjoys, the compensation she is able to offer to family for expense she 'causes' (mainly at childbirth), psychological well-being, moral uprightness and avoidance of sexual temptation and gossip, good physical health, and becoming an exemplary model for all others around her (Amma 1927–28: 52). In short, performing the new maternal responsibility was not always seen as incompatible with income-generating work by women. The times were such that the non-contradiction may indeed have been a necessity. After the late 1920s, the economic distress brought about by the Great Depression pushed many of the first generation of modern-educated women, especially of the land-owning joint families, into the labour market, a process well documented by many celebrated autobiographies (for example, Cherukad 1981). Joint families came to be increasingly partitioned in the wake of legislation (Saradamoni 1999; Velayudhan 1999), and changing marriage practices, especially the rise of dowry among even the matrilineal communities, put pressure on privileged-caste women to seek paid work.

But women's domestic labour and paid work outside were regarded as incompatible and corrosive of women's essential 'femininity'; the entry of unmarried women into the labour market, it was feared, would expose them to sexual predators outside the home and community in the wake of the difficulties inflicted by the Great Depression (Amma 1930). The first-generation feminists in Kerala met these salvos with two arguments: one, they insisted that feminine qualities were associated with not so much a space, the home, as a form of power, which was relevant to all spaces that sought to shape subjectivities through non-coercive techniques. This 'gentle power' portrayed as quintessentially feminine could therefore be exercised by the women in spaces of paid work such as in schools, hospitals, reform institutions – even in public policing. Second, they argued that if a woman sought work for wages outside the home, it was usually to support her family and ensure its upward mobility and subject to the cultural docility the latter entailed (for a detailed account, see Devika 2007). Women did enter the service sector workforce in this period (Devika 2007: 198); those who did work deemed 'unfeminine' faced social humiliation, but this did not deter them.[5] These arguments were to become widespread among privileged-caste communities in the post-independence decades. While working-class women were gradually interpellated into the new maternal responsibility by the end of the 20th century (Lindberg 2001), in general, women's economic autonomy declined considerably with declining employment from failing agriculture and traditional industries and dowry becoming near universal (Arun 2018).

Strikingly, the early 20th-century advocates of the nuclear family never failed to emphasise the thrift as fundamental, implying that as a family form, it required significant investment of commitment, energies, and material resources as well; later commentators note that the expenditure necessary to lead such family life was higher (Devika 2005). The labour of children was lost when they were sent to school, and new kinds of materials and supervision were integral to it. The very nature of the dominant family-form, the nuclear family which requires relatively more resources to be stable, may indeed be one of the prominent pillars of the persistence of dowry and its steady growth in 20th-century Malayali society and after – the patrilineal and patrifocal nuclear family bolstered by transfers of wealth from the bride's family to the bridegroom's as dowry. This implies that those who have less wealth to transfer during marriage and are less subject to the ideology of marriage may face marital instability and family insecurity.[6] These changes may be considered fairly complete, even among many historically disadvantaged social groups in Kerala (Puthenkalam 1977; Osella and Osella 2000).

The labour migration from Kerala to the Gulf countries in response to demand accelerated from the 1970s after the monogamous nuclear family form had become the norm here. The estimated stock of emigrants from Kerala in West Asia grew from .34 lakh in 1973 to 11.40 lakhs in 2000 (Kannan and Hari 2002: 223). The immediate trigger for the outflow was the oil price boom of 1993. The volume of remittances from West Asia to Kerala is estimated to have risen from Rs 11,302 crores in 1997–98 to Rs 14,158 crores for 1999–00, and these were probably underestimates (*ibid*.: 211). Average per capita consumption expenditure here, which was below national average in 1977–78, rose to above 41 per cent of it by 1999–2000; family savings also rose considerably (*ibid*.: 201). It was also estimated that by 2000, the Kerala workforce abroad equalled the organised sector workforce at home in size (*ibid*.: 217). Migration from Kerala to West Asia continued to grow since, and in 2007, there were an estimated 18.5 lakh emigrants, and 9.8 lakh return-migrants.

Over time, migration came to be valued deeply as the key path to upward mobility (Osella and Osella 2000; Chua 2014; Gulati 1993), and Zachariah and colleagues (2002) noted a rise in confidence among women who had now to manage their households since men were away. Gulati (1993) tracks the different ways in which men retained control while women's workloads as well as their skills and confidence, increased. Already, in Gulati's work, one can discern that the nature of women's responsibilities changed from caregiver to supervisor overseeing the children's education (*ibid.*: 128). In their study on the social consequences of migration based on the Kerala Migration Study of 2000, Rajan et al. noted that migrant households consumed much more than non-migrant ones (2000: 67) and that there was a strong preference emerging for the more expensive private unaided schools and self-financing colleges and the tendency to pay more in private tuition fees among the former (*ibid.*: 75). Nevertheless, most scholars who have researched Gulf migration have reflected on the consequences of the uncertainty – which, as Gulati (1993: 13) notes, might be why households rarely risk investing their savings in businesses and instead invest in children's education and building homes. By 1993 already, it was being noted that 'Migration to West Asia is now Kerala's biggest industry' (Gulati 1993: 10). This is confirmed more recently (Planning Commission 2008; Raman 2010).

This growing prosperity-in-uncertainty in migration, coupled with greater dependence on it for socioeconomic upward mobility, coincided with the gradual withdrawal of the welfare state in Kerala post-liberalisation. The general fall in public service provisioning in health and education in the post-liberalisation years (Oommen 2010) has been noted, and since education that enables migration continues to be the goal, it is not surprising that micro-credit loans used by the poorest, the overwhelmingly unemployed Dalit and Adivasi women, are hugely for children's education and healthcare expenses (Nair, 114–15). In other words, by the new millennium, the family burdens, economic and otherwise, carried by mothers, especially of poor households, may have risen considerably. Research from the first decade on women's work and childcare arrangements among the poor in Kerala revealed the changing composition of women's work, their continuing and rising responsibilities as caregivers for children, and the increasing share of expenditure for children from the incomes of mothers (Thampi 2007).[7] However, the declining proportion of women in Kerala's labour force has been noted (Abraham 2013; Arun 2018).

These increasing responsibilities perhaps indicate major shifts in both quantity and quality of women's labour in/for the family. In quantity it now includes governmental labour – participation in self-help groups (SHGs), financial management, accounting, reporting work, presence in government and NGO events, and voluntary welfare work, as well as microenterprises (Neysmith et al. 2012). This is confirmed by a field study of SHGs in three districts of Kerala, in which the huge majority of respondents claimed that attending SHG meetings has become a 'routine activity which they have internalised as part of their domestic chores' (Nair 2015: 89–90).

In quality, performance of 'affective labour' in families cutting across class and caste hierarchies is evident. By 'affective labour', I mean the work that goes into the management of emotions. Earlier feminist theorisation, notably by Arlie Hochschild (1983), identified similar characteristics in certain corporate-sector jobs that required treating clients as guests. The production of appropriate emotions is removed from the home and family and becomes part of a corporate job managing client relations.[8] I claim that given the high investment in children's education as the main perceived pathway to furthering family upward mobility across the class-caste divide in present-day Kerala, the deployment of appropriate emotions in managing the time and energy of children by mothers has become a key component of feminine caring labour.[9] This is not a local phenomenon; it has been observed in contexts of high inequality in which education is the key path towards social and economic upward mobility, in which 'emotional capital' is deployed in childcare (Reay 2000).

Research into the changing nature of maternal labour seems to indicate that categories of work that may be classified under this form of labour, such as assisting children with their studies, putting them to sleep, and enhancing their verbal abilities, are performed overwhelmingly by mothers. For example, in such a study of activities mothers perform in the childcare regime, the percentage of mothers who took on themselves the task of teaching children ranged from 58 to 74 between women performing different combinations of labour types (Thampi 2007: 85). For women who limited themselves to domestic work and SHG activities, the share of traditional maternal responsibilities like cooking and these relatively new ones seemed more or less even (Thampi 2007; Arun 2018). Earlier responsibilities, for example, engaging in 'family status production', continue (Papanek 1979; Arun 2018).[10] This seems confirmed by recent studies of even the poorest, for example, of extremely underprivileged Dalit mothers in Kerala (Mathews 2016) and of the middle-class as well (Chua 2014). Recent fieldwork among Dalit agricultural workers in Kuttanad indicates that younger women do seek paid work but insist that it does not interfere with the many forms of domestic labour that they identify as 'women's work' (Sunny 2016) – a view confirmed by my own recent field work at a fisher village in Kerala (Devika 2017). It also seems that when women are able to entrust children and their education to other institutions, they do perform gainful labour in and around the home (Abraham and Devika 2014; Devika 2017).

The previous account reveals that women's labour within families in Malayali society has changed dramatically over the course of a century and a half. Towards the end of the 20th century, studies indicate a possible transformation of the role of the mother/housewife as a response to global migration and liberalising state policies. This seems implied in both the intensification of women's affective labour, its further entrenchment as feminine labour, and the general increase in the amounts and types of labour poor women have to perform to maintain family living standards. It is now well recognised in the feminist literature on care work that unpaid care work in general includes many different components that involve distinct labour processes and connect differently to the market; also, that it calls for synergies between different kinds of social, environmental, and human capital in particular contexts (Folbre 2006). Also, vital components like supervision of children, central to the affective labour that Malayali women perform, are often not construed as an activity at all (Budig and Folbre 2004). In Kerala, better-earning families, particularly of migrants to the Gulf, are more able to purchase non-nurturant care services, while the women who deliver them are more likely to leave a care deficit in their own homes. Thus, economically well-off women are more able to engage paid care workers, while most poorer women who offer such services have little community or family support (Mathews 2016). Paying attention to the invisibility of affective and governmental labour and exploring the local 'care-chain' may throw up interesting hypotheses to answer the question of poor women's labour market presence as well as rising inequalities among women here – in other words, the specific shape of what Palriwala and Neetha (2011) call 'stratified familialism' in the Indian context.[11]

## Resisting 'domestication': feminism in Kerala[12]

There is hardly a coherent feminist movement in contemporary Kerala, but feminist ideas, of varying provenance, circulate everywhere. The presence of global flows in feminism is very apparent both in the state's policies for women's – and more recently, the transgender groups' – empowerment as well as in civil social protests over gender injustices. The spread of global governance world-wide in the wake of Third Wave democratisation and the calls to deepen democracy; the effects of structural adjustment policies; and the often-intersecting discourses of UN-centred human development, World Bank-centred good governance, and the rhetoric of economic growth, is now well known. It incorporates the views of hegemonic US feminism and installs them in positions of legal-institutional power (Halley et al. 2006: 340). Governance feminism increasingly homogenises the needs and interests of women around the world, transferring the power to define these to global policy arenas (Baksh and Harcourt 2015; Mukhopadhyay 2015). Transnational feminisms, however, are perceived as

> a conceptual framework that seeks to liberate itself from the political and intellectual constraints of international feminisms and global feminisms. Whereas international feminisms are seen as rigidly adhering to nation-state borders and paying inadequate attention to forces of globalisation, global feminisms have been subjected to critical scrutiny for prioritising northern feminist agendas and perspectives and for

> homogenising women's struggles for sociopolitical justice, especially in colonial and neocolonial contexts.
>
> (Nagar and Swarr 2010: 4)

The literature on the ways in which feminism travels globally highlights the non-linearity of its spread. There is now evidence that the flow of feminist ideas was neither mediated exclusively by multilateral agencies, nor was it a one-way traffic from the West to the rest; also, the 'sponge/additive' approach to understanding the spread of feminism is critiqued (Lal et al. 2010: 37; Shohat 2001); this seems important for Kerala. For what we see is multiple strands of feminism, shaped also by the regional and national contexts. It is also true that global governance feminism in Kerala was interpreted in unique ways. The crucial point is precisely this: both global governance feminism and various transnational feminisms came to be interpreted and relayed in unique ways, but while the interpretation of the former did not help to make visible or politicise the emerging shape of patriarchy in 21st-century Kerala, the latter was more successful. In order to illustrate this, I offer a brief account of the articulation of feminism in Kerala in the 1980s.

Given the hegemonic status of the organised left in formal politics in Kerala, at least until the mid-1980s, second-wave feminism was a relatively late entrant to the political field here, though the early 20th century had seen a first wave of feminists who were inspired, among other things, by women's rights struggles in the West (Devika 2005). The former took root, braving the fiercest opposition from both the left and right political parties and their women's mass organisations and even the oppositional civil society (Erwer 2003). These feminists had roots in the ex-Naxalite radical groups in Kerala that chose to now move into civil social activism in the context of the 1980s in which post-Emergency, radical leftists moved into civil society to organise oppressed groups to shape a broader social left (Kumar 1989).

Generally, one may speak of these as two distinct strands of feminism of different political provenance, drawing equally but differently on Indian and Western intellectual resources. I have elsewhere called them 'political feminism' and 'developmentalist' feminism (Devika 2016a). Political feminism drew from Marxist feminism and ex-Naxalite political and intellectual formations. It envisaged patriarchy as a structure straddling family, civil society, political society, and the market (Devika 2016a). Political feminism undertook much-reported campaigns against domestic violence and dowry and was connected with the national women's movement. It ripped off the benign mask of the 'Kerala Model' discourse on socially developed femininity. 'Developmentalist' feminism had its roots in the people's science movement of Kerala, the Kerala Sastra Sahitya Parishat. The women who gathered around it were often middle-class leftists who sought a more flexible, pedagogic, and civil platform more in tune with the refined, modernised elite femininity they embodied. The universalist public activism of 'development' sounded far less iconoclastic; it took gradualist and reformist positions even as the structural dimensions of patriarchy were acknowledged (Erwer 2003; Devika and Thampi 2012).

In the same time-period, the mid-1990s, was the thrust towards 'deepening democracy' in Kerala, part of post–Cold War 'Third Wave' democratisation in India, complete with its deep investment in neoliberalised gender mainstreaming in decentralised governance through Panchayati Raj. This flow of welfare was mediated here by Kerala Sastra Sahitya Parishath's developmentalist feminism decisively, hitching the potentials of the discourse on 'women's empowerment' to livelihood-oriented, mostly economistic development directly (Parameswaran 2004). Gender mainstreaming post the Fourth World Conference of Women at Beijing in new dispensation through reservations and the Women's Component Plan in local-level planning held the liberal possibility of regarding women as a specific interest group. However, since women were not inducted into political decentralisation as political subjects, they were not regarded as an interest group but as a passive governmental category receiving welfare (Devika and Thampi 2012). Feminists soon were drawn into this new field, that of 'local governance', where they were relatively more welcome than in high politics, where they had fought relentlessly against the sexual violence of powerful politicians (Devika and Kodoth 2001). Here feminists of all stripes were welcomed as 'gender trainers' and adapted smoothly to the People's Planning Campaign's liberal political language in which women did not figure as subjects of counter-hegemonic politics. Elected women representatives, therefore, were not viewed as potential subjects of self-transformative politics but as agents of gender-equal development who needed 'capacity-building'. The 'gender' that the gender-trainer feminists deployed was yet another rehashed version of the male–female binary, already rampant in developmentalism. Not surprisingly, then, women gained a great deal of visibility and access to the public through both reservation in the local bodies as well as the statewide network of SHGs in Kerala, known as the Kudumbashree. It is also true that the 'unintended consequences' of such mobilisation have evoked interesting challenges to reigning patriarchies in micro-sites (Devika 2016b). However, the fundamentals of the new patriarchy were not affected. In sum, global governance feminism had decisively shaped local feminism by the early years of the new millennium. Interventions in high politics required an at-best ambiguous position on sexuality, sexual pleasure, and choice (Erwer 2003). Interventions in local governance required reinstating 'gender' as the male–female binary, albeit socially constructed, and 'women' as a governmental category. The flexibility necessary to meet emergent voices and challenges was depleted.

This was distressingly apparent when strands of transnational feminisms – mainly around organising sex workers and LGBT activism – made their appearance in the early years of the new millennium. Around 1999, sex workers began to be networked by NGOs in Kerala (Sreedhar 2011:

84–85); however, their public presence came from a determined bid they made to break away from being subjects of the global governmental regime set up around AIDS and assert themselves as speaking subjects and public–political beings (Menon 2005). The sex workers' refusal to accept an assessment of their work in moral terms led to an irresponsible conflation of sex work with the 'sex-rackets' – organised criminal networks – that feminists were fighting. In other words, the moral language that mainstream feminism had adopted in its struggles within the field of high politics continued to dominate its response to new formations and subjectivities in oppositional civil society (Devika 2016a).

In other words, local manifestations of transnational feminisms now often stand in distinction to governance feminisms in Kerala. The recent hightide of Hindutva aggression at the national level reveals this in stark relief. The Kiss of Love (KOL) protests that began from Kerala in 2014[13] were in resistance to the normalised abjection of the sexuality and the body and thus indebted to transnational feminisms around sexuality. The emphasis on touch in the KOL – the insistence on its heterogeneity, the refusal of the idea that all loving public touch must be asexual – is a clear defiance of naturalised gender (which also reinforces secularised caste) at the core of Kerala's experience of modernity. It appears that this activism that draws from transnational feminisms is more able to challenge the Victorian-brahmanical gender values that are advanced as 'truly Indian nationalist' by the agents of Hindutva, while governance feminism's neoliberal agenda seems to be increasingly dovetailing with, or at least not confronting, Hindutva's gender neoconservatism.

Second, the Kiss of Love protests also revealed the extent to which the abjection of sexuality and desire and forced heteronormativity are necessary conditions for the continuation of Kerala's export of human power, definitely the most important contemporary economic activity here. That is, the repression of all that may divert energies and attention from the task of turning the 'raw material' – young people – into the 'finished product' or 'human capital' – skilled labour for global job markets to be exported or invested – has been normalised in Kerala's present. In other words, if the version of governance feminism institutionalised in Kerala through gender mainstreaming has exacerbated women's labour burdens and failed to reduce the affective component in it, transnational feminisms manifest here seemed to have generated resistance to it, as evident in the KOL protests.

However, the present includes women's open and veiled struggles against patriarchal control that are far away from these streams of feminist activism and largely unaddressed by them. The most spectacular of these developments was undoubtedly the massive struggle launched by women plantation workers at the Kannan Devan tea estates in Munnar who have borne the worst effects of economic liberalisation, when six thousand women workers struck work on their own in defiance of their (male) trade union leaders (Mathew 2015). Also, women's struggles against ecological devastation caused by predatory growth have remained largely outside the concerns of the many strands of feminisms and local women's organisations (Binoy 2014).

## Conclusions

It is clear from the previous that it may be possible that we can no longer expect to find an answer that emphasises endogenous factors to utterly 'local' questions, for instance, about why the work participation rate of Malayali women continues to be abysmally low despite the fact that women students outnumber men in higher education (Kodoth 2010) here. In this chapter, I sought to move away from the tendency to identify women and their labour as stereotyped 'local' – that is, static and cut off from socioeconomic processes – still prominent in recent academic discussion on women's labour in Kerala. Sonia George (2013) for instance, argues, rightly, that paid labour carries negative connotations for women in Kerala and that women's work here is trapped within the framework of reproductive responsibilities. But she tends to ignore the implication of women's affective and governmental labours in processes initiated by economic liberalisation and decentralised governance. This seems to locate patriarchy in 21st-century Kerala as essentially a 'local'-familial phenomenon. I have, on the contrary, tried to trace its contours as shaped by both pre-existing forms and practices and through a complex intertwining of local, national, and global processes. Also, what is interesting about the Kerala case in the gender, labour, and globalisation literature is perhaps that it shows how the effects of globalisation need not always fall into the pattern of globally mobile capital drawing poorer local women into labour-intensive labour (for example, Collins 2003; Lynch 2007); it could well be the effects of migration-dependence in the economy having a transformative effect on women's family labour. Further, the national shift towards neoliberalism in welfare policies, and the regional version of it, affect women independently of globalisation. In other words, the contemporary transformation of women's labour in Kerala requires multiscalar research.

It is clear that the nature of labour identified as 'women's work' in Kerala has changed over the 20th century in response to the shifts in the manner of the region's integration with the world outside. As the 20th century progressed, and as the housewifisation of women workers proceeded apace, affective labour came to be demanded from women across widely distanced social and economic groups. Besides this, neoliberalised welfare sought to transform poor women into productive subjects; it also added governmental labour. Both of these may be important reasons for women's continuing peripheral status in Kerala's labour market. If prevailing Victorian-brahmanical domestic ideologies keep women's affective labour invisible, the discourse of women's empowerment keeps invisible the governmental labour that they perform as participants in neoliberal welfare governance.

It may also be noted that recent research into reproductive choices of women here reveals a dismal picture, revealing very poor autonomy within the household and meagre information (Jissa 2017), and this seems to be the continuation of a pattern observed earlier (Thampi 2007).

I have argued that in the recent decades, the Malayalee family has been drawn closer to the global market: the affective labour of (mainly) the mother, along with the parents' material investment in education and training of children, plays a central role in converting them from 'raw labour power' to saleable skilled labour. In any case, even a preliminary inquiry into the educational network in present-day Kerala would reveal that now there is an entire apparatus – in which homes, schools, tuition centres, skill-building programmes, coaching classes, self-financing and government institutes of technical education, placement centres, and the regulatory machinery of the government form interconnected sites and nodes – which is now fully entrenched in our growing market economy.[14] In other words, there are enormously powerful vested interests that would actively work to suppress young people's citizenship impulses through an array of instruments and turn them into docile bodies and tamed procreative beings, saleable labour power. Given the rising investment in (the increasingly few) children in families, the interest in shaping them into saleable labour is also high. The focus on migration for work and rising dowry demands by men with globally saleable qualifications may have effects that are as yet unexplored in contemporary Kerala. For instance, how to make sense of the 'structural worthlessness' of the young daughter in a family which has no resources to turn her into a migration-worthy worker through education foreseeing the huge dowry payments she would require? Does this have anything to tell us about the many recent instances of the trafficking of young girls of poor and lower middle-class families by their close family members?[15] There is much work to be done in re-examining the mutations of patriarchy in Malayalee families today.

The resistance to this refurbished patriarchy does not flow from the local – the feminisms that now circulate in Kerala are surely not endogenous in any simple sense. Governance feminism seems to have had a depoliticising effect despite the fact that it opened the gates for many women to enter the lower levels of formal politics; in sharp contrast, transnational feminist flows have politicised sections that were hitherto voiceless, especially those which challenge dominant neo-Victorian-brahmanical gender values directly and explicitly. Not surprising, then, is the shift in the discourse of feminist liberation – identified by the cultural mainstream as 'dangerous' – towards a young and queer generation. This leaves the older women more or less with a much-governmentalised notion of 'empowerment', which increasingly renders their rising burdens of labour invisible. But if feminism adequate to the local must be forged, perhaps the public and domestic ideologies which deny women's affective and governmental labours should be exposed.

It is true, as Kathi Weeks reminds, that it is no longer easy to perceive the 'private' and the 'public' components of women's work and even between 'work' and 'life' – especially in affective labour and governmental labour. However, as she reminds, '[W]hat counts as work and as life, and the border between them, are not pregiven; they are, rather, matters of political determination and . . . important points of focus for feminist struggles' (2007: 247). This is the necessary precondition for the formation of new alliances between feminist women workers' organisations, such as SEWA Kerala and the mobilisations of women workers exploited under the current regime of flexible work such as the Asanghatithamekhala Tozhilali Union in Kozhikode (Neethi 2015; George 2013; Binoy 2018)[16] and women workers rendered abject by economic liberalisation, such as those who work in plantations and traditional industries.

Also, the feminism that informs the anti-moral policing struggles in contemporary Kerala which generate resistance to the abjection of sexuality and desire needs to be understood as in essence opposed to the regime of 'child-crafting' for the global job market that calls for women's affective labour at home. Sexuality and desire, after all, are attributes of life and not of inert raw materials for production, and affirming it is surely resistance to an order that seeks to prune life into docile labour power. It is, then, possible to imagine fruitful alliances between the local manifestations of transnational feminisms that fuel resistance to the policing of sexuality and desire and feminist trade unionism that addresses local complexities adequately. It is also possible to imagine a coming together of the local resistance to majoritarian Hindutva and the struggle against new regimes of labour exploitation proceeding from neoliberal welfare policies and economic liberalisation.

## Notes

1 An earlier version of this chapter has appeared in the *Review of Development and Change* 24 (1), 2019, 79–99.

2 Work participation of women in Kerala is just 28 per cent, compared to 47 for all India. The rural figures are 33 and 58 per cent, respectively, and the urban figures 14 and 20 per cent. From the *Human Development Report of India*, 2010, cited by Neethi 2015: 7.

3 Jack Goody (2003) argues that trade and interaction generated social similarities around the world long before globalisation, especially in family, marriage, and the demographic transition.

4 Such understanding is pervasive in research and journalism in Kerala. For a critical analysis of dystopic narratives focused on Kerala in the 1990s, see Sreekumar 2009. Also, Chua 2014.

5 Femininity and success in police duties, for example, appeared to be inversely proportional. See, Sundaram, 'Penpolice Geetha' [Song of the Female Police] (*Naradar* 1, 9, 1941: 12–13).

6 Elsewhere, such situations of striking difference in instability and poor material endowments of families have been observed to have grim implications, pointing to the widening of the gap between children of better-endowed/stable marriages

and those of less-endowed/less-stable marriages in the access to resources and opportunities available (McLanahan 2004).

7 Buvinic and Gupta point to two factors that may accelerate this phenomenon. Of these, the first is the disruption of traditional patriarchal governance in families which 'weakens implicit and explicit contracts that enforce income transfers from fathers to mothers and their children' (Buvinic and Gupta 1997: 262–63). They quote Nancy Folbre, who remarks that this is a converging issue for women in the developing societies and in the industrialising world and that it is indexical not so much of women's choice not to depend on men as of a forced independence (*ibid.*: 263). The second trend they identify relates to declining real incomes in the wake of economic crises which prompt men to give up supporting families (*ibid.*: 263).

8 Hardt (1999) however, theorises affective labour as an essential component of all immaterial labour (that produces knowledge, services, and so on) in the post-Fordist labour regime. For him, this is a component of all labour – shaping networks, community, biopower. However, critics like Oksala (2016) point out that such over-broad theorisation of affective labour makes us lose sight of the fact that not all forms of affective labour command the same biopolitical power and recognition, and therefore the distinctions between reproductive labour and affective labour need to be fully recognised. This is a point stressed, rather differently, by neo-Marxist feminists like Kathi Weeks (2007), too. She endorses Hardt and Negri's claim that all of social life has become a productive machine but nevertheless insists on the gendered organisation of work that continues to persist within the new regime and that it is imperative to examine unwaged caring domestic work to see what component of it would constitute work under contemporary capitalism and what part constitutes life, which may be 'potentially set against the spaces, relations, and temporalities now dominated by work' (p. 247). I agree with Oksala and Weeks.

9 To reinforce what I argued before, it is worth stressing, as Aruzza (2014) does, that the labour of managing the emotions is not specific to late capitalism, and reinforcing her cautioning that 'It is not a matter of defending private authenticity versus social reification, but rather of mediating, shaping, and managing our affects through more humane social relations'.

10 Hannah Papanek (1979) defines 'family status production' as the totality of labour the elements of which include support for the paid work of other family members, the future paid work and status ambitions of children, ensuring status through social activities, and religious activity.

11 Studies elsewhere have also explored the specifics of affective labour that parents undertake. For example, see Lareau (2002), which examined white and black middle-class parenting styles in the United States, which reveals different patterns of affective labour in child care.

12 Parts of this section rely on my earlier work (Devika 2016).

13 See http://timesofindia.indiatimes.com/india/the-kiss-of-love-campaign/photostory/45109061.cms (accessed on 22 September 2016).

14 For an account of entrance coaching centres, see T. Ramavarman, 'Entrance Coaching – A Success Story', *The Hindu*, 22 April 2005, Thiruvananthapuran edition, www.thehindu.com/2005/04/22/stories/2005042200520500.htm (accessed on 10 September 2015).

15 See, 'Parents force their 13-year-old daughter into prostitution', 9 July 2015, www.newsgram.com/parents-force-their-13-year-old-daughter-into-prostitution-in-kerala/. Also, 'Father rapes daughter, pushes her into prostitution: 29 arrested', *India Today*, 23 June 2011, http://indiatoday.intoday.in/story/rapist-father-29-others-arrested-in-kerala/1/142512.html and 'Woman held for pushing daughters into

prostitution', 25 July 2015, www.thehindu.com/news/national/kerala/woman-held-for-pushing-daughters-into-prostitution/article7462954.ece.

16 Recent women workers' struggles in Kerala also include protests by nurses against poor pay and working conditions as well as harassment of many sorts, often leading to suicides (Jacob 2016).

## References


Abraham, Vinoj. 2013. 'Missing Labour or Consistent "Defeminisation"?', *Economic and Political Weekly*, 48: 31.

Abraham, Vinoj and J. Devika. 2014. 'Poverty and Women's Livelihood in Kerala: A Comparison of Two Sites', *Labour and Development*, 21(2): 1–29.

Amma, B. Kalyani. 1930. 'Streevidyabhyaasathinte Matruka' (The Model of Women's Education), *Malayalamaasika*, 1(1): 14–15.

Amma, L. Meenakshi. 1927–28. 'Streekalute Tozhhilillaaima' (Women's Unemployment), in J. Devika (ed.) *Kalpanayute Mattoli: Malayala Adhunikatayute Streepaksham*, pp. 47–63. Thrissur: Kerala Sastra Sahitya Parishat.

Arun, Shoba. 2018. *Development and Gender Capital in India: Change, Continuity, and Conflict in Kerala*. New York and Oxford: Routledge.

Aruzza, C. 2014. 'The Capitalism of Affects', *Public Seminar*, August. Available at: www.publicseminar.org/2014/08/the-capitalism-of-affects/#.V-EXYeZGRg6 [Last accessed September 20, 2016].

Baksh, Rawwida and Wendy Harcourt (eds.). 2015. *The Oxford Book of Transnational Feminist Movements*. London: Oxford University Press.

Binoy, Parvathy. 2014. 'Struggling Against Gendered Precarity in Kathikudam, Kerala', *Economic and Political Weekly*, XLIX (17): 45–52.

Binoy, Reshmi. 2018. 'P Viji Fights for a Fair Deal for Women in Kerala', *The Hindu*, Thiruvananthapuram edition. Available at: www.thehindu.com/society/p-viji-one-of-the-100-women-in-the-bbc-list-of-inspiring-and-influential-women-in-the-world-in-2018-was-selected-for-her-gritty-battle-to-secure-a-fair-deal-for-women-labourers-in-kerala/article25557501.ece [Last accessed November 23, 2018].

Budig, M. and N. Folbre. 2004. 'Activity, Proximity, or Responsibility? Measuring Parental Child Care Time', in N. Folbre and M. Bittman (eds.) *Family Time: The Social Organisation of Care*, pp. 51–68. New York: Routledge.

Buvinic, Mayra and Geeta Rao Gupta. 1997. 'Female-Headed Households or Female-Maintained Families: Are They Worth Targeting to Reduce Poverty in Developing Countries?', *Economic Development and Cultural Change*, 45(2): 259–80.

Chang, Kimberly A. and L.H.M. Ling. 2000. 'Globalisation and Its Intimate Other: Filipina Domestic Workers in Hong Kong', in Marianne H. Marchand and Anne Sisson Runyan (eds.) *Gender and Global Restructuring: Sightings, Sites and Resistances*, pp. 27–43. London: Routledge.

Cherukad Govinda, Pisharody. 1981. *Jeevitapatha*. Thiruvananthapuram: Chintha Books.

Chua, Jocelyn L. 2014. *In Pursuit of the Good Life: Aspiration and Suicide in Globalising South India*. Berkeley: University of California Press.

Collins, Jane L. 2003. *Threads: Gender, Labor, and Power in the Global Apparel Industry*. Chicago: Chicago University Press.

Connolly, William. 2000. 'Speed, Concentric Cultures, and Cosmopolitanism', *Political Theory*, 28 (5): 596–618.
Devika, J. 2005. *Her-Self: Early Writings on Gender by Malayalee Women*. Stree: Kolkata.
Devika, J. 2007. *En-Gendering Individuals: The Language of Re-Forming in Early Twentieth Century Keralam*. Hyderabad: Orient Longman.
Devika, J. 2008. *Individuals, Householders, Citizens: Malayalees and Family Planning, 1930s–1970*. New Delhi: Zubaan.
Devika, J. 2015. *Kulasthreeyum Chanthappennum Undaayathengane?* Thrissur: KSSP.
Devika, J. 2016a. 'Feminism and Late Twentieth-Century Governmentality in Kerala, India: Towards a Critical History', in Maitrayee Mukhopadhyay (ed.) *Feminist Subversion and Complicity: Governmentalities and Gender Knowledge in South Asia*, pp. 123–46. New Delhi: Zubaan.
Devika, J. 2016b. 'The "Kudumbashree Woman" and the Kerala Model Woman: Women and Politics in Contemporary Kerala', *Indian Journal of Gender Studies*, 23 (2): 1–22.
Devika, J. 2017. 'Surviving in Contemporary Kerala, India: Reflections from Recent Research in a Fisher Village', *Development and Change*. https://doi.org/10.1111/dech.12299
Devika, J. and Praveena Kodoth. 2001. 'Sexual Violence and the Predicament of Feminist Politics in Kerala', *Economic and Political Weekly*, 36 (33): 3170–77.
Devika, J. and Binitha V. Thampi. 2012. *New Lamps for Old? Gender Paradoxes of Political Decentralization in Kerala*. Zubaan: New Delhi.
Erickson, R. 2011. 'Emotional Carework, Gender, and the Division of Household Labor', in A. Garey and K. Hansen (eds.) *At the Heart of Work and Family: Engaging the Ideas of Arlie Hochschild*, pp. 61–73. New York: Rutgers University Press.
Erwer, Monica. 2003. *Challenging the Gender Paradox: Women's Collective Agency and the Transformation of Kerala Politics*. Goteborg: Department of Peace and Development Research, Goteborg University.
Folbre, Nancy. 2006. 'Measuring Care: Gender, Empowerment, and the Care Economy', *Journal of Human Development*, 7 (2): 184–99.
Freeman, Carla. 2001. 'Is Local: Global as Feminine: Masculine? Rethinking the Gender of Globalization', *Signs*, 26 (4): 1007–37.
Ganesh, K.N. 1997. *Kunjan Nambiar: Vaakkum Samoohavum*. Edappal: Vallathol Vidyapeetham.
George, Sonia M. 2013. 'Enabling Subjectivities – Economic and Cultural Negotiations: A Gendered Reading of the Handloom Sector and the Special Economic Zone of Kerala', *Indian Journal of Gender Studies*, 20 (2): 305–34.
Goody, Jack. 2003. 'Globalisation and the Domestic Group', *Urban Anthropology and Studies of Cultural Systems and World Economic Development*, 32 (1): 41–55.
Gulati, L. 1993. *In the Absence of Their Men: The Impact of Male Migration on Women*. New Delhi: Sage Publications.
Halley, J., Prabha Kotiswaran, Hila Shamir and Chantal Thomas. 2006. 'From the International to the Local in Feminist Legal responses to Rape, Prostitution/Sexwork, and Sex Trafficking: Four Studies in Contemporary Governance Feminism'. Available at: www.policeprostitutionandpolitics.com/pdfs_all/

Academics%20Research%20Articles%20Support%20Prostitution%20%20Decriminalization/2006%20Harvard%20Law%20Governance%20Feminism.pdf [Last accessed September 22, 2016].

Hardt, Michael. 1999. 'Affective Labour', *Boundary*, 26 (2): 89–100.

Hochschild, Arlie. 1983. *The Managed Heart: Commericalisation of Human Feeling*. Berkeley: University of California Press.

Jacob, Sajimon P. 2016. 'Nursing as "Decent Work": Questions of "Rights" and "Equity" in Care Profession'. Available at: http://kile.kerala.gov.in/malayalam/images/Research/Saji%20P.%20Jacob.pdf [Last accessed September 22, 2016].

Jeffrey, Robin. 2003. *Politics, Women and Well-Being: How Kerala Became a 'Model'*. New Delhi: Oxford University Press.

Jissa, V.T. 2017. 'A Study on Reproductive Rights and Choices among Young Women (18–28 Years) in Trivandrum District, Kerala', Paper presented at the Achutha Menon Centre for Health Science Studies, Sree Chitra Institute of Medical Sciences and Technology, Thiruvananthapuram, May 22.

Kannan, K.P. and K.S. Hari. 2002. 'Kerala's Gulf Connection: Emigration, Remittances and their Macroeconomic Impact, 1972–2000', CDS Working Paper Series 328, Centre for Development Studies, Thiruvananthapuram.

Kim-Puri, H.J. (Hyun Sook Kim, Jyoti Puri). 2005. 'Conceptualising Gender-Sexuality-State-Nation: An Introduction', *Gender and Society*, 19 (2): 137–59.

Kodoth, Praveena. 2010. 'Globalisation and Higher Education in Kerala: Access, Equity, and Quality', Report submitted to the Sir Ratan Tata Trust. Available at: http://srtt.org/institutional_grants/pdf/globalisation_higher_education.pdf [Last accessed August 10, 2016].

Kumar, Radha. 1989. 'Contemporary Indian Feminism', *Feminist Review*, 33: 20–29.

Lal, Jayati, Kristin McGuire, Abigail J. Stewart, Magdalena Zaborowska and Justine M. Pas. 2010. 'Recasting Global Feminisms: Toward a Comparative Historical Approach to Women's Activism and Feminist Scholarship', *Feminist Studies*, 36 (1): 13–39. Available at: www.jstor.org/stable/40607998 [Last accessed May 12, 2020].

Lareau, Annette. 2002. 'Invisible Inequality: Social Class and Childrearing in Black Families and White Families', *American Sociological Review*, 67(5): 747–76.

Lindberg, Anna. 2001. *Experience and Identity: A Historical Account of Class, Caste and Gender among the Cashew Workers of Kerala, 1930–2000*. Lund: Department of History, University of Lund.

Lynch, Caitlin. 2007. *Juki Girls, Good Girls: Gender and Cultural Politics in Sri Lanka's Global Garment Industry*. New York: Cornell University Press.

Marchand, Marianne H. and Anne Sisson Runyan (eds.). 2000. *Gender and Global Restructuring: Sightings, Sites and Resistances*. London and New York: Routledge.

Mathews, Binu. 2015. 'A Green Blood Women's Revolution in Munnar', *Countercurrents*, September 13. Available at: www.countercurrents.org/mathew130915.htm [Last accessed September 22, 2016].

Mathews, Leya. 2016. 'Aspiring India: The Politics of Mothering, Educational Reforms, and English', Unpublished PhD dissertation submitted to the University of Pennsylvania.

McLanahan, Sara. 2004. 'Diverging Destinies: How Children Are Faring under the Second Demographic Transition', *Demography*, 41(4): 607–27.

Menon, Bindu M. 2005. 'Identification, Desire, Otherness: *Susanna* and Its Public', *Deep Focus*, January–March: 61–69.

Mohanty, Chandra T. 2006. *Feminism without Borders: Decolonising Theory*, Fifth edition. Durham: Duke University Press.

Mukhopadhyay, Maitrayee. 2015. 'Gendered Citizenship in the Postcolony: The Challenge for Transnational Feminist Politics', in Rawwida Baksh and Wendy Harcourt (eds.) *The Oxford Handbook of Transnational Feminist Movements*. London and New York: Oxford University Press. Available at: www.kit.nl/gender/wp-content/uploads/publications/55ccac716a40e_Gendered_Citizenship_in_the_Postcolony.pdf [Last accessed September 22, 2016].

Nagar, Richa, Victoria Lawson, Linda McDowell and Susan Hanson. 2002. 'Locating Globalization: Feminist (Re)readings of the Subjects and Spaces of Globalization', *Economic Geography*, 78 (3): 257–84.

Nagar, Richa and Amanda Swarr (eds.). 2010. *Critical Transnational Feminist Praxis*. New York: SUNY Press.

Nair, Jyothi S. 2015. 'Social Capital Creation through Self-Help Groups in Kerala: A Multiple Organisational Analysis', Report submitted to ICSSR, New Delhi.

Nair, Jyothi S. 'Dalit Women in Self-Help Groups in Kerala: Instrument for Social Exclusion or Inclusion?', Report submitted to UGC, New Delhi.

Neethi, P. 2015. *Globalisation Lived Locally: A Labour Geography Perspective*. New Delhi: Oxford University Press.

Neysmith, Sheila M., M. Reitsma-Street, S.B. Collins and E. Porter. 2012. *Beyond Caring Labour to Provisioning Work*. Toronto: University of Toronto Press.

Oksala, Joanna. 2016. 'Affective Labour and Feminist Politics', *Signs*, 41(2): 281–303.

Oommen, M.A. 2010. 'Freedom, Economic Reform, and the Kerala "Model"', in K. Ravi Raman (ed.) *Development, Democracy, and the State: Critiquing the Kerala Model of Development*, pp. 71–86. London and New York: Routledge.

Osella, Filippo and Caroline Osella. 2000. *Social Mobility in Kerala: Modernity and Identity in Conflict*. London: Pluto Press.

Palriwala, Rajni and N. Neetha. 2011. 'Stratified Familialism: The Care Regime in India through the Eyes of the Caregivers', *Development and Change*, 42 (4): 1049–78.

Papanek, Hannah. 1979. 'Family Status Production: The "Work" and "Non-Work" of Women', *Signs*, 4 (4): 775–81.

Parameswaran, M.P. 2004. *Nalam Lokam: Swapnavum Yadharthyavum*. Kottayam: D.C. Books.

Planning Commission. 2008. *Kerala Development Report*. New Delhi: Academic Foundation.

Puthenkalam, J. 1977. 'Marriage and Family in Kerala with Special References to the Matrilineal Castes', in George Kurien (ed.) *Journal of Comparative Family Studies Monograph Series*. Alberta: University of Calgary.

Raman, K. Ravi (ed.). 2010. *Development, Democracy, and the State: Critiquing the Kerala Model of Development*. London and New York: Routledge.

Reay, Diane. 2000. 'A Useful Extension of Bourdieu's Conceptual Framework? Emotional Capital as a Way of Understanding Mothers' Involvement in their Children's Education', *Sociological Review*, 4 (4): 568–85.

Saradamoni, K. 1999. 'Kerala Model: Time for Rethinking', in M.A. Oommen (ed.) *Rethinking Development: Kerala's Development Experience*, pp. 159–74. New Delhi: Institute of Social Research and Concept Publishers.

Shohat, Ella. 2001. 'Area Studies, Transnationalism, and the Feminist Production of Knowledge', *Signs*, 26 (4): 1269–72.

Sreedhar, Darshana. 2011. 'Theorising Female Same-Sex Sub-Culture: Dissident Voices in 21st Century Kerala', Unpublished MPhil dissertation submitted to CSSS, Kolkata.

Sreekumar, Sharmila. 2009. *Scripting Lives: Narratives of 'Dominant Women' in Kerala*. New Delhi: Orient Blackswan.

Sunny, Yemuna. 2016. 'Social Relations, Environmental Discourses and Region Formation: The Case of Kuttanad in Kerala', Unpublished PhD thesis submitted to Tata Institute of Social Sciences, Bombay.

Thampi, Binitha V. 2007. 'Economic Role of Women and Its Impact on Child Health and Care: A Study in Kerala', PhD thesis submitted to ISEC, Bangalore.

Tharayil, Muraleedharan. 2014. 'Shifting Paradigms: Gender and Sexuality Debates in Kerala', *Economic and Political Weekly*, 49 (17): 70–78.

Velayudhan, Meera. 1999. 'Reform, Law and Gendered Identity', in M.A. Oommen (ed.) *Rethinking Development: Kerala's Development Experience*, pp. 60–72. New Delhi: Institute of Social Research and Concept Publishers.

Weeks, Kathi. 2007. 'Life within and against Work: Affective Labour, Feminist Critique, and Post-Fordist Politics', *Ephemera*, 7 (1): 233–49.

Zachariah, K.C. and S. Irudaya Rajan. 2012. *A Decade of Kerala's Gulf Connection*. New Delhi: Orient Blackswan.

Zachariah, K.C., E.T. Mathew and S. Irudaya Rajan. 2002. 'Impact of Migration on Kerala's Economy and Society', CDS Working Paper No. 297, Centre for Development Studies, Thiruvananthapuram.

# Part 4

# State, citizenship and the global connection

# 8 Unequal and gendered

## Notes on the coloniality of citizenship[1]

*Manuela Boatcă and Julia Roth*

Time and again, canonical sociology has presented and analysed citizenship as a counterbalance to social inequalities. Most sociology classics have seen the institutionalisation of citizenship as part of a sequence of social change characteristic of the West, which entailed progress from bondage to freedom and from ascribed to achieved positions in the inequality structure, ultimately defining the alleged transition from tradition to modernity. By contrast, the present chapter argues that a global perspective on citizenship reveals that its institutionalisation in the West has gone hand in hand with the legal (and physical) exclusion of non-European, non-white, and non-Western populations from civic, political, social and cultural rights. Both within and outside the West, women have been granted such citizenship rights only gradually, while populations of other regions have been gendered along colonial lines. On the one hand, the chapter draws on recent legal and sociological scholarship on global inequalities which has pointed to the ascribed character of citizenship and its key role in maintaining high inequalities between countries in the modern world (Korzeniewicz and Moran 2009; Shachar 2009). On the other hand, it builds on the literature on coloniality (Quijano 2000; Mignolo 2000; Lugones 2008) in order to reveal the structural distribution of unequal and gendered citizenship rights as a crucial component of modernity/coloniality, or what we call the coloniality of citizenship.

### Coloniality of citizenship and the colonial traffic in women

From a global perspective, the institutionalisation of citizenship rights in Western nation states coincided with the legal (and physical) exclusion of non-European, non-white, and non-Western populations from social and cultural rights. The Western construction of gender in the course of European colonial expansion (McClintock 1995; Oyewumi 1997; Stoler and Cooper 1997; Lugones 2007) has shaped the modern/colonial institution of citizenship since it came into existence. Inside and outside the West, citizenship rights were granted to women only gradually, while men and women of other regions were en-gendered along colonial lines. In line with the literature on coloniality (Quijano 2000; Mignolo 2000; Lugones 2007, 2008), we view the structural distribution of unequal and en-gendered citizenship rights as a crucial component of coloniality/modernity. Not only the naturalisation of women but also that of peasants and enslaved workers in the colonies occurred temporally and (ideo)logically parallel to the process of housewifisation of bourgeois women and to that of the proletarianisation of male non-wage workers in the industrial centres. Both were conceived as dimensions of the larger civilising process (von Werlhof et al. 1983; Mies 1996). Pnina Werner and Nira Yuval-Davis accordingly describe the exclusion of women from citizenship rights as 'intrinsic sign of their naturalisation and as embodiment of the private, the family and the emotional' and thus as 'crucial for the construction of the public space as masculine, rational, responsible and respectable' (1999: 6, our translation). By relegating women, children and foreigners to the (however recent) past of the civilising process that adult men had presumably accomplished, the implementation of seemingly universal principles of citizenship created constantly racialised and gendered particularisms. The corresponding exclusions historically ranged 'from colonial subjects to women, particular classes and racialised minorities, up to people with different sexualities and abilities' (Dobrowolsky and Tastsoglou 2006: 10). Gender positions have been racialised and ethnicised along colonial patterns, creating the image of the white virtuous woman and 'mother' of the race/nation – and later housewife – to be monitored and protected from black male aggression or of the sexually threatening, eroticised, and permanently available black female body, accordingly deprived of (the right to) protection and motherhood. It is at this juncture of gender, race and ethnicity as products of the colonial crucible that the institution of citizenship is revealed to be a key element in the maintenance of the coloniality of power of the modern/colonial world-system (Mignolo 2000). It is the specific mechanisms of its functioning throughout the history of the system that we refer to as the coloniality of citizenship.

By targeting the racialised and eroticised body, the coloniality of citizenship has made the circulation of the female body as a commodity a central part of the colonial order of gender relations ever since its emergence. In her 1975 essay 'The traffic in women', Gayle Rubin described the 'sex/gender system' as a 'set of arrangements' through which sex is translated into gender and which serves as a prototype of all social and economic relations. In this system, men exchange women among themselves on a continuum ranging from prostitution to marriage (Rubin 1975). In turn, Jean Franco maintained that particular forms of the 'exchange' of colonised women – such as enslaved indigenous women given as a gift to the Spanish conquerors or being exchanged between Aztecs and Spanish men – were already part and parcel of the Conquest of the Americas (Franco 1999: 71ff.). Gender has thus informed the modern/colonial institution of citizenship from its emergence, while gender and citizenship have been entangled in complex ways with other dimensions of stratification and inequality such as racialisation and enslavement that placed men, women and transgender persons at very different positions in racialised colonial hierarchies.

## Constructing a universal Occidental norm

The nineteenth century saw Europe's expansion into Asia and Africa, Darwinian evolutionism, and theories of the racial superiority of the white male (having the 'beastliness' of the African woman as a counterpart) eventually coalesce into scientific racism (Quijano and Wallerstein 1992: 551; Mies 1996: 95). The mechanisms of othering that were thus employed blended the logic of gendering into those of racial and ethnic inferiorisation by equating primitiveness and exoticism with femininity and puerility. What Edward Said had identified as the set of features used in describing the Orient as Other – 'its eccentricity, its backwardness, its silent indifference, its feminine penetrability, its supine malleability' – applied to slightly varying degrees to African women, Oriental men, and the non-Western more generally.[2]

The social construct of race had gradually replaced religious denomination as an identity marker and also as an indicator of a person's position within the hierarchy of methods of labour control outside Europe. At the same time, citizenship, initially defined in relation to (male) gender, property status, and literacy but not least social and ethnic extraction, fulfilled the same function in the newly emerging secular nation states of Western Europe. While the typologies thus established legitimised the hierarchy of labour payment according to a person's degree of proximity to this standard of citizenship, institutional mechanisms ensured the normalisation of the resulting 'Others'. The work of the Africans and Native Americans in the colonies, like that of women and children in the entire world economy, was treated as inferior and that of housewives as 'non-work' and was therefore either non-wage or unpaid labour. National constitutions, schools, hospitals, prisons, and guidebooks were in charge of emphasising the universal norm, isolating or treating deviation, and preparing the young generation for the role of the citizen as defined by Occidental standards. As decolonial philosopher Santiago Castro-Gómez has argued for Latin America, the disabled, homosexuals, and dissidents fell just as much short of the economically profitable and socially compliant national subject, as women, the illiterate, non-whites, or the enslaved:

> The acquisition of citizenship is . . . a filter through which only those are allowed to pass, whose profile fits the type of citizen required by the project of modernity: male, White, paterfamilias, Catholic, property-owner, literate and heterosexual. Those who do not meet these requirements (women, servants, the mentally ill, the illiterate, Blacks, heretics, slaves, Indians, homosexuals, dissidents) remain outside the 'lettered

> City' . . ., sentenced to punishment and therapy by the same law that excludes them.
>
> (Castro-Gómez 2000: 149, our translation)

Especially in those parts of Latin America that had previously been central to the Spanish empire before the eighteenth century, and which still had a sizeable indigenous population – such as Mexico, Central America, and the Andean region – the inculcation of Western norms through public education was part of extensive policies of cultural assimilation that largely built on modified versions of the former colonial policies.[3] In contrast, in Argentina, Chile, and Uruguay, but also in the Unites States, the virtual physical extermination of the natives and the conspicuous absence of Blacks from state discourse silenced the question of the political participation and social enfranchisement of the non-White population (Quijano 2006: 199ff.). Thus, the civilising mission brought about a dual pattern of hierarchisation of difference according to racial and ethnic criteria, both of which were moreover gendered (e.g. depicting indigenous men as feminised and lacking Occidental masculinity while positioning enslaved Africans as hypermasculine, threatening, and thus to be controlled). In turn, the respective gender positions have been racialised and ethnicised along colonial patterns.

## Global perspectives on citizenship

More recently, legal and sociological analyses of global inequalities have pointed to the ascribed character of citizenship and its key historical role in distributing unequal opportunities on a global scale (rather than its levelling effects within the boundaries of nation-states). In her 2009 book 'The Birthright Lottery. Citizenship and Global Inequality', legal scholar Ayelet Shachar has traced the Western institution of citizenship back to the feudal entail, a legal means of restricting future succession of property to the descendants of a designated estate-owner practised in medieval England. The entail of property offered a tool to preserve land in the hands of dynastic families by entrenching birthright succession and forbidding future generations to alter the estate inherited from their predecessors. It was this feudal institution that, according to Shachar's analysis, shaped the modern principle of citizenship allocation of Western European states in both jus soli or jus sanguinis arrangements. The entail of citizenship helps preserve the state's wealth in the hands of designated 'heirs of membership titles' – the state's citizens – by allocating political membership at birth in dramatically different opportunity structures and excluding non-citizens from the same opportunities (Shachar 2009: 38ff.).

In Shachar's gripping comparison, for a girl born in 2001 in Mali, one of the poorest countries in the world, the chances of surviving to age five, having access to clean water, or getting an education were incomparably lower than for a baby born at the same time in the United States, where chances for boys and girls on all these counts are nearly identically high. Contrary to an entire Western tradition of citizenship theory from Max Weber through T.H. Marshall (1973) and Talcott Parsons (1971) to Bryan Turner (1996), citizenship and gender, the most decisive factors accounting for these extreme inequalities between individuals in poor and rich countries in the twenty-first century, are both statuses ascribed at birth. Thus, citizenship functions as a kind of inherited property that restricts membership in well-off polities to a small part of the world population, additionally divided along gendered lines (Shachar 2009). Moreover, both inherited property and birthright citizenship are automatically transferred from one generation to the next according to ascriptive principles – either descent from citizen parents in the case of *jus sanguinis* or birth in the national territory in the case of *jus soli*. For individuals without birthright privilege in a wealthy state, international migration accordingly becomes a 'lifeline', 'a possible way to attain the precious and globally scarce good of citizenship in a stable and well-off polity' (Shachar 2009: 83).

At the same time, solid evidence for the fact that national citizenship represents the best indicator of an individual's position within the world's inequality structure has come from sociological analyses of the global income distribution. Using the Gini coefficients of 96 countries, Korzeniewicz and Moran (2009) have shown that national inequality patterns can be grouped into two distinct clusters. In the high inequality cluster (above a Gini of 0.5), containing the bulk of Latin America, the Caribbean, and Africa, *systematic exclusion* on the basis of ascriptive criteria such as race, ethnicity, and gender has historically served to limit access to economic, social, and political opportunities to a tiny elite. In turn, the low inequality cluster (below a Gini of 0.3), which encompasses the whole of Western Europe and parts of Eastern Europe, as well as Australia, Japan, and Canada, has involved widespread *relative inclusion* of the population through the extension of property and political rights increasingly derived from achieved (rather than ascribed) characteristics, such as education, and has facilitated the development of welfare states. The authors find that membership in both clusters goes back in time to the eighteenth century, and they clearly trace the origins of the institutional arrangements typical of high inequality patterns back to colonial slavery (Korzeniewicz and Moran 2009: 31). The long-term stability of low inequality levels, they argue, has been safeguarded by restricting physical access to these regions on the basis of ascribed categories, especially national identity and citizenship, through the control of immigration flows – not by achieved characteristics such as one's level of education or professional position or the economic growth of the country or region itself.

In this case, too, the logical (and radical) conclusion is that international migration, which entails gaining access to at least the average income of the poorer country deciles of a much richer nation-state, becomes the 'single most immediate and effective means of global social mobility for populations in most countries of the world' (ibid. 2009: 107). Thus, migration not only represents a strategy of upward mobility for populations of former colonial countries who possess metropolitan citizenship but also a means of eluding the ascribed position derived from the national citizenship of a poor state for populations able and willing to risk illegal, undocumented, or non-citizen status in a rich state.[4]

The possession of the citizenship of the former metropole remains to this day a crucial factor deciding the timing and the destination of former colonial subjects' emigration as well as the struggle for independence in the remaining colonial possessions. This has been documented for the postcolonial migration flows between several Western European countries and their former colonies or current overseas departments, as well as for the United States and its 'protectorates': thus, fear of losing Dutch citizenship has led to an unparalleled increase in Surinamese emigration to the Netherlands in the years preceding Surinam's independence from the Kingdom of the Netherlands (1974/75) and is the main reason behind the lack of political pressure for independence in the Dutch Antilles and Aruba in recent times (van Amersfoort and van Niekerk 2006). Likewise, the extension of United States citizenship rights to the populations of all Caribbean colonies after World War II triggered a massive transfer of labour migrants from the Caribbean to the United States.

This world-systemic reconceptualisation sheds new light on the workings of the institution of modern citizenship from its very emergence in the context of the French Revolution: on the one hand, the gradual extension of citizenship rights from propertied white males to all white males and to white women accounted for the development of low inequality within continental France as of the eighteenth century. On the other hand, the categorical exclusion of Saint-Domingue's black and mulatto population from French citizenship, irrespective of their property status, ensured the maintenance of high inequality between France and Saint-Domingue/Haiti, as well as between other Western colonial powers and their colonial possessions more generally. It thus becomes clear that the entail of property that Shachar used as an analogy to the entail of citizenship was a colonial entail and that both helped preserve inherited property, both in the form of material goods proper and of *rights to* goods, state support, social services, and infrastructure in the hands of the (racially, ethnically, and geopolitically) designated heirs to the Western colonial enterprise for several centuries.

## The commodification of citizenship

The global perspectives detailed previously reveal the ascribed characteristic of citizenship to be as important for worldwide stratification as class and international migration as crucial for worldwide social mobility. Yet (upper) class membership at the global level comes with the significant benefit of being able to sidestep both ascription and the actual migration. Whether or not the social mobility achieved through gaining legal status in a wealthy country counts as or actually constitutes migration depends not only on one's citizenship status but essentially also on one's financial resources. Resorting to market mechanisms in order to elude the ascription of citizenship is therefore an increasingly visible, yet rare, option available only to the wealthy few, whose mobility, however, is seldom described as migration. They are instead referred to as 'global investors', 'expats', or 'foreign residents for tax purposes', while their migration process is more often referred to as 'relocation' or qualified as 'business migration'. The growing commodification of citizenship rights across the world in recent years, that is, the possibility of literally purchasing residence and citizenship in certain countries, not only makes the similarity between citizenship and the entail of property particularly salient. It also prompts the realisation that the ascription of citizenship represents no exception to a modern trend away from ascriptive mechanisms but a core principle of global stratification in the capitalist world-economy.

Conferring citizenship to investors who reside on a country's territory has been common practice in a number of states, including the United Kingdom, the United States, Canada, Belgium, and Australia. The by far less common but recently growing practice consists of extending citizenship status to investors without them even having to set foot in the country. Firmly implemented in St. Kitts and Nevis and the Commonwealth of Dominica since 1984 and 1993, respectively, the so-called citizenship by investment programmes have recently proliferated in Southern and Eastern Europe (Boatcă 2015). For the first states implementing them, the programmes were meant to bridge the transition from the export monoculture of the colonial economy to more diversified production after independence: St. Kitts and Nevis, a federation of two islands in the Caribbean, established its program one year after the islands gained independence from the United Kingdom in 1983. Similarly, the Commonwealth of Dominica, which gained independence from the United Kingdom in 1978, established an investor citizenship program after adverse weather conditions and the decrease in the world prices of bananas, the country's primary crop, seriously damaged its economy (Dzankic 2012). Within Southern and Eastern Europe, citizenship and residency programs have emerged especially as a result of the 2008 financial crisis. A real estate investment ranging from 250,000 to 1,150,000 EUR buys foreigners residency rights and, in some cases, full European Union citizenship in Latvia, Hungary, Ireland, Spain, Portugal, Greece, Cyprus, Macedonia, Bulgaria, and Malta, whose investment programs have all been implemented since 2010 (CNN Money 2013; BBC News 2013). Visa-free travel to core countries, citizenship of a Schengen zone state, or even the right to work in the European Union thereby become available for the (moderately or very) wealthy, consequently linking the inequality of income and property to the access to property commodified in the form of citizenship. However, the commodification of citizenship does not represent a viable option for most of the world's population. Instead, it is either an option purposely designed for a very select few or – more frequently – is scandalised, stigmatised, and, ultimately, criminalised when it threatens to become available to a wider number of people. In most cases, the declared goal of economic citizenship programs is to attract wealthy investors, especially from China but also, and increasingly, from Russia and the Middle East. Yet it is only the citizenship of few states that lends itself to being commodified by virtue of being a scarce good awarding (relatively) rare benefits. From this point of view, states whose citizenship includes the advantage of the previously mentioned visa-free travel to Western countries or even the right to legal employment in them offer what could be referred to as 'premium citizenship' that is attractive to investors. States that are not part of the wealthy core may, as in the case of St. Kitts and Nevis, use the residual benefits of having once been a British colony and that today consist of being a member of the Commonwealth of Nations – which share, among other things, a visa-free travel area. This, however, hardly compares to the rights accruing from EU citizenship. The European Union is home to eight out of the ten countries worldwide whose citizens enjoy the most freedom of visa-free travel (International Business Times 2013). At the same time, it is the historic heir to Western colonial states whose colonial possessions covered almost half of the inhabited surface of the non-European world as late as the 1930s and who today control 28 out of the remaining 58 colonial possessions (Böröcz and Sakar 2005; Dependencies and Territories of the World 2013). In accordance with the worldwide division of labour, wealthy individuals in high positions through which they enjoy access to 'buying into' a privileged citizenship are predominantly male. The colonial entail of property thereby helps perpetuate the colonial entail of premium citizenship for Western states alongside the gender dividend of citizenship worldwide.

## Tourism, marriage, and motherhood as (fast) tracks to citizenship

As investor citizenships and visas proliferate, naturalisation and visa requirements for the majority of the world's migrants become more restricted and are criminalised as well as met with gendered forms of racialisation and precarisation. This double standard runs through the global logic of the coloniality of citizenship. While both investor citizenship and labour migration are geared towards more people gaining access to premium citizenship, the racial criminalisation of migrants to core regions – most prominently the European Union and the United States – only targets the latter: For labour migrants, inherited citizenship and lengthy naturalisation procedures are legally (re)inforced as the only legitimate options. In addition, the curtailment of women's rights, mobility, and access to capital, which has historically made them more vulnerable to physical and sexual violence in Western societies and all the more so in the context of colonialism and enslavement, continues to do so today. Currently, non-Western women – and other marginalised persons of non-conforming gender performance – still are the most vulnerable migrants. Their precarious position at the crossroads of multiple axes of inequality requires them to negotiate their options for global mobility along the continuum ranging from prostitution to marriage into which they have been defined since the sixteenth century. The title of Barbara Ehrenreich and Arlie Russell Hochschild's 2003 book *Global Woman: Nannies, Maids, and Sex Workers in the New Economy* keenly summarised the main options that the increasing feminisation of migration offered to racialised women. As Anca Parvulescu argues, today, East European women and women from the global South are ' "exchanged" so that they can do a lot of the physical household work and the immaterial, caring labor traditionally performed by a wife within the institution of marriage' (Parvulescu 2014: 2).

Unlike predominantly male wealthy investors, who can achieve global mobility in exchange for a check, predominantly poor women, transgender persons, and racialised Others exchange themselves, that is, offer their bodies, their emotional labour, housework, or all of the above, in exchange for upward mobility through citizenship. Since marriage to the owner of a Western passport provides one of the few legal and comparatively easy means of access (as opposed to life-threatening illegal border-crossings), in some regions, tourism serves as platform of options for all parties. Yet North-South tourism – and sex or 'romance' tourism in particular – is based on deeply unequal power structures. Who can be a tourist and where to, and by whom s/he is being served, is related to highly asymmetrical and colonial axes of stratification, deeply marked by racial and gendered dimensions. Owners of a Western passport (with a medium or high income) can use their citizenship privilege to travel to racially eroticised 'fantasy islands', for example, to the Caribbean (O'Connell Davidson and Sánchez Taylor 1999). In most formerly colonised regions, highly dependent on the tourism industry, romance and/or sex are often part and parcel of the package dream holiday of Western tourists of all genders.[5] Against the backdrop of a long tradition of exoticising and sexualising of the colonial 'Other' (McClintock 1995), Western men and women's disadvantageous age, gender and/or class positions are crisscrossed with the 'cultural/racial capital of whiteness' (Shohat and Stam 2012: 191) derived from their class and citizenship privilege as sex tourists to a poorer country. Sex workers in the Caribbean, in turn, can transform their class and citizenship disadvantage into erotic capital rooted in colonial and racialised erotic imaginations of the black body and thereby gain financial advantage in a structurally unequal encounter (Roth 2013). In many places, tourism provides one of the few ways of access to hard currency, consumer goods, or luxury products. In some cases, encounters with tourists even result in such global mobility prospects as a holiday abroad through a tourist visa, permanent residence, up to marriage and a Western passport. However, the non-Western partners are highly dependent on their privileged passport partners, and women are, again, particularly vulnerable to physical, psychic, or sexual violence.[6]

In numerous European states – among them Germany, Greece, Denmark, Estonia, Lithuania, and Latvia – the legal residence permit of both partners is the precondition for marriage or same-sex partnership in case one partner is a EU citizen and the other is not. Nevertheless, in most Western countries, bi-national couples have to face permanent suspicion, control, and illegalisation for years after marriage, which patently violates international human rights standards, especially the right to family life and privacy (Messinger 2013: 377). Under the headline 'Heiraten für den deutschen Pass' (Getting married for the German passport), the German daily newspaper *Der Tagesspiegel* (5.7.2015) recently reported the case of a Jamaican woman who came to Germany on a tourist visa and got married to a German citizen, thus obtaining permanent residence for herself and Schengen tourist visas for her two daughters in Jamaica. The *Tagesspiegel* reporter accordingly compared the German husband to the winning of the global mobility 'jackpot': 'From waitress or maid in Jamaica to fully provided-for housewife – social ascent on the fast track, overtaking all the refugees who often have to dwell in barracks for years and cannot work' (*Der Tagesspiegel*, 5.7.2015, our translation).[7] For the Jamaican woman, who successfully combined the strategy of international migration with the use of the racial and sexual capital of Western colonial fantasies, the ascription of citizenship through the 'birthright lottery' (Shachar 2009) is transformed into the achievement of citizenship through the marriage lottery. For the (white) German man, 'the commodification of his marital options' (Parvulescu 2014: 115) is a combined effect of EU immigration policies, centred around family values and of German citizenship law, largely based on the right of blood. The report thus provides an exemplary case for the workings of citizenship under jus sanguinis arrangements, which offers low-income migrants few possibilities to take up residence and in which seeking asylum is rarely successful. In this context, getting married or having a child with a EU passport holder provides a more secure option. 'The German authorities downright force us to get pregnant or married', the *Tagesspiegel* quotes the Jamaican woman.

It is, however, precisely such strategies of social mobility through marriage that become the object of state sanctions and are criminalised as a type of 'forged descent' (from a bloodline community of citizens) in jus sanguinis arrangements (Boatcă 2014). In Germany and Austria, matrimonies between EU and non-EU citizens with the objective of obtaining a residence permit are pejoratively referred to as 'Scheinehe' (sham marriage). The fact that the term is never applied to pragmatic unions between two Western passport holders – who might aim to save taxes or enjoy other privileges provided to married couples by the state – reveals a high level of institutionalised racism (Messinger 2013: 386)[8] made possible by the double standard of the coloniality of citizenship. Suspected matrimonies are likely to be exposed to degrading controls by the state – for example, in the form of unannounced visits to prove the 'real' nature of the relationship. Irene Messinger's (2013) analysis of the Austrian case draws a clear connection between the tightening of migration controls in many EU states and the legal situation of bi-national couples in which one is a non EU-citizen, noting that a clause on 'marriages of convenience' was included for the first time in the 2005 Austrian Alien Law Act. The deeply gendered, racialised, and class-biased dimension of such state surveillance of bi-national marriages that serves to reinforce immigration controls is blatantly obvious: most suspected couples are Austrian women of low income married to African men who did not enter the country legally, while the equally large group of Austrian men married to Asian women is not listed as suspicious and is hardly exposed to observation and intrusion. Moreover, age difference is only listed as suspicious when the Austrian woman is considerably older than her partner, revealing a deeply patriarchal bias. The fact that, since 2006, the couple has to prove a regular income of more than 1,200 Euros per month worsens the chances for low-income groups.

If Germany and Austria provide examples for the criminalisation of migrant practices to subvert jus sanguinis arrangements, the Americas, where jus soli has historically underpinned colonial settlement, offer a different set of possibilities to migrants. Marriage is a particularly attractive option for women in border regions, such as those crossing the Southern border to Mexico from Guatemala. Many of them eventually abandon their initial plan to continue all the way to the United States along highly insecure paths and therefore are increasingly exposed to sex crimes and enforced prostitution. Women stuck in the border region between Guatemala and Mexico often work as 'ficheras' in bars, which not only offers them more money than other available jobs to pay for their further journey or send remittances to their families back home but also increases the possibility of meeting a potential husband with a Mexican passport (Quintino et al. 2011: 107). Women stuck in a migrant shelter in this border region get pregnant, as a baby born on Mexican ground promises permanent residency for the mother (and the father), as well as access to healthcare and education (Guevara González 2015, n.p.). In the United States, the same strategy is currently sanctioned and criminalised through the ethnic and racial profiling of immigrants who come to the country to give birth, who are accused of having abused the right of soil. Immigration hard-liners describe a wave of migrants crossing the Mexican-U.S. border in the advanced stages of pregnancy to have what are dismissively called 'anchor babies' (Lacey 2011). The term refers to the automatic granting of U.S. citizenship, in virtue of the 14th Amendment, to children born on U.S. soil, who can in turn secure citizenship for their parents upon reaching the age of 21, depicting immigrant mothers as a monstrous 'threat to the nation'. However, many immigrants arriving to give birth in the United States are frequent border crossers with valid visas who travel legally in order to take advantage of better medical care. Moreover, although the total U.S. immigration population continues to grow, unauthorised immigration has slowed in the past decade (Pew Research Center 2013). Nevertheless, several Republican attempts at amending the U.S. constitution since 2010 have mobilised terms like 'anchor babies', 'birth tourism', and 'accidental citizens' in order to end the automatic granting of citizenship, arguing that the provision attracts high numbers of unauthorised migrants (Feere 2010; Huffington Post 2013). In 2014, the state of Texas has stopped issuing birth certificates to children born on its territory to undocumented migrants and bearers of a Mexican passport without a valid U.S. visa, making it impossible for parents to authorise medical treatment for their children or enrol them in daycare or school (Texas Observer 2015). States are highly active and creative in restricting immigration – often abusively, as shown in the case of the violation of the right to family life and privacy for binational couples in Austria and Germany or of existing citizenship law for Mexican mothers in the United States. By withholding social protection, health services, and other rights from undocumented migrants and other non-citizens, states perpetuate the colonial entail of citizenship rights for their own nationals, while the highly unequal global system of social reproduction keeps producing 'stratified workers and stratified mothers' (Herrera 2010).

## Outlook

Investor citizenships and the commodification of marital options outlined previously are similar strategies of eluding the ascription of citizenship through recourse to the market. Attempts to beat the ascriptive logic of citizenship at its own game – that is, by undermining the institution of birthright citizenship through migration – meet with critique, sanctions, and criminalisation from supra-state and financial institutions; encounter legal countermeasures; and are policed along racial, ethnic, and gender lines. Citizenship, based on colonial racial and ethnic constructs, and gender, which has been reconfigured during colonialism, are key components of the persistence of global inequalities today. Currently, the gendering of globalised domestic work or globalised social reproduction requires the global North to take on 'the role of an old-fashioned male, provider and successful in the public sphere but in need of care in every other way, while countries of the South take on the role of the traditional female, caring and nurturing and even sexually available, filling in the "care deficit" that has emerged in the North' (Dobrowolsky and Tastsoglou 2006: 17).

The birthright transmission of citizenship, just like the gendered division of labour (reinforced in form of global care chains, transnational adoption, surrogacy, and sex tourism), is therefore no striking exception to a trend away from ascription but a key mechanism of global stratification. It is the very coloniality of these mechanisms that makes their modernity possible. It is in the context of global colonial capitalism and its corresponding logic of accumulation that the institution of citizenship emerged; the economic and political interests of the main European colonial powers that pioneered it were essential in defining its central features, particularly its gendered and racialised dimensions. As long as the gendered and racial dividend of citizenship allocation still translates into the systematically unequal allocation of life chances, the modernity of the institution of citizenship will be the very proof of its coloniality.

## Notes

1 This is a considerably abridged version of the article by the same title published in *Current Sociology* 64 (2), 2016, 191–212.

2 'Along with all other peoples variously designated as backward, degenerate, uncivilised, and retarded, the Orientals were viewed in a framework constructed out of biological determinism and moral-political admonishment. The Oriental was thus linked to elements in Western society (delinquents, the insane, women, the poor) having in common an identity best described as lamentably alien. Orientals were rarely seen or looked at; they were seen through, analyzed not as citizens, or even people, but as problems to be solved or confined' (Said 1979: 207).

3 As noted, these policies were not straightforwardly assimilationist but retained their colonial overtones: 'However, said strategy never ceased to alternate and combine with discriminating policies against the "indio" as well as with the othering of the "indio". In this way, de-Indianisation could not encompass the majority of the "Indian" population, which could only incorporate itself or be incorporated to a partial, precarious and formal extent in the process of nationalising society, the culture, and the state' (Quijano 2006: 201, our translation).

4 Using the inequality data for six countries interlinked through considerable migration flows, Korzeniewicz and Moran are able to show how anyone in the poorest seven to eight deciles of Bolivia or Guatemala can move up several global income deciles by migrating to Argentina or Mexico, respectively, and gaining access to the average income of the second poorest decile there. Even more strikingly, anyone but people in the wealthiest decile in both Argentina and Mexico is able to skip several global income deciles by entering Spain or the United States' second-poorest decile through migration (Korzeniewicz and Moran 2009: 108f.). In all these cases, the upward mobility of migrant populations is considerably higher than either the within-country educational attainment or the economic growth of one's country of origin would have allowed during a lifetime (judging by the most successful examples of economic growth, such as South Korea in the 1980s or China today).

5 See Sánchez Taylor 2010 on sex tourism research and sex tourism and inequalities.

6 There are also marriage agencies offering the 'racial, erotic' capital of (mostly) females from poor countries in exchange for the 'citizenship' capital of men (and women) in the global North who do not easily find a partner back home or are looking for specific characteristics in a partner (e.g. a decisively younger, devoted, caring, sexy partner to be chosen from the agencies' catalogue).

7 Dobrowolsky and Tastsoglou underscore the experience of gender exclusion shared by women despite 'women's multiple, intersecting identities (such as race, ethnicity, class, ability, sexual orientation, age, religion and so on)'. For migrant women in particular these exclusions come with limited citizenship rights: '[W]omen (im)migrants frequently find themselves in citizenship limbo, or with various kinds of "partial citizenship" as is the case for temporary workers. . ., with very few if any rights to draw upon. This, in turn, can lead to further deprivation and impoverishment, and an array of abuses or forms of exploitation. . . . They

are affected by structural processes (global, transnational, national and local) as they seek safe passage across borders, or eke out an existence in borderlands, or struggle to re-establish professional careers in new contexts when immigration regulations construct them as dependents on a male breadwinner. (Dobrowolsky and Tastsoglou 2006: 5, 6).

8 Interestingly, marriages between German (or other) citizens and persecuted Jews (who were deprived of their citizenship) are now being referred to as 'Schutzehe' ('protective marriage'). (see Messinger 2012).

## References

'The Best Passports to Have for Unrestricted Travel around the World'. 2013. *International Business Times*. Available at: www.ibtimes.com/best-passports-have-unrestricted-travel-around-world-1422038 [Last accessed May 1, 2014].

Boatcă, Manuela. 2014. 'Commodification of Citizenship. Global Inequalities and the Modern Transmission of Property', in Immanuel Wallerstein, Christopher Chase-Dunn and Christian Suter (eds.) *Overcoming Global Inequalities*, pp. 13–28. Boulder, CO: Paradigm Publishers.

Boatcă, Manuela. 2015. *Global Inequalities Beyond Occidentalism*. Farnham: Ashgate.

Böröcz, J. and M. Sakar. 2005. 'What Is the EU?', *International Sociology*, 20 (2): 153–73.

Castro-Gómez, S. 2000. 'Ciencias sociales, violencia epistémica y el problema de la invención del otro', in E. Lander (ed.) *La colonialidad del saber: eurocentrismo y ciencias sociales. Perspectivas latinoamericanas*, pp. 145–61. Buenos Aires: CLACSO.

Dependencies and Territories of the World. 2013. *Worldatlas.com*, January. Available at: www.worldatlas.com/dependtr.htm [Last accessed May 8, 2014].

Dobrowolsky, Alexandra and Evangelia Tastsoglou. 2006. 'Crossing Boundaries and Making Connections', in A. Dobrowolsky and E. Tastsoglou (eds.) *Women, Migration and Citizenship: Making Local, National, and Transnational Connections*, pp. 1–35. Hampshire: Ashgate.

Dzankic, J. 2012. 'The Pros and Cons of Ius Pecuniae: Investor Citizenship in Comparative Perspective', EUI Working Papers, RSCAS, 2012/14, 1–18.

Ehrenreich, Barbara and Arlie Russell Hochschild. 2003. *From Global Woman: Nannies, Maids, and Sex Workers in the New Economy*. New York: Henry Holt Company.

'Europe's Golden Visas Lure Rich Chinese'. 2013. *CNN Money*, November 26. Available at: http://money.cnn.com/2013/11/26/news/europe-golden-visas/ [Last accessed April 2, 2014].

'EU Shrugs off European Race to Woo Rich Foreigners'. 2013. *BBC News*, November 18. Available at: www.bbc.com/nws/world-europe-24940012 [Last accessed April 2, 2014].

Feere, J. 2010. 'Birthright Citizenship in the United States: A Global Comparison', *Center for Immigration Studies Backgrounder*, August: 1–20. Available at: www.cis.org/sites/cis.org/files/articles/2010/birthright.pdf [Last accessed May 2, 2014].

Franco, Jean. 1999. 'La Malinche: From Gift to Sexual Contract', in Mary Louise Pratt and Kathleen Newman (eds.) *Critical Passions: Jean Franco: Selected Essays*, pp. 66–82. Durham and London: Duke University Press.

Guevara González, Yaatsil. 2015. 'Transit Itineraries: Migrant's Experiences and Interactions in Mexico's Southern Border', Unpublished dissertation Project.

Guevara González, Yaatsil. 'Migración de tránsito y ayuda humanitaria: Apuntes sobre las casas de migrantes en la ruta migratoria del pacífico sur en México', *fiar* 8.1, *Transcultural Mobility*'.

'Heiraten für den deutschen Pass' (Getting married for the German passport). 2015. Der Tagsspiegel, July 5 by Benedict Wermter.

Herrera, Gioconda. 2010. 'Stratified Workers, Stratified Mothers: Migration Policies and Citizenship among Ecuadorian Immigrant Women', in Wendy Chavkin and Jane Maree Maher (eds.) *The Globalization of Motherhood: Deconstructions and Reconstructions of Biology of Care*, pp. 55–76. New York: Routledge.

Korzeniewicz, R.P. and T.P. Moran. 2009. *Unveiling Inequality. A World-Historical Perspective*. New York: Russell Sage Foundation.

Lacey, M. 2011. 'Birthright Citizenship Looms as Next Immigration Battle', *New York Times*, January 4. Available at: www.nytimes.com/2011/.

Lugones, María. 2007. 'Heterosexualism and the Colonial/Modern Gender System', *Hypatia*, 22 (1): 186–209.

Lugones, María. 2008. 'The Coloniality of Gender', *Worlds & Knowledges Otherwise*, 2: 1–17.

Marshall, T.H. 1973. *Class, Citizenship and Social Development: Essays*. Chicago: University of Chicago Press.

McClintock, Anne. 1995. *Imperial Leather: Race, Class and Sexuality in the Colonial Context*. London and New York: Routledge.

Messinger, Irene. 2012. *Schein oder nicht Schein. Konstruktion und Kriminalisierung von "Scheinehen" in Geschichte und Gegenwart*. Reihe Kritik and Utopie, Vienna: Mandelbaum.

Messinger, Irene. 2013. 'There Is Something about Marrying . . . The Case of Human Rights *vs*. Migration Regimes Using the Example of Austria', *Laws*, 2: 376–91. doi:10.3390/laws2040376

Mies, Maria. 1996. *Patriarchy and Accumulation on a World Scale*. London: Zed Books.

Mignolo, Walter. 2000. *Local Histories/Global Designs: Coloniality, Subaltern Knowledges, and Border Thinking*. New Jersey: Princeton University Press.

O'Connell Davidson, Julia and Jacqueline Sánchez Taylor. 1999. 'Fantasy Islands: Exploring the Demand for Sex Tourism', in Kampala Kempadoo (ed.) *Sun, Sex and Gold: Tourism and Sex Work in the Caribbean*, pp. 37–54. London: Boulder.

Oyewumi, O. 1997. *The Invention of Women: Making African Sense of Western Gender Discourses*? Minneapolis, MN: University of Minnesota Press.

Parsons, Talcott. 1971. *The System of Modern Societies*. Englewood Cliffs: Prentice Hall.

Parvulescu, Anca. 2014. *The Traffic in Women's Work: East European Migration and the Making of Europe*? Chicago: University Press of Chicago.

Pew Research Center. 2013. 'Unauthorized Immigrants: How Pew Research Counts Them and What We Know About Them', April 17. Available at: www.pewresearch.org/2013/04/17/unauthorized-immigrants-how-pew-research-counts-them-and-what-we-know-about-them/ [Last accessed May 6, 2014].

Quijano, Aníbal. 2000. 'Coloniality of Power: Eurocentrism, and Latin America', *Nepantla: Views from South*, 1 (3): 533–74.

Quijano, Aníbal. 2006. 'El "Movimiento Indígena" y las Cuestiones Pendientes en América Latina: Review', *Journal of the Fernand Braudel Center*, XXIX (2): 189–220.
Quijano, Aníbal and Immanuel Wallerstein. 1992. 'Americanity as a Concept, or the Americas in the Modern World-System', *International Journal of the Social Sciences*, 134: 549–57.
Quintino, Frida et al. 2011. 'Trabajadoras sexuales en la frontera México-Guatemala: Migración y salud sexual y reproductiva en la frontera sur de México, vulnerabilidiad y acceso a servicios de salud sexual y reproductivo', *Instituto Nacional de Saludos Pública*, 107–26.
Roth, Julia. 2013. 'Entangled Inequalities as Intersectionalities: Towards an Epistemic Sensibilization', Working Paper No. 43, desiguALdades.net. Available at: www.desigualdades.net/bilder/Working_Paper/43_WP_Roth_Online.pdf?1367229865
Rubin, Gayle. 1975. 'The Traffic in Women: Notes on the "Political Economy" of Sex', in Rayna Reiter (ed.) *Toward and Anthropology of Women*, pp. 157–210. New York: Monthly Review Press.
Said, Edward. 1979. *Orientalism*. New York: Vintage Book.
Sánchez Taylor, Jacqueline. 2010. 'Sex Tourism and Inequalities', in S. Cole and N. Morgan (eds.) *Tourism and Inequality: Problems and Prospects*. Boston: CABI.
Shachar, Ayelet. 2009. *The Birthright Lottery: Citizenship and Global Inequality*. Cambridge and London: Harvard University Press.
Shohat, Ella and Robert Stam. 2012. *Race in Translation: Culture Wars around the Postcolonial Atlantic*. New York: New York University Press.
'Steve King Introduces Bill to Stop "Anchor Babies"'. 2013. *Huffington Post*, January 4. Available at: www.huffingtonpost.com/ 2013/01/04/steve-king-anchor-babies_n_2411989.html [Last accessed July 5, 2013].
Stoler, A.L. and F. Cooper. 1997. *Tensions of Empire: Colonial Cultures in a Bourgeois World*. Berkeley: University of California Press.
Texas Observer. 2015. Available at: www.texasobserver.org/children-of-immigrants-denied-citizenship/
Turner, B.S. 1996. 'Introduction. Marx and Nietzsche', in *For Weber: Essays on the Sociology of Fate*. London: Sage.
van Amersfoort, H. and M. van Niekerk. 2006. 'Immigration as a Colonial Inheritance: Post-Colonial Immigrants in the Netherlands: 1945–2002', *Journal of Ethnic and Migration Studies*, 32: 323–46.
Werbner, Pnina and Nira Yuval-Davis. 1999. 'Introduction: Women and the New Discourse on Citizenship', in P. Werbner and N. Yuval-Davis (eds.) *Women, Citizenship, and Difference*. London and New York: Zed Books.
Werlhof, Claudia von, Maria Mies and Veronika Bennholdt-Thomsen. 1983. 'Frauen, die letzte Kolonie (Women: The Last Colony)', *Technologie und Politik*, November 20.

# 9 Particular universalities

## Imagining the nation at its borders

*Sudha Vasan*

### Sindhu Darshan: performing a nation at a globalised border

'*Kuch Indians aajathe hain*' (Some Indians come for it), said Tashi, a taxi driver in Leh, when I asked him about a festival called Sindhu Darshan in April 2018. Singhe Khababs, a Ladakhi name used earlier for Sindhu Darshan, was initially not familiar to him, although he made the connection later. Other taxi drivers in Leh that I spoke to also showed familiarity with the event but little enthusiasm.

This was reflected on the official website of the Leh Autonomous Hill Development Council (LAHDC), which described it in two lines: 'Sindhu Darshan Festival has in-fact become a movement signifying National Integration and unity among diversity. Sindhu Darshan festival is held on 12th, 13th, and 14th, of June every year' (LAHDC 2018). It was missing in the calendar of (Ladakhi) festivals, and there was no mention of Singhe Khababs.

The Jammu and Kashmir government tourism website showed more enthusiasm:

> Also called Singhe Kabaab Festival, Sindhu Darshan is a festival that focuses on river Sindhu, also known as the Indus. The Government of Jammu and Kashmir organizes the Sindhu Darshan festival at Leh in the month of May-June. In this festival, people come for a Darshan and Puja (worship) of the River Sindhu (Indus). The Sindhu River is regarded as a symbol of the rich culture, communal harmony and peaceful co-existence in India. It also acts as a tribute to the brave soldiers of India who have bravely fought for their country. This Festival is celebrated on the full moon day (Guru Poornima) in the month of June. It stretches on for three days. The main reason behind the celebration of the Festival is to endorse the Indus River (Sindhu River) as an icon of the communal harmony and unity of India.
>
> (JK Tourism 2018)

Sindhu Darshan is a self-consciously invented tradition, started in 1997, and traces the evolution of relations between Ladakh, the latest Union Territory of India carved out of the state of Jammu and Kashmir, and the Indian nation in the last two decades. It is shaped by the interaction of the resources of the nation-state, micro-politics of an emerging aspirational local elite, and regional geopolitics. It plays out the relationship between radicalism of dominant and minority identities and (re)construction of local identities forged under globalisation. It highlights most of all the malleability of identities and the agency of borders in particularising the nation. This chapter examines Sindhu Darshan and its transformation over two decades from 1997 to 2017 to understand the interweaving of nationalism, regionalism and identity in the context of a globalised border. It is based on participant observation, individual and group interviews conducted with residents in Leh over five visits between 2008 and 2018 and analysis of media reports on Sindhu Darshan.

Ladakh, a border region that recently became a Union Territory of India, presents a border animated variously by globalisation. With a history of being at the crossroads of thriving trade routes, Ladakh is far from a culturally insular border. Historically, it has been recognised as a cultural melting pot with a unique amalgamation of diverse trading cultures. In terms of religion, most of the population is either Buddhist or Muslim, with a slim majority being Buddhists. There are a sprinkling of Christians, Sikhs and Hindus concentrated in Leh, the main town of the region. Ladakh has two distinct regions, which are also separate administrative divisions, Leh and Kargil, where Buddhists and Muslims, respectively, are overwhelming majorities.[1] This religious and cultural diversity has a long history dating back to the early 15th century, when Sikander's army entered the Ladakhi kingdom (Dollfus 1995), and the later importance of Ladakh as a major stop in the trading route that connected Central Tibet to South Asia. Moravian missionaries reached Leh in 1884, setting up a dispensary and the still-popular Moravian Mission School in 1887, although the spread of Christianity has been limited. Ladakh was, and still is, the meeting point of the Islamic and Buddhist worlds and of the Tibetan and Indic cultures (Pirie 2007: 1). In recent decades, the religious demography of Ladakh has been a major point of political tensions (see Aengst 2013, for instance). There is little consensus on Ladakh's population figures, and the difficulty of data collection adds to this tension. According to the 2011 census, 66.4% of the population of Leh district is Buddhist, 14.28% Muslim and 17.14% Hindu. Kargil district returned 76.87% Muslim, 14.29% Buddhist and 7.34% Hindu. The rest include Christians, Sikhs and Jains in both districts. From a region where people were mainly agro-pastoralist, Ladakh has changed into a region whose economy is driven by the presence of armed forces and tourism. While the number of army personnel stationed in Ladakh is not officially revealed, it is widely accepted that this is the major source of income and market access for Ladakh. Ladakh is located at a tri-junction of India's borders with Pakistan and China. Its eastern borders with China see active military patrolling and claims and counterclaims on disputed territories through armed incursions. Siachen Glacier in the North has remained a site of active military engagement between India and Pakistan since the mid-1980s. The Kargil war of 1999 with Pakistan was the first televised war of India; it not only saw large-scale army mobilisations in this region but also brought the Ladakh region into the popular culture of 'mainland' India. One estimate places the number of army personnel in Ladakh in 1998 at 30–40,000 (Angeles and Tarbotton 2001), and another suggests that army personnel outnumber Ladakhi civilians five to one during the summer months (Powell 1992: 157). In addition to direct employment in the Ladakhi Scouts, Angeles and Tarbotton (2001) estimate that one in every three Ladakhi men has paid employment related to the military, either as sub-contractors, service providers or suppliers of goods.

Ladakh was considered a sensitive border by the Indian government, as it shares borders with both Pakistan and China. Access to civilian outsiders (Indians from outside the state of Jammu and Kashmir) and foreigners to this region was restricted until the 1970s. The loosening of this control began in the 1970s when tourists were allowed to travel to a few parts of Ladakh after getting permits from the administration. Road connectivity was still poor, and Ladakh was cut off from the rest of India for up to eight months in a year. More areas of Ladakh are still being opened to tourists, and tourist infrastructure is rapidly expanding. Tourism has emerged as the second major sector of the economy.

Until the 1990s, 80% of tourists who visited Ladakh were from affluent countries, particularly North America and Western Europe (Michaud 1991). Scholars have pointed out a particular character of this Western tourism in Ladakh, which constructed it as a proxy for Tibet. In global geopolitics, Tibet forms an important imagined cultural landscape for the West. Many scholars have shown how Tibet has been an exemplar of Orientalism (Said 1978), and this has considerably shaped the political trajectory of Tibet (Anand 2007; Neuhaus 2012). 'Tibet is, in Foucault's terms, a heterotopia, a plurality of often contradictory, competing, and mutually exclusive places simultaneously positioned on a single geographical location' (Bishop 2001: 204, cited in Anand 2007: 38). The construction of the 'Other' relies on fantasies of the Self, and in the case of Tibet, the lack of European-style 'development' is an important element of the construction of this utopia.

Given the lack of access to Tibet, Ladakh has often served as a proxy for Tibet for Western tourists. The cold desert landscape of Ladakh, located at the eastern end of the Tibetan plateau, the presence of Tibetan Buddhist monasteries and visits by the Dalai Lama, who took refuge in India, reiterated the global image of Ladakh as a mini-Tibet. The global image of Ladakh as 'Little Tibet' or 'Shangri La', populated by innocent and peaceful Buddhists who are cut off from modern global, political and technological change, continues to be a powerful motivator of international tourism (Fewkes 2009). While this distorted romanticisation is resented and resisted by many local communities as denying their true and unique identity, it has paved the way for tourist income. Deboos (2013) also points out its significance in drawing Western non-governmental organisation (NGO) funding for Buddhist social and cultural heritage associations and Buddhist schools.

While Ladakh was historically connected to the Tibetan kingdom and had strong trading links, the similarity and connections are at present fairly limited. In contemporary Ladakh, while this stereotype brings some benefits through tourism and NGO funding, there is often explicit resentment at the stereotyping. The development and connectivity aspirations of many Ladakhis are at odds with the exotic insular image of tradition portrayed globally. As young elite Ladakhis increasingly consider themselves part of the cosmopolitan global elite, defining Ladakhi identity gains significance locally (Vasan 2017). The fact that outsiders, particularly powerful outsiders, do not recognise the distinctiveness of Ladakh rankles (ibid.).

Inter-sect rivalry within Buddhism also plays a role in this assertion of Ladakhi distinctiveness. Observers claim that China has been using 'soft power' to infiltrate Ladakh through skilfully exploiting inter-sect rivalries (Raman 2016; Patil 2018). In group meetings in April 2018, local community leaders affiliated with the Drukpa lineage emphasised Ladakhi distinctiveness in contrast to Tibet and emphasized cultural connections to India. The Drukpa lineage is one of the branches of the Kagyu school (one of the New Translations school) of Tibetan Buddhism that was founded in West Tibet By Tsangpa Gyare (1161–1211 CE). Some of the early disciples of this sect are recorded to have meditated in the Ladakh region and were invited by Ladakhi kings to give spiritual guidance and propagate the teachings of the Drukpa lineage in Ladakh. The first monastery of this lineage was founded at Hanley in 1624 by Tagshang Repa, and the currently most famous one, Hemis monastery, was built in 1630.[2] It is the most prevalent sect of Buddhism in Ladakh and the dominant school and state religion in Bhutan.

In meetings in 2018, Drukpa community leaders expressed dismay that Indian political leaders did not recognise this. Even the *Incredible India* campaign of the tourism department of Government of India, they said, did not know the difference; the campaign images while advertising Ladakh used Tibetan instead of Ladakhi iconography. Ladakhi Buddhists generally revere the Dalai Lama, and some monasteries in Ladakh profess allegiance to Tibetan Buddhism and the Dalai Lama's Gelugpa sect. However, there is rarely any intermarriage between Ladakhis and the Tibetans settled here, and many traditions within Buddhism (e.g. Drukpa, followed by the majority in Ladakh) actively distinguish themselves from Tibetan Buddhism. Tensions between different Buddhist sects competing for control over monasteries and followers is not uncommon.

Ladakh, at the geographical and cultural margin of the Indian nation, has always been a globalised space. The 1990s marked a distinct transition in the reciprocal relation of the Indian nation with this border region. India's first televised war at Kargil brought Ladakh centrally into the national imagination, although the images focused exclusively on the Indian army in this spectacular landscape, and local people remained invisible. Ladakh became the backdrop for a few popular Hindi films, most notably *Lakshya* and *Three Idiots*. This framed Ladakh in a dual frame – as a landscape of patriotism and spectacular and exotic beauty. As it coincided with the formation of the new middle classes in liberalised India, domestic tourism began picking up. Domestic tourist figures to Ladakh consistently increased and soon overtook the number of foreign tourists. In 2009, for instance, Leh recorded 48,517 domestic tourists and 30,570 international tourists (LAHDC 2010).

Ladakh's internal politics also took a turn around the same period. In 1989, local mobilisation to assert autonomy from the Jammu and Kashmir (J&K) state, which has always been perceived as step-motherly, took an assertively communal turn. Religion and politics have always interacted in Ladakh (van Beek 1998, 2000; Bray 2007). The year 1989 was marked by scuffles between Buddhist and Muslim youths, which led to an agitation led by the Ladakh Buddhist Association (LBA) and firing by security forces, killing three men. The LBA agitation raised the demand for Union Territory status for Ladakh, citing discrimination of 'Buddhist' Ladakh by the 'Muslim' J&K state government, directly instrumentalising religion for a political demand. LBA also called for an economic and social boycott of all Muslims in Ladakh, clubbing together Kashmiri Muslim traders and Ladakhi Muslims. The boycott, which officially lasted for three years, divided Ladakhi society significantly and perhaps irreparably. Communal rhetoric on fertility and demography, consensual relationships and marriages being labelled 'stealing of women' and accusations and professions of loyalty to India/Kashmir have remained undercurrents in the everyday life in Ladakh. Communal tensions have risen periodically, most recently in 2017, protesting an inter-religious marriage of a couple in their thirties. In 1995, after a prolonged struggle, Ladakh became an autonomous region with the setting up of two Autonomous Hill Development Councils in Leh and Kargil. And in October 2019, Ladakh (and Jammu) was made a Union Territory to be centrally administered, severing its administrative links with Jammu and Kashmir.

In this context, Ladakhi response to Sindhu Darshan, and its transformation, bears significance. On the one hand, Sindhu Darshan as an event emerges in the context of broader geopolitical movements, the rise of Hindu nationalism and changes in the imagination of the Indian nation. Ladakh becomes an important cultural object for India within these tendencies. However, with its own emerging elite, Ladakh is not a passive object incorporated into India's Hindu nationalism. The Indian cultural nation encounters an agential elite at this border, with local, regional, national and global interests negotiating cultural space in the performance of Sindhu Darshan. This research focuses on Sindhu Darshan from the vantage point of Ladakhi politics, allowing us to understand what the nation is, does and becomes at its borders in the era of globalisation. It reflects on the complex process of globalisation that co-evolves with regional and national processes, resulting in a universal process (globalisation) with particular local characteristics.

## Global nations as assemblages of power

Benedict Anderson's (1983) widely used conception of the nation as an imagined sovereign community has proved robust over time, although critically appropriated sometimes in ways much different from his initial formulation. It has allowed us to understand the nation as emerging from but also being created and recreated from the ground up through the agency of people who imagine it into existence, who of course exercise that agency within structural conditions available to them. The constant work of (re) creating the nation has become more intensive in the phase of capitalist globalisation. For all its initial predicted potential of making nation-states irrelevant, globalisation has actually made the nation a central mooring within the global economy, and nationalism has resurged across the world. The cultural nation has emerged as central to and in the global economy.

The character of nation and nationalism under globalisation, however, has distinct features compared to its earlier avatar. The (re)emergence of the nation under globalisation can be characterised as a political assemblage, the coming together of disparate power centres, sometimes contradictory to or competing with each other, but acting together in the present. The Indian nation in Ladakh provides one such complex power assemblage, with the coming together of religion, ethnicity and geopolitics. Its location in the state of Jammu and Kashmir, and at a contested international border that garners much global attention, makes it particularly central in the Indian political imagination.

Engaging with the nation as assemblage (Deleuze and Guattari 1988) offers the possibility of grasping how something as heterogeneous as nations, for instance, or regional political formations, hold together without actually ceasing to be heterogeneous (Allen 2011). Institutional arrangement of power can more or less hold together, despite being made up of a co-existence of diverse logics and priorities, often pulling in different directions (ibid. 155). Assemblage is a useful concept to understand the nation in times of globalisation, as it emphasises both spatiality and temporality simultaneously. It elaborates on how elements are drawn together at a particular conjecture, only to disperse or realign. Even tangible material social relations are not always organic wholes, where the differences of the parts are subsumed into a higher unity (Anderson and McFarlane 2011). Bennett (2005) says that the concept allows us to name an uneven topography of trajectories that cross or engage each other to different extents over time and that themselves exceed the assemblage. This raises questions about where agency, causality and responsibility lie in assemblage and about how they should be conceived. Further, unlike Foucauldian notions like apparatus, regime or governmental technology, assemblage connotes emergence rather than the resultant (Li 2007).

Borders are liminal spaces where the nation is experienced most intimately, and Aggarwal (2004), in her ethnographic study of Ladakh, shows how they are spaces that are carefully performed, contested, produced and maintained and therefore constitute the heart of national identity. Cultural performances and state festivals provide a space through which official versions of nationalism are simultaneously questioned and reinforced. Ladakhis 'fiercely claim Indian identity, not only by resisting or accommodating centralised ideologies, but by seeing themselves as central to the national project' (ibid.: 29). Everyday practices transform the 'imagined' nation into lived experience, as Bhan (2008) elaborates in a study of the Brogpas of Ladakh. These mundane, multiple, contradictory everyday practices, driven by instrumental interests of its multiple actors, continuously constitute and transform the nation. While these ideas are reinforced in the performance of Sindhu Darshan, its transformation over the years illuminates how the very location at the border means that the nation is also vulnerable and has to be flexible to elicit allegiance to a particular nation. This internal vulnerability of the nation at its borders is central to its constitution and border politics.

Sindhu Darshan represents one performative space where the relations between nation and region are negotiated. The fortunes of this event over the two decades unravel the entanglement of Ladakhi regional politics with Indian politics and reveal layers of the political assemblage that form the nation at the border on one hand and Ladakhi identity on the other.

## Nationalism as tourist spectacle

Four busloads of tourists from Gujarat disembark on the shores of Indus river at Sindhu Ghat, just outside of Leh, in June 2009. Loud music, mainly A.R. Rehman nationalist songs, blares from the temporary stage as boisterous men and their families occupy the plastic chairs arranged facing a makeshift stage on the banks of the river. There are a few large cloth banners fluttering desperately in the cool and intense wind. The most prominent one has a classic picture of mother India in a sari bedecked with a golden crown with the Indian flag in her hand, an iconic representation familiar to most 'mainstream' Indians, tracing its origins to the early twentieth century. Other prominent banners speak of national integration, the grandeur of the Indian nation and bravery of Indian soldiers – all written in Hindi. The oxygen-thin cold air, clear blue sky and sharp sun in the treeless ochre mountain landscape where the sparkling blue Indus flows remind us that this is in trans-Himalayan Ladakh. Except for this, the cultural iconography could place us anywhere in the northern plains of India. About a dozen Ladakhis are seated in the chairs – either political leaders or tourism organisation heads. Another two dozen are working to manage the stage. The rest of the crowd for whom this show is put up are mostly from Gujarat and a few tourists from other parts of India. It is the period before the start of the main tourist season, and other than the Gujarati tourists who planned their tour specifically around this program, the others have mainly heard about this after they reached Leh and decided to include this in their tour itinerary at the last moment.

The audience is urged to discipline by the programme conductor as leaders from Delhi and Kashmir arrive in a flurry of cars. While political speeches on stage talk about the valour of Indian soldiers at the border, army personnel are busy watching the tourists, who seem keen to wade into the cold waters of the Indus. Ladakhis who are not on the stage are mostly amused by these efforts. The group of Ladakhi taxi drivers who have brought tourists to this programme discuss the event. 'It used to be much bigger when big leaders from Delhi came', recollects Padma Tashi, '(N)ow only few buses come. You should have come some years ago. The government had a big programme. All our leaders were here'. In response to why the event was more subdued now, most drivers were hesitant to respond, but another taxi driver, also named Tashi, said, '*Delhi me sarkar badal gaya*' (the government changed in Delhi). Most drivers felt Sindhu Darshan was good for tourism, since it brought Indian tourists to Ladakh slightly before the busy tourist season started, but none saw it as a Ladakhi festival, although most of their elected representatives religiously attended it over the years. Some saw it as a Hindu festival – 'they worship the Sindhu', said Spalden, '*nadiko puja karne aathe hai Sindhi log*' (Sindhi people come to worship the river): It is sacred river for the Hindus'. 'It is also celebrating the army and India', added another driver. Asked if they participate, Tashi quipped, 'we bring them here'.

Ladakhi relationship to the Indian nation and to Hinduism retains a tension even as they have been in close interaction in the last two decades. Ladakh has a long history of appealing to the Indian state to delink it from the dominance and perceived discrimination of Kashmir. These appeals have highlighted Ladakh's distinctiveness from Kashmir in many ways, including its distinct history, culture and religion. In the context of partition of the subcontinent and rise of separatist movements in Kashmir, the emphasis on Ladakhi patriotism has held much appeal. This narrative has been revitalised since the 1990s (van Beek 1998, 2000). Recent interviews in Ladakh also reinforced this perspective. In a discussion with local leaders (April 2018), Stobdan, a government contractor, said, 'We are patriotic Indians. Even in the Kargil war, it was Ladakhis who helped the Indian army to take all the supplies in this high altitude. We are on the border. We are always loyal to India. It is important that India should not neglect us'. What is notable in these protestations of patriotism is that these statements come with the unselfconscious use of 'India' as the other. Visible and cultural ethnic distinctiveness of Ladakh from 'mainstream' India and racist experiences of Ladakhis living in other parts of India reiterate their otherness (Vasan 2017). At the same time as Ladakh defies conventional ideas of Indianness, it 'embodies Indianness with an immediacy that is alien to outsiders'

(Aggarwal 2004: 13). Aggarwal (ibid.) quotes an unnamed politician who claims, 'We are more Indian than Indians'.

The foray of Hindutva cultural nationalism into Ladakh needs to be situated in this context. While the attention that Sindhu Darshan drew to Ladakh was welcome, it was also met with suspicion, anxiety and resentment. According to Cheering Dorjee, Leh president of Bharatiya Janata Party (BJP), anti-Rashtriya Swayamsevak Sangh (RSS) hostility grew during the first phase of Sindhu Darshan. 'We had to assure people that, unlike some Christian NGOs, we are not here to convert people from Buddhism to Hinduism' (Ladakh RSS member Dhaniram, quoted in Deshmane 2014). van Beek (2004), commenting on the early years of Sindhu Darshan in Leh, opines that while local Buddhists were sceptical of this festival with its quasi-Hindu symbolism, it also generated anxiety as it appears to be an attempt to incorporate Ladakh and Ladakhi Buddhism into a wider Hindu agenda. This tension during the initial phase of Sindhu Darshan is reiterated by Bray (2007): 'Ladakhis are pragmatic enough to welcome the tourist income from *tamashas* such as the Sindhu Darshan, but it is doubtful whether many of them take the festival's claim to serve as a symbol of national and religious unity at face value'.

Ideas of nation and community, however, do not flow only from centre to periphery. This is reflected in the evolution of Sindhu Darshan in Ladakh. The discourse of nation and patriotism has played a significant role in the politics of Ladakh in its relationship with India. Interestingly, while Ladakhi elite proactively construct this discourse, they do not passively accept ideas of the nation that are thrust on them. They retain their agency to negotiate, and the nation, too, does not follow a unitary script but adapts, especially at its borders.

## The many lives of Sindhu Darshan

Sindhu Darshan has evolved in three distinct phases that parallel the rise in fortunes of right-wing nationalism in Delhi but also mark the transformation of Ladakhi regional politics' association with the Indian nation. From 1997, when it was first celebrated, to 2003 marks the exploratory honeymoon phase, when Sindhu Darshan carried tremendous political symbolism and expectation from both Indian and Ladakhi political perspectives. It marked the initial forays of Hindu right-wing RSS into Ladakh and received a cautious and mixed welcome from Ladakh religious and political leadership. The overt Hindu symbolism, tight central control over its organisation and rapid pace of development were viewed with scepticism and anxiety within Ladakh. Simultaneously, as the internal hesitation was growing, the power equation in Delhi changed, and Sindhu Darshan underwent a period of secularisation from 2004 to 2013. This also coincided with the expanding phase of domestic tourism in Ladakh, and Sindhu Darshan emerged as a domestic tourism extravaganza promoted as a part of *Incredible India* tourism campaigns. The revival of right-wing fortunes in Delhi after 2014 meant a renewed interest in Sindhu Darshan. The new Sindhu Darshan, however, is different from earlier versions, with more local influence and assertion, reflecting changes in Ladakhi society and its relationship with India.

The first phase of Sindhu Darshan marked the initial attempts by right-wing Hindu organisations to gain a foothold in this border region. Ladakhi elite, fresh from the formation of the Autonomous Hill Councils, found it prudent to engage with the right wing rising in India. Dalliance with communalism already appeared to have brought some benefits, and many in Ladakh read the formation of the Autonomous Hill Council as a concession given to the Ladakhi Buddhist elite in exchange for reigning in communal violence. There was a welcoming of the overtures of Hindutva organisations, as it was seen as a strategic partnership.

Sindhu Darshan remained marginal in the lives of ordinary Ladakhis, including Lehpas (residents of Leh). While the Indus is central to habitation in Ladakh, worship of the river did not form part of Ladakhi Buddhist or other local cultural traditions (Bray 2007). However, it was an important event for the new political class in Leh. Political leaders from Delhi were visiting Leh, often for the first time, and it presented an opportunity for the political elite of Leh to strengthen their networks. The inauguration of Sindhu Darshan always had politicians and religious leaders in attendance. The event was promoted as a multi-religious event, and apart from Hindu priests brought in by the RSS, the local Buddhist and Christian clergy, Shia and Sunni Muslim clerics and Sikh Gurudwara office bearers were the main invitees.

For many ordinary Ladakhis, such as Phunsuk, the owner of one of the guesthouses in Leh, this was merely an event where '*kuch Sindhi aake pooja karthe hai*' (some Sindhis come and offer prayers; interview October 2008). The event was always touted by its organisers as a multi-religious and nationalist festival. However, its core symbolism remained Hindu. Phunsuk, a devout Buddhist, was not happy with the Buddhist monks attending Sindhu Darshan. 'They are just for show', she complained in July 2009, 'they are just made to chant something on the side'. This perception of marginality of Ladakhis to the entire show was also reiterated by other Ladakhis in 2009. While many of the LAHDC members were present at the inauguration, news reports of the event focused on leaders from Delhi and Srinagar.

According to the organisers' lore, Sindhu Darshan began when L. K. Advani, then a leader of the BJP, who is a Sindhi himself, 'discovered' on a visit to Ladakh in 1996 that a section of the Sindhu or Indus river flows through the Ladakh region of India. Sindhis derive their name from their origins in Sindh province, eponymous with the river, now in Pakistan. Tarun Vijay, editor of *Panchajanya*, the magazine of Rashtriya Swayamsevak Sangh – the Hindu nationalist right-wing volunteer organisation, seen as the parent organisation of the Bharatiya Janata Party – along with L.K. Advani, established and promoted the idea of a festival to celebrate the Sindhu river as a symbol of India. Since the BJP-led coalition, the National Democratic Alliance (NDA), was in power in Delhi, this was quickly brought to fruition, and in 1997, the first Sindhu Darshan was celebrated on the banks of the Sindhu river. Organised in October, primarily by the RSS, it was attended by L.K. Advani, Indresh Kumar and other RSS leaders. While the central government did not participate, Chief Minister Farooq Abdullah and Ladakh Hill Council Chief Councilor Thupstan Chhewang were prominent dignitaries who attended the function. A major boost to Sindhu Darshan came after the skirmish between India and Pakistan at Kargil. This televised war brought Kargil into drawing rooms in Delhi, symbolically establishing Ladakh as a border bravely guarded by the Indian army. Nationalist fervour was whipped up considerably in India, and Sindhu Darshan served this symbolic popular assertion. National unity and integration could be asserted at a site close to and in a state where secessionist movements have long thrived, and tribute could be paid to the soldier near a site where India won a war with Pakistan. In this symbolism, Ladakh remained an empty strategic space that could be appropriated for celebrating the nation.

The Sindhu Ghat was built with great speed at Shey Manla, a village on the shores of the Indus, adjacent to the Dalai Lama's summer residence and practically opposite the large new Shi'ite mosque at Chushod. The ghat drew little from local architectural styles, built of red sandstone from Rajasthan and elements such as the three *chattris*. A large plot of land for the construction of a Sindhu Sanskriti Kendra was also sold to the Sindhu Darshan organisation by the monastery of Sankar, the seat of Kushok Bakula Rinpoche. The event itself was replete with Hindu religious symbolism mixed with a discourse of nationalism that had catapulted the BJP to power. These rapid expansion plans of the Sindhu Darshan organisation were met with some consternation in Ladakh. Some sections began to fear that this process of discovery and appropriation of pilgrimage sites would turn Ladakh into another Lahaul – a Buddhist region in Himachal Pradesh where local religion is seen as gradually marginalised by Hinduism (van Beek 2004: 209).

From 1997 to 2003, each year Sindhu Darshan emphasised religious nationalism and was heavily promoted by the Indian government. In 1998, for instance, the Indian army provided logistics to the festival by erecting platforms and pavilions. The 3rd Infantry Division in Ladakh hosted over 500 RSS workers who attended (Swami 1999). This continued in 1999, and the Postal Department of the government of India issued a commemorative postage stamp on 28 July 1999 on the occasion of the Sindhu Darshan Festival (Abhiyan). With a picture of the upper reaches of the Sindhu river and an inset of the Vrishaba (bull) seal of the Indus valley civilisation, the 3-rupee stamp also had an inscription from the Rig Veda describing the Indus river. Ladakh again represented only an empty geography that could be inscribed with a particular national imagination. Apart from these symbolic assertions, the event also created bitterness through its neglect of local people. Tremendous animosity was caused, for instance, by the requisitioning of seats for the yatris on Indian Airlines flights out of Leh after flights had been cancelled for a week due to bad weather, leaving large numbers of locals stranded (van Beek 2004: 209).

The presence of national leaders at Sindhu Darshan created some anticipation of developmental schemes for Ladakh, but often the visiting dignitaries were more concerned with their constituencies back home. In 2000, the Sindhu Darshan Festival was inaugurated by the prime minister of India, Atal Behari Vajpayee, and he laid the foundation stone of the Sindhu Cultural Center. The highlight of the year was the mixing of waters of other Indian rivers in the Indus, inaugurated with the chief minister of Arunachal Pradesh, Mukut Mithi, bringing water from the Brahmaputra river, which also has its source in the Manasarovar Lake in Tibet. The very next year, Union Home Minister L.K. Advani poured water brought from the Sindhu river into the Dibang stream in Arunachal Pradesh, which meets Lohit downstream and becomes the Brahmaputra in the plains of Assam. In 2001, an organisation called Himalaya Parivar was set up highlighting the expansionary goals of the Hindu right wing in the Himalayan region. The Sindhu Darshan was officially treated as a Hindu pilgrimage by the Gujarat government, and a state subsidy of up to Rs. 15000 each was provided for up to 200 pilgrims, partly explaining the predominance of Gujaratis at these events.

Doordarshan telecast live the proceedings of the Sindhu Darshan festivities of 2002. Forty-five non-resident Indians from twelve different countries were reported to have participated and also donated money for the construction of a Sindhu Cultural Center at Leh (PTI report cited in van Beek 2004). The Indo-Tibetan Border Police and the state police were conspicuous at the event, providing security and logistical support.

Sindhu Darshan seemed to have little relation to Ladakh, being a site for symbolic contestations and expression of the politics in Delhi. The success of the festival in 2003 was read as the strength of L.K. Advani's authority within his party (Outlook 2003). A large entourage of ministers participated in the festival, each vying to outdo each other in promoting Sindhu Darshan. Tourism minister Jagmohan announced that he would build a stadium on the banks of the Indus, minister of state for civil aviation Rajiv Pratap Rudy said it was the mission of the ministry to propagate this festival, minister of state (home) Swami Chinmayanand suggested that Sindhu should become the fifth site for the Khumb Mela and urban development minister Ananth Kumar offered land for a Sindhu Darshan trust in Delhi (ibid.).

Members of the LADHC attended the festival every year, but they clearly appeared to have no control over the proceedings. One of the justifications of the Sindhu Darshan was its ability to boost tourism that was critical to the local economy. Some leaders claimed, as Thopstan Chhewang, Congressman and chairman of LADHC, did in 2003: 'Earlier, only foreigners came to Ladakh. Now Indians come too . . . it makes us feel connected to the rest of the country' (Outlook 2003). But given the centralised organisation of the event and the army and state machinery providing logistics, actual local tourism benefits from Sindhu Darshan were meagre.

The year 2004 marked a turning point since the BJP-led coalition lost the general election, and the Congress-led coalition came to power in New Delhi. The changed political climate in Delhi also provided more space for local criticism of Sindhu Darshan. But given its potential to bring domestic tourism, it was taken over by the government and modified rather than abandoned. Changes focused on making it more Ladakhi and multi-religious in form and content and expanding its tourism potential. By 2006, the festival was renamed 'Ladakh Singhey Khababs Festival' by the Ladakh Hill Development Council. Singhey Khababs translates as 'the river that comes out of the lion's mouth'. It was advertised as the spring festival of Ladakh by the Government of Jammu and Kashmir and the Union Tourism Ministry to bring in more Ladakhi flavour and local involvement. Leaders of the tourism industry were prominently invited, and more Ladakhi folk dancers and popular bands were invited as part of the three-day program. 'This year's festival is not a Hindu darshan; it is a national darshan. We have turned around what was meant to be a saffron statement to an event symbolising national integration', said Renuka Choudhary, the Congress tourism minister who choreographed the event in 2004 (Ganesh 2004). RSS cadres, a preponderance of saffron robes and Hindu rituals were noticeably marginal in that year's Sindhu Darshan.

In this phase, Sindhu Darshan was specifically constructed as a Ladakhi tourism festival that was celebrated to extend the short tourist season in Ladakh. The Hindu and Sindhi connection was downplayed, and the celebration of India was sustained. It still generated limited enthusiasm among Leh's public, but tourist operators associated tours with it. The earlier RSS-based Sindhu Darshan organisation committee was sidelined in the new dispensation. This committee and the Himalaya Parivar during this period decided to organise their own Sindhu Darshan separately, on a much smaller scale without state support. So, for a few years, two Sindhu Darshans were held in Ladakh – one the official Sindhu Darshan/Singhe Khababs and the other the Sindhu Darshanyatra/pilgrimage, both claiming continuity.

The fortunes of right-wing parties in India changed again in 2014, with the BJP-led coalition coming back to power in Delhi and later the Mehbooba Mufti government was formed in coalition with BJP in Jammu and Kashmir. The Hindu nationalist Sindhu Darshan was revived. But the new version of Sindhu Darshan was different in significant ways. The discomfort of the Buddhist Ladakhi elite with the earlier domination of Hindu nationalists and resentment had an effect on their functioning. Adapting to this resistance, the RSS gradually built its local base in Ladakh. By 2014, the RSS had not only a much stronger presence in Ladakh but a Buddhist face in the local community. Ladakh Phande Tsogspa (LPT), or Ladakh Welfare

Society, headed by a practicing Buddhist, Ringzhen Tundup Shastri, was an organisation that gained tremendous goodwill through its relief work after the devastating floods of 2010 in Leh. The Ladakh Phande Tsogspa became the organiser of Sindhu Darshan along with the Sindhu Darshan Yatra Samiti, and the parallel state-sponsored Singhe Khababs festival was ended. Buddhist clergy was won over by the organisation and were now given pride of place at Sindhu Darshan. H.E. Skyabje Togdan Rinpoche, a Buddhist monk, was made the chief guest, although the Union minister of state for home affairs, Kiren Rijju, and a Ladakhi member of parliament (MP) were also on the stage.

The Ladakh Phandey Tsogspa played a role again in 2017, organising the Sindhu Darshan program along with the Sindhu Darshan Yatra Samiti. The program was again inaugurated by a Rimpoche, H.E. Thuksey Rinpoche, who was the chief guest. He inaugurated the festivities by offering prayers to the Indus River and appealed for peace and harmony. Indresh Kumar, RSS veteran and chief patron of the Sindhu Darshan yatra, spoke almost entirely about cow protection and against anti-nationals, clearly addressing a non-Ladakhi Indian audience. The member of parliament from Ladakh raised the demand for inclusion of Bhoti language in the 8th Schedule of the Indian Constitution and on the importance of opening the route through Ladakh for the Kailas-Manasarovar yatra.

The renewed Sindhu Darshan is now symbolically organised by Ladakhis and inaugurated by Buddhist clergy. The RSS shares the stage and addresses its core Hindu constituency outside Ladakh, while political leaders from Delhi praise the martyrs of the armed forces and announce schemes for Ladakh. Ladakhi political leadership uses the stage to place demands to the government in Delhi and address their local constituency. The audience, still mostly RSS cadres and Indian tourists, responds to the slogans raised by the RSS and BJP leaders. Still the only Ladakhis present are the organisers, performing cultural troupes and invited religious and political leaders, and of course the taxi drivers who are bringing them all to Sindhu Ghat from Leh. Stobden, owner of a tourist resort and an active member of the tourist association, described Sindhu Darshan in an interview in April 2018 thus: 'Sindhu Darshan is organised by Ladakhis for Indians'.

The festival appears to have completed the full circle. From being organised by outside Hindu religious forces and seen as an attempt to appropriate Ladakh, the festival is now seen by Ladakhis as being organised by them. However, the otherness of Indians who are the main audience for this event is maintained, reflecting the complex play of Ladakhi self-identity and agency. It maintains a relationship with Hindu nationalist government at the centre and the RSS but perceives itself as controlling the form of this relationship. Global exoticisation of Ladakh, as discussed earlier, relies on its Tibetan connection, invisibilising its historical and contemporary links to South Asia and India. The Indian nation, on the other hand, offers a different narrative, one that emphasises Indian roots in Ladakh through the

Indus. Sindhu Darshan exemplifies the latter, and the fate of the event, as discussed in this chapter, embodies the tension between global forces, the needs of the nation and transforming Ladakhi politics.

## Particular universalities: Ladakhi identity and the Indian nation

Ladakh has always been at the confluence of global flows – economic, political and cultural. From a hub on caravan routes, to a transition zone of Himalayan cultures, to a line of control between India, Pakistan and China, to Western and Indian tourism. The conundrum of this socio-political location is that external forces have often attempted to define Ladakh in their own terms, most recently as 'Little Tibet', 'Shangri La' and border with 'Patriotic Indians'. Ladakhi response to these assertions has brought together contradictory tendencies of appropriation and resistance, allowing them to retain their distinctiveness even as they become part of the globalised world.

In more recent history since Indian independence, globalisation has been an important aspect of the economy of Ladakh. According to government records, the number of tourist arrivals rose from a mere 527 in 1974 to 79,087 in 2009 (Pelliciardi 2010: 15). While both international and domestic tourist numbers have increased over this period, domestic tourism has increased at a faster rate (ibid.). While the tourist economy has brought much-needed income and aspirations for development, it has also brought attention to Ladakhi identity. Tendencies in Indian nationalism have pushed another image of Ladakh, linking it to the Indian nation, through the invocation of its landscape, particularly the Indus river. While the Ladakhi political elite found the Sindhu Darshan a medium to engage with the Indian elite and secure their own positions, this does not enthuse most Ladakhis.

As forces of globalisation reach Ladakh through multiple channels – economic transformations, tourist flows, migration – concern with defining Ladakhi identity has become more important in public discourse (Vasan 2017). Youth culture in Ladakh, particularly in the capital city of Leh, remains in constant tension between the forces of nationalism and globalisation. On the one hand, the global stereotyping of Ladakh as a traditional Buddhist land brings in the most profitable tourism and NGO funds. The strengthening of various cultural identities (religious, national, ethnic, geographic and gender, among others) has accompanied the process of globalisation, not simply as a coincidence but through a systematic relationship between the two (Castells 2006). While this may be a global trend, the forms identities take is particular to a social context. Sindhu Darshan marks a performative space where contestations over Indian and Ladakhi identity in a globalised world come into contact. The identity of Indian nation and communalism, at one level universal and dependent on dominant transformations at the nation's power centres, is nonetheless particularised within the context of Ladakh. The communal idiom of Indian politics clearly influenced Sindhu

Darshan. However, it is significant how this intervention was co-opted and transformed within the politics of Ladakh. Sindhu Darshan marks the success of the Hindu nation in its ability to be malleable and to draw in local initiative and identity. Simultaneously it marks the maturation of Ladakhi elite in their ability to transform outside forces into their own. Herein lies the character of globalisation, in strengthening the nation precisely through its weakening, in holding together contradictory tendencies, allowing the nation to exist as an assemblage.

Ladakh's engagement with dominant cultural tendencies reveals the non-linear and contingent nature of processes of globalisation. Ladakh's tryst with global economic and cultural processes pre-dates the globalisation of the last century. As an important node in the trans-Himalayan trade, Ladakh was always exposed to global cultures and economies. Even as it became a contested border of India, located at the confluence of three modern nations, tourism brought in Western cultural exposure to this 'remote' region in the Himalayas. In the era of contemporary globalisation, Ladakh has seen the rise of a local politics centred on redefining identity in the context of religious right-wing Indian nationalism. This ethnography of Sindhu Darshan as an instance of Ladakh's engagement with the Indian cultural nation embedded in globalisation illustrates the processes through which dominant cultures are transformed even while they are assimilated by the local. Global and particular cultures are not mutually exclusive processes; cultures are and can be simultaneously global and particular.

## Notes

1 Ladakhi elite discussed in this essay are Leh centred and Buddhist. While there are Muslim elite and leaders, some of them also in Kargil (the eponymous capital of Kargil district), Leh and Buddhism claim, in power and popular discourse, the mantle of 'Ladakhi' politics.

2 For more on the history of the Drukpas and sects within Buddhism, see www.chinabuddhismencyclopedia.com/en/index.php?title=Drukpa_Lineage_Explained.

## Bibliography

Abercrombie, T.J. 1978. 'Ladakh – The Last Shangri-la', *National Geographic Magazine*, 153: 332–59.

Aengst, Jennifer. 2013. 'The Politics of Fertility: Population and Pronatalism in Ladakh', *Himalaya, the Journal of the Association for Nepal and Himalayan Studies*, 32 (1): Article 11.

Aggarwal, Ravina. 2004. *Beyond Lines of Control: Performance and Politics on the Disputed Borders of Ladakh, India*. Durham, NC: Duke University Press.

Allen, J. 2011. 'Powerful Assemblages?', *Area*, 43 (2): 154–57.

Anand, D. 2007. *Geopolitical Exotica: Tibet in Western Imagination*. London and Minneapolis: University of Minnesota Press.

Anderson, B. 1983. *Imagined Communities: Reflections on the Origins and Spread of Nationalism*. London: Verso.

Anderson, B. and C. McFarlane. 2011. 'Assemblage and Geography', *Area*, 43 (2): 124–27.

Angeles, L.C. and R. Tarbotton. 2001. 'Local Transformation through Global Connection: Women's Assets and Environmental Activism for Sustainable Agriculture in Ladakh, India', *Women's Studies Quarterly*, 29: 99–115.

Bennett, J. 2005. 'The Agency of Assemblages and the North American Blackout', *Public Culture*, 17: 445–65.

Bhan, Mona. 2008. 'Border Practices: Labour and Nationalism among Brogpas of Ladakh', *Contemporary South Asia*, 16 (2): 139–57.

Bishop, P. 2001. 'Not Only a Shangri-La: Images of Tibet in Western Literature', in T. Dodin and H. Rather (eds.) *Imagining Tibet: Perceptions, Projections and Fantasies*. Boston: Wisdom.

Bray, J. 2007. 'Old Religions, New Identities and Conflicting Values in Ladakh', Paper presented at the International Conference on "Religion, Conflict and Development", University of Passau (Germany), June 25–27. Available at: www.phil.uni-passau.de/fileadmin/dokumente/lehrstuehle/korff/pdf/conferences/paper_j._bray.pdf [Last accessed July 1, 2018].

Castells, M. 2006. 'Globalisation and Identity', *TRANSFER, Journal of Contemporary Culture*, 1: 56–66.

Deboos, S. 2013. 'Religious Fundamentalism in Zanskar, Indian Himalaya', *Himalaya*, 32 (1). Available at: https:/ https://digitalcommons.macalester /digitalcommons.macalester.edu/himala. edu/himalaya/vol32/iss1/12 ol32/iss1/12.

Deleuze, G. and F. Guattari. 1988. *A Thousand Plateaus: Capitalism and Schizophrenia*. London: The Athlone Press.

Deshmane, A. 2014. 'Ringzhen Tundup Shastri: The Devout Buddhist Who Helped RSS Reach Ladakh', *The Economic Times*, September 12. Available at: https://economictimes.indiatimes.com/news/politics-and-nation/ringzhen-tundup-shastri-the-devout-buddhist-who-helped-rss-reach-ladakh/articleshow/42305697.cms [Last accessed July 1, 2018).

Dollfus, Pascale. 1995. 'The History of Muslims in Central Ladakh', *The Tibet Journal*, 20 (3): Tibetan Muslims, Autumn, 35–58.

Fewekes, J.H. 2009. *Trade and Contemporary Society along the Silk Road. An Ethnohistory of Ladakh*. London and New York: Routledge.

Ganesh, Narayani. 2004. 'Sindhu Darshan No Longer a Hindu Darshan: Renuka', *TNN*, June 19. Available at: https://timesofindia.indiatimes.com/india/sindhu-darshan-no-longer-a-hindu-darshan-renuka/articleshow/745646.cms [Last accessed June 2, 2018]; www.chinabuddhismencyclopedia.com/en/index.php?title=Drukpa_Lineage_Explained [Last accessed March 1, 2019]; www.census2011.co.in/data/religion/district/622-kargil.html [Last accessed March 1, 2019]; www.census2011.co.in/data/religion/district/621-leh.html [Last accessed March 1, 2019].

Jina, P.S. 1994. *Tourism in Ladakh Himalaya*. Delhi: Indus Publishing Co.

JK Tourism. 2018. Available at: www.jktourism.org/index.php/cultural/festivals [Last accessed May 31, 2018].

LAHDC (Leh Autonomous Hill Development Council). 2010. *Statistical Handbook*. District Statistics and Evaluation Office, Leh, LAHDC.

LAHDC (Leh Autonomous Hill Development Council). 2018. Available at: http://leh.gov.in/tourist/mfestival.html [Last accessed May 31, 2018].

Li, T.M. 2007. 'Practices of Assemblage and Community Forest Management', *Economy and Society*, 36: 263–93.

Michaud, J. 1991. 'A Social Anthropology of Tourism in Ladakh', *Annals of Tourism Research*, 18: 605–21.
Neuhaus, Tom. 2012. *Tibet in the Western Imagination*. New York: Palgrave Macmillan.
Outlook. 2003. 'Splitting the Waters. Advani's 'Sindhu Darshan' Is Now a Symbol of His Hold Over the Party', *Outlook India News*, June 16, 2003. Available at: https://www.outlookindia.com/magazine/story/splitting-the-waters/220422 [Last accessed May 12, 2020].
Patil, S. 2018. 'China Targets India's Ladakh', *Gateway House: Indian Council on Global Relations*. Available at: https://www.gatewayhouse.in/china-targets-indias-ladakh/ [Last accessed May 11, 2020].
Pelliciardi, Vladimiro. 2010. 'Tourism Traffic Volumes in Leh District: An Overview', *Ladakh Studies*, 14–23.
Pirie, F. 2007. *Peace and Conflict in Ladakh: The Construction of a Fragile Web of Order*. Leiden and Boston: Brill.
Powell, A. 1992. *Heirs to Tibet: Travels Among the Exiles in India*. London: Heinemann.
Raman, S. 2016. 'Ladakh Should Not Go Unheard', *Gateway House: Indian Council on Global Relations*. Available at: https://www.gatewayhouse.in/ladakh-not-go-unheard/ [Last accessed May 11, 2020].
Rizvi, J. 1983. *Ladakh: Crossroads of High Asia*. Delhi: Oxford University Press.
Said, E. 1978. *Orientalism: Western Conceptions of the Orient*. New York: Penguin.
Swami, Praveen. 1999. 'The Kargil Conflict: Other Engagements', *Frontline*, 16 (16).
van Beek, M. 1998. 'True Patriots: Justifying Autonomy for Ladakh', *Himalayan Research Bulletin*, 18 (35).
van Beek, M. 2000. 'Beyond Identity Fetishism: "Communal" Conflict in Ladakh and the Limits of Autonomy', *Cultural Anthropology*, 15: 525–69.
van Beek, M. 2004. 'Dangerous Liaisons: Hindu Nationalism and Buddhist Radicalism in Ladakh', in *Religious Radicalism and Security in South Asia*, Eds. Limaye, Satu P., Malik, Mohan and Wirsing, Robert G. pp. 193–218. Honolulu, HI: Asia-Pacific Center for Security Studies.
Vasan, S. 2017. 'Being Ladakhi, Being Indian: Identity Formation, Culture and Community', *Economic and Political Weekly*, 52 (14), April 8: 43–49.
Wison-Smith, Henry. 2015. 'More Religious and Less Moral: The Changing Face of Religious Coexistence in Ladakh', Independent Study Project (ISP) Collection. Paper 2225. Available at: http://digitalcollections.sit.edu/isp_collection/2225 [Last accessed July 2, 2018].

# Part 5

# Media, borders and emergent subjects

# 10 Are we all pirates?

## Film and TV distribution on the Internet

*Patricia Ferrante*

What does it mean to be a pirate in the contemporary (digital) world we all inhabit? For sure, sea pirates are still the subjects of a definition much older than that of copyright or patent but, as Johns points out in his history of piracy (Johns 2009), the concept has sailed turbulent waters and reached a new condition in the 21st century. Today, anyone can be a pirate. It only takes a device connected to the Internet and some kind of interest in sharing what is read, listened to or watched. For almost the last 30 years, cultural and entertainment industries (TV, film, music, books, videogames, among other products) have faced a deep change in the distribution economies which organised them. The digital domain, in which physical supports and contents are separated and copies are, for the first time in history, identical to originals (Bunz 2007), brought a new scenario, with new media affordances (Gitelman 2006) in which users are enabled to access, copy, share, reuse and modify any content from a connected device.

But even when practices with media have undergone a deep transformation process, they still occur under the complex intellectual property rights regulatory framework that defines a global regime for the protection of cultural industries. Not only the Trade Related Aspects of Intellectual Property Rights (TRIPS) agreement but also public and corporate regulations shape the ways of participating in digital culture (Gillespie 2007) to a global extent, spreading what can or can't be done as defined by different actors in a global informational network (Castells 2011).

In this chapter, the concept of digital piracy is analysed into a broader concept, not defined by criminal discourses but as related to media practices in a digital landscape. It mainly focuses on practices that occur in the global south, usually lagging in the global distribution economies of film and TV.

### Users, producers, audiences . . . and pirates

Connected to the Internet, what we used to call users or audiences can be described as *prosumers* (Jenkins 2006) or *produsers* (Curran et al. 2012), a figure that is no longer depicting a person who is consuming culture but describing a more active engagement. The active dimension of *prosumers* is the one that clashes against a regulatory framework that mainly considers rigid roles in practices of cultural reproduction.

To define digital piracy then requires bringing together a global regulatory regime that determines which things are illegal and why, as well as an analysis of practices that shape digital culture. From this perspective, piracy is above all a global, social, political and cultural phenomena, as well as an everyday practice (Frederiksson and Arvanitakis 2014: 3). To define piracy, then, it will be necessary to approach the concept of digital culture, a very much used but maybe underdefined idea of the ways in which contemporary culture is being produced, shared, distributed, engaged with. While some authors describe this transitional stage of cultural practices as the information society (Castells 1997, 2011), the algorithmic revolution (Bunz 2014), the convergence culture (Jenkins 2006), the networked economy (Benkler 2006) or the augmented reality era in which we digitally manage our lives (Sadin 2017), Doueihi defines digital culture in terms of challenges:

> What is digital culture, nowadays so omnipresent, dominant and familiar? It is a series of combined technologies that have produced and continue to produce social practices that, at least to these times, threaten or question the viability, or even the legitimacy, of established socio cultural rules and the legal frameworks related to them. . . . Digital culture is built upon modes of communication and information exchanges that displace, redefine and remodel knowledge into new forms and formats and by new methods to acquire and transmit that knowledge.
>
> (Doueihi 2010: 35)

Doueihi defines digital culture in terms of the fractures it inscribes in the ways of cultural practices. One of these fractures is the legal one: on the one side, there are millions of connected people globally distributed sharing content, knowledge and information and, on the other, a series of legal dispositions that condemn a large part of those practices as criminal.

The clash between the 20th-century model of media, culture and entertainment, production and distribution – solidly protected by a series of legal and technological instruments that enabled or disabled access – that still persists and the contemporary ways of cultural engagement in a connected world produces a global rise in what the industry calls digital piracy, in many cases involving people that are not even aware of this pirate condition.

Lev Manovich proposes that contemporary cultural practices are transforming mass media into mass production media. Everyday media practices (Manovich 2008) involving the consumption and sharing of audiovisual content entail a pirate function (Philip 2005) that, even when regulation with global reach considers it a crime, can be studied as a powerful way of access to movies and TV shows (Karaganis 2011) built upon specific affordances of new media (Gitelman 2006) and the possibility to unlimited copying while keeping the quality intact (Bunz 2007). People's practices, technological capabilities and the expansion of a global network of participatory users build up a distribution model in a changing media economy (Curran et al. 2012). This model is inhabited by traditional actors – media companies that distribute movies and TV – and new actors: technological companies that provide search engines or platforms for sharing content, nowadays as powerful as highly concentrated media corporations, coexisting with just simple users that, even when power disparities prevail, can also assume a distributive role while sharing or posting any content. Users/audiences also become distributors and key actors in this scenario that involves legal and illegal actors, as well as actors that stand in a grey zone that constitutes a shadow economy circuit (Lobato 2012). Shadow economies – as we will see in the next section – have played a vital role in the history of film distribution, and what happens in that zone is currently reshaping the media landscape.

## Online film and TV distribution: from the Pirate Bay and YouTube to Netflix and other platforms

'Me at the Zoo' is a 19-second video, first published in 2005 and watched by more than 40 million people worldwide. It is also the first video uploaded to YouTube, which back then launched its platform for sharing amateur video in a community-driven platform with a clear slogan: broadcast yourself. Such an uneventful video – a guy stands in front of the elephants and describes the long trunks, rather poorly shot – triggered an enormous change in the ways we watch, share and produce audiovisual content. A year later, in 2006, another short amateur video showed YouTube founders announcing its sale to tech giant Google. As Snickars and Vonderau point out, the peculiarity of YouTube lies in the way the platform has been negotiating and navigating between community and commerce. If YouTube is anything, it is both industry and user driven (Snickers and Vonderau 2009: 6). In this journey, the platform had great impacts in the ways in which TV and audiovisual content is thought of as a medium, as an archive, as an industry.[1]

At first planned to be a platform for uploading and sharing amateur video, YouTube quickly became the most popular video server and distributor worldwide: to be seen, you needed to be on that screen more than any other. Accordingly, with the apparent absence of hierarchy other than popularity, on YouTube, different actors coexisted: cinema studios and distribution companies uploading trailers, electronic press kits and other videos associated with a film; complete films uploaded by users (from fans to French director Godard); TV channels; regular people showing their everyday lives to whomever wanted to watch; parodies; pet videos, bloopers and so on. . .

With no time schedule or limits in the number of times you can watch the same video, YouTube inaugurated an era named by Stiegler 'the carnival of the new screen' (Stiegler 2009). This new screen at first operated besides media regulation other than the terms and conditions of use established by the company itself and ended up with the traditional ways of watching TV (in a TV set, at certain moments, throughout a regulated system).

YouTube expanded enormously the access to audiovisual content that otherwise wouldn't be available in many countries and confirmed the computer connected to the Internet as a key device to watch and share videos. Other platforms such as Dailymotion or the Pirate Bay were also important for the shaping of the audiovisual digital landscape, but undoubtedly YouTube propelled new ways of seeing, pushing legal actors to reshape their distribution strategies to seriously consider the online circuit, in which they entered with much more resources but later than the 'new' actors, such as technological companies and prosumers.

While YouTube started the era of mass streaming, the Pirate Bay was a key actor in the era of mass downloading BitTorrent archives, maybe as important as Napster, the music-sharing platform that ignited the digital music revolution. Based on a model of peer-to-peer (P2P) sharing technologies, it launched in 2003 and quickly formed a mass of global users eager to share, upload and download books, music, film and TV shows, translated or subtitled and available for global distribution, circumventing the corporate circuits that historically divided the world into regions cultural products were delivered to.

Established as a global market divided into regions, the economies of TV and film distribution in the pre-Internet days were pretty much the same in every country: once a film was launched in its country of production, the rights to show copies were sold to cable networks in movie fairs. The movies could then be shown at limited times in what is called 'the windows policy' in which the first window/screen is at the movie theatre, the second is the DVD launch for home video consumption and the third is the TV (mostly cable networks). None of this circuit contemplated the chance to distribute on video-sharing platforms nor considered the computer, a tablet or a cell phone as a device on which people watch movies or TV.

TV series were managed by a similar cycle: launch in country of origin, international sales throughout cable networks and, in the last years, online distribution via video platforms. This was done mostly throughout pay-per-view services such as Netflix, broadcasting companies that enable cable users to watch online or geo-localised players such as the BBC Iplayer – restricted to users connected in the geographical area of the United Kingdom – or Hulu, a platform that streams original content and TV series produced by the major broadcasters in the United States and for US territory.

The system worked upon an idea of a controlled audience, organised in very clear time schedules and geographical spaces. The corporate model of media distribution that dominated the 20th century – as Benkler or Jenkins describe it (Benkler 2006; Jenkins 2006) – sought to reach audiences as wide and as homogenous as possible, guaranteeing a dominant presence of the most powerful markets – for example, the Hollywood model – worldwide.

But if, as suggested by Lobato, we widen our scope and understand distribution as the movement of media through time and space, this enlargement opens the study to an array of informal channels that are rarely documented but allow us to insert into the distribution circuits actors that are not frequently considered by industry or media studies as capable of agency and hence placed on the same level analytically as their formal counterparts (Lobato 2012: 2). In a study with historical perspective, Lobato describes the three main dynamics in the economies of film distribution that we extend into the TV series distribution as well: the formal, the informal the shadow economies.

In the digital domain, formal economies are inhabited by actors – enterprises, public institutions, public and private TV channels, conglomerates, corporations – that offer audiovisual content for free or by a pay-per-view model that complies with local and international regulations of intellectual property. Though formal, these actors can spend some time in the grey zone – that of the shadow economy.

The economics of online TV and film distribution is a hybrid formed by a formal market inhabited by giant media and technological actors and small ventures that seek to create a niche market (auteur cinema, LGBT content); the informal market, inhabited by platforms and search engines that offer access to stream or download movies and series and the grey zones in which legality or illegality is not clear. For instance, it is not illegal to offer a VPN service, but it is or it might be considered illegal to watch a TV show that is not being distributed in your region by the legal circuits.

This economy of film distribution happens in the shadow of legality, developing a network that challenges formal distribution circuits while opening new opportunities for global audiences.

Some actors operate in the three zones, like YouTube, where amateur and professional videos coexist. Even though protected content is removed, users are noticed if they upload content that circumvents intellectual property rights, and there is an ongoing negotiation about intellectual property rights and the genres of amateur media (for example, parodies, movie re-enactments or music video clips that use personal photos or video shoots in specific songs).[2] In the case of Netflix, the platform keeps adjusting its programming to national rules and agreements. For instance, when Netflix first arrived in Argentina (2011), the film and TV series offered were different from those of other countries, and users frequently used a VPN[3] in order to circumvent the technical patch that regulates what can or cannot be distributed in different countries. The company has been seeking to harmonise a global catalogue, even though it has to strongly negotiate with production and distribution companies in order to sustain user engagement.

Informal actors include a wide array of platforms, websites and users: from a kid posting a link through social media to platforms for sharing content using peer-to-peer technologies or cyberlockers such as Megaupload:[4] individuals and small and big organisations found themselves in the position of being *de facto* distributors, generating new kinds of viewing practices and modes of consumption (Lobato 2012: 13). Users operate simultaneously in the three dimensions, and these are the practices that seem to be reshaping the movie and TV distribution economy and the cultural and media landscape as a whole.

The digital media landscape introduces affordances and agency capabilities that are mainly considered piracy by local and global regulation. In Argentina, as well as in every country throughout the region, so-called digital piracy is a phenomenon of rising concern for media corporations, reflecting locally a global war against content sharing that goes underneath or beside the commercial structures for participating or consuming. But who defines who the pirates are and how regulation adjusts/shapes global sharing networks? We will discuss these issues in the following section.

## 'Piracy' and the pirate function in the digital domain

As stated previously, defining digital piracy is a complex issue, necessarily related to who defines it. As it happened throughout history, intellectual property regulation is attached to power structures, private interests and public law, and it expresses socio-historical definitions of public policy about what kind of knowledge/ideas should be protected (Sell and May 2006). The global stage of intellectual property protection began with the TRIPS agreement, transforming behaviours that were legal into illegal practices. Approaching piracy from a legal perspective, even from a critique to intellectual property rights, falls short in describing a much larger phenomenon. For instance, anthropologist Brian Larkin studies pirate infrastructures in Nigeria and defines piracy as first and foremost a system of reproduction and transmission of goods that generate social action and aesthetic forms. The legal/illegal dichotomy leaves aside a more complex study of cultural practices.[5]

The Internet expansion since the beginning of the 1990s and the cultural practices associated with the digital distribution that spread along with the technology challenged the whole regulatory infrastructure, triggering a set of regional or local regulations that can impact globally the ways in which everybody participates in digital culture.

The WTO Glossary defines piracy as the unauthorised copying of materials protected by intellectual property rights (such as copyright, trademarks, patents, geographical indications etc.) for commercial purposes and unauthorised commercial dealing in copied materials. Paradoxically, this definition turned out to be more benevolent than those proposed by the Stop Online Piracy Act (SOPA) or Protect Intellectual Property Act (PIPA), the two US acts that did not pass as laws in 2012 but expressed the fierce stance of media and entertainment lobbies against digital sharing.

Media corporations have frequently associated piracy with crime, even though it is interesting to point out what Tim Wu notices in his book *The*

*Master Switch: The Rise and Fall of Information Empires* (Wu 2010): that media and communication corporations have a shared life cycle that goes from an experimental–innovative phase, in which regulation is somehow lax; to a series of steps of increasing power – oligopoly, monopoly, empire – that entail the capacity of lobbying for more restrictive regulations involving media and intellectual property.

Even though the Internet revolution expanded an ideal of a more free, open, global and democratic media architecture, contemporary media corporations are undergoing a cycle of concentration (Freedman 2012), operating in a regulatory architecture that reflects their power much more than that of the audiences, users or prosumers. Under this perspective, to download a song or stream a movie from a noncommercial site is still considered analogous to, for example, the theft of a car or a purse,[6] and they frequently report digital piracy in terms of loss: of jobs, of money, of security (piracy is also frequently associated with terrorist networks).

As Susan Sell and Karaganis demonstrate (Sell 2003; Karaganis 2011), reports about piracy by media corporations or media alliances and associations (both local and global) are the key ones taken into account by the yearly Special 301 Report of the United States Trade Representative (USTR) that informs, according to US standards, how different countries are complying with intellectual property protection. Like other countries, Argentina is an ongoing presence in the priority watch list, and for some years, the report stated that there was an almost 100% digital piracy rate.[7] Scholars such as Sell and May (2006), May (2006), Sell (2003), Drahos (2010), Drahos and John Braithwaite (2002) and Correa (2016) have thoroughly studied the sanction of the TRIPS regime, the power disparities that the treatment expresses and the new division of labour it establishes between developed and developing countries. The TRIPS agreement operates in a global regime in which national regulations are also entangled. The frequent presence in a Priority Watch List of the USTR enables commercial retaliations, pushing the countries that are listed to adapt their intellectual property laws to US commercial policy objectives.

The conception of piracy that appears in the Special 301 reports can tell us a lot about how power structures define and distribute rights and wrongs and how copyright regulation constructs piracy in this era. But it falls short when describing the digital media landscape, and it leaves aside a set of practices that are triggering innovation: instead of thinking of piracy as a singular practice, it is necessary to think in terms of piracies. Depending on the context, piracy may be theft or a legitimate business practice, a free speech act or a form of political resistance. Sometimes it is all these things at once (Lobato 2012: 70). The digital domain requires rethinking piracy as a cultural practice, not only in order to study the ways in which people consume, produce and share culture in a connected world but also to better rethink regulation.

Crossing the legal perspectives with cultural practices allows us to rethink about piracy in ways that can better explain contemporary transitions in media. As Brian Larkin proposes,

> piracy is a technical infrastructure, and like all such infrastructures it influences and shapes the forms of sociability, aesthetic production, and economic organisation that mark urban life. While it is understandable that questions of law should dominate the debate about piracy, we also need to place piracy into a history of infrastructures. . . . Examining piracy as a technical mode rather than a legal one helps pull into focus the form of piracy rather than its content. It looks at what piracy does and its resulting effect on people's experiences of temporality and subjectivity, on practices of watching and using technology, on the new forms of leisure and sociability, and in the forging of new aesthetic forms.
>
> (Larkin 2007: 77)

Film and TV distribution in Argentina has an unwritten 'pirate' history: during the 1976–83 dictatorship, in which there was no freedom of speech and censorship ruled cultural, information and media distribution, there were pirate networks distributing censored films (Almodóvar and Bertollucci films, for example).

In recent years and previous to the platform expansion, international film and TV releases were attached to global rules that organised the world into zones. For instance, Argentina belonged to region 4 for DVD distribution, which indicated a specific time and space for legal distribution, associated with the technological devices that read VHS, DVD and other forms of predigital storage. Movies and TV series were usually distributed one year later, and a copying practice expanded: if able to catch a copy of an unreleased movie or series, changing the zone or modifying the VHS with a short piece of tape would make the content readable.

When video content was available on the Internet (post-2005), different practices to get delayed or unreleased content expanded: searching a global network suddenly made access much more easy. In Argentina, different projects seeking to organise the chaos of Internet audiovisual content searches were developed (and will be described next).

Going beyond the legal/illegal dichotomy to approach piracy as a digital culture phenomenon allows one to see a wider landscape in which it can also be approached as a way of access and sharing of cultural goods, in which income may be a key variable or not. Karaganis (2011) explored how income is a key determinant, but not the only one, of access to culture and media in emerging economies. In those economies, copy expands and persists because of low incomes, but also for other reasons (such as not being relevant markets for media industries, for example). Later he also demonstrate how sharing culture is a strong practice among people in middle- to high-income economies (Karaganis and Renkema 2013). People copy because they cannot afford to buy, and they also do so because they want/need to share with others. De Kosnik also describes personal archival and fan practices as part of a copy culture that exceeds the idea of piracy as a legal problem (De Kosnik 2016). Access, from these perspectives, needs to be understood not only as an economic concept but a cultural one: access implies satisfying a cultural need but also the need to archive or share what you like with others.

Kavita Phillip, a feminist post-colonial scholar, analyses piracy discourses in the 21st century and transfers Foucault's question about authorship – what is an author? – to a question about piracy – what is a pirate?:'

> I attempt to suggest an understanding of the pirate function, analogous to Foucault's author function. The figure of the pirate seems to emerge, at the turn of the 20th century, as a key component in the shaping of early 21st century bourgeois law. At this historical moment, a particular confluence of digital copying, its affiliated modes of creativity, a 'crisis' in bourgeois legalities and culture apparently precipitated by the telecom and digital revolutions, and the space-time compression of global cultures and economies, creates the conditions for the public recognition of the fragmented 'author functions' that Foucault identified. At the same time, shifts – both conservative and progressive – in bourgeois legalities seek to preclude the apparently chaotic fragmentation of the author into its component author functions.
>
> (Philip 2005: 207)

Philip subverts the legal bourgeois definition of piracy and, instead, asking about the technological author, identifies how piracy is currently defining authorship: How does the digital revolution, with its mantra of rip/mix/burn and its interpellation of high-bandwidth multicultural youth, make a difference to how we read modern authorship? (207). The pirate function, in the contemporary media landscape, is a key component of technical authorship and creative agency in the film and TV distribution circuits.

## Formal, informal and blurred circuits

*Breaking Bad* was a huge success worldwide, and Argentina was no exception. The story of a chemistry teacher turned designer drug lord was watched, talked about and shared on every social media platform, and mainstream media echoed this success in different stories (the series is frequently mentioned in the stories of drug dealing and trafficking in Argentina). But *Breaking Bad* was mostly an internet phenomena. The regional cable network AXN (property of Sony Networks) offered it in its programming . . . at 3 AM. As the series became more and more popular worldwide, the channel rescheduled it for prime time but airing old episodes.

Two years after the final season, a local network bought the rights to air the series in Spanish, but it could only deliver the show for the city and province of Buenos Aires, because the rights were only bought for that scope, leaving out most of the country.

There was no possible way for a fan to adapt to this legal scheme. The Television 2.0 that Bury and Li describe (Bury and Li 2013) has become spreadable. Along with the formal channels – cable networks, local and global channels and streaming platforms – and the different variety of informal ones – pirate platforms and sites, links shared in social media – there are millions of fans sharing information about cultural goods and how to reach them. The networks of online TV and movie distribution are inhabited by the formal, the informal and the blurred zone in which the experience goes beyond regulation. For instance, if somebody wanted to watch *Breaking Bad* in the formal market in Argentina and was not living in an urban area, there was no other chance than looking for the show online and watching it. No other market options were available.

## Online sharing vs. online piracy in Argentina

Online sharing culture evolved into a constant flow of recommendations and the interchange of cultural goods, sometimes clashing against intellectual property regulation, and it is in these cases that we can better see how regulation is in constant tension/negotiation with extended cultural practices, trying to shape digital culture and adapt it to the formalities of laws that were sanctioned in and for an analogous world.

In Argentina, these tensions can be seen in two sound judiciary cases. Taringa! (www.taringa.net) is a virtual community with more than 28 million registered users, accused of circumvention of the local copyright law (Law 11.723) because of users sharing links to download books. The claim was set in 2009 by a pool of publishing houses. Some of them reached a private agreement with Taringa! owners, and the case continued to the Supreme Court. The three Taringa! owners were absolved in 2018 (almost 10 years later) in a verdict that states that the verification of intellectual property compliance of every user post prior to the publication would constitute previous censorship. The case brought up a common issue when discussing digital piracy: Is the intermediary responsible? How and why? Can the intermediary – in this case Taringa!, but the question is also valid for search engines, social networks and cloud computing platforms – be accused of circumventing IP regulation because of allowing the technical capacity to share a link between users?

The other sound case is Cuevana, a platform that aggregated links to streamed TV series and movies that faced a court case introduced by Turner Corporation, Fox, Paramount, Columbia, Warner Bros, Universal and Disney because of the circumvention of copyright law of TV shows. Cuevana is pointed out in at least three Special 301 reports as a major concern for international media corporations.

While formal actors were designing their TV on-demand strategies, a young student developed Cuevana, a streaming platform that reached 2 million daily users in 2011 and enabled access to copies made by someone else through links to content that was not hosted on the web page but somewhere else. The site ordered, indexed and organised content but did not copy, store or host this content. Tomás Escobar, Cuevana founder, summarised to the press what he understood the conflict was all about: 'For the industry, Cuevana is the voice of the user'.[8]

These cases did not change regulation but seeded a debate about how people are sharing audiovisual content and how media corporations are expanding their offers into the digital domain.

As stated previously, shadow economies are not new in Argentina: in the scenario regulated by the 20th-century media distribution model and prior to the Internet expansion, there were specific distribution channels for 'other cinemas': cine clubs, festivals, enthusiast clubs and fans of European or oriental film that managed to share their love for movies with people alike, not only because the market was divided between Hollywood and national production[9] but also because 'pirate' distribution was the only way to circumvent censorship, a very common practice in Argentina's media regulation history, most of all during dictator regimes.[10]

As has happened in other cultural industries such as publishing or recording throughout time, piracy has been an important force against censorship and the regulation of content distribution and consumption based upon moral, political or religious standards, and this was no exception in Argentina. While commercial, regulatory and political standards shaped the audiovisual market, piracy somehow emerged as a resistance to the media capitalism trend and forged an anarchic market based on sharing practices.

Besides this pirate function as a way to guarantee free speech and the diffusion of specific ideas that were prohibited because of political, moral or religious standards, what we are interested in approaching in this chapter is the expansion of piracy as a complex phenomena as it operates in the digital domain that entails a range of definitions that goes from global crime or, at least, misdemeanour, to an efficient way – perhaps the most efficient – of distributing films and TV series with a global reach, hitching in a virtuous way the different affordances of new media and participatory culture.

Crisscrossing the formal and the informal, there is this blurred area – the grey zone, the shadow economy – in which access and a culture of sharing are shaping new ways in which we watch movies and TV shows.

During the 20th century media distribution model, content was being delivered, while content, in the digital domain, is a constant flow that can be transformed, shared, recommended, talked about, related to some other content.

Following Jenkins, we are trying to understand the global spread of 'digital piracy' – for whatever that means for whomever defines it – not by reflecting what media can/could do to the people but what people are doing with media in these networked societies. From this perspective, we consider Gitelman's definition of media as 'socially realised structures of communication, where structures include both technological forms and their associated protocols, and where communication is a cultural practice, a ritualised collocation of different people on the same mental map, sharing or engaged with popular ontologies of representation' (Gitelman 2006: 7).

In the new media shared mental map, one feature of the newness is related to the media affordances: for the first time in media technology history, in the digital domain, a copy is identical to the (digital) original – somehow abolishing the distinction – it's easy to do and it's cheap (Bunz 2007). The historical practice of recommending or talking about a movie now includes the actual possibility of sharing a copy by sharing a link. Throughout different platforms, media and apps, there is a model of distribution 'from below' that is a central rather than marginal feature of film (and TV) culture (Lobato 2012: 19).

In the convergent media ecology[11] we increasingly inhabit (even in middle- to low-income countries), this distribution model from below expands itself enormously, and each and every one of us sharing some link to a movie or TV show is assuming a distribution position, an agency to distribute content that was previously a domain of media industries. And this is one of the reasons even industry lobbies, technological fixes (Gillespie 2007) and debates about the extension of terms of intellectual property rights are completely unable to prevent, stop or reconvert cultural practices. As long as there is a chance to share a link to any given audiovisual content, protected or not, there is a distribution agency happening.

As regards film and TV distribution, participating in digital culture – which is what transforms a user in a produser/prosumer – entails different ranges of engagement, from merely sharing a link on social media to uploading or downloading content, streaming from a specific site or subtitling entire episodes, films or series.[12]

These (audiovisual) participatory culture practices evolve in a convergent media ecology, not because contents run or may run on different devices, but because convergence is embedded in social cultural practices. Convergence should not be understood as a technological process bringing together multiple media functions within the same devices. 'Instead – proposes Henry Jenkins – convergence represents a cultural shift as consumers are encouraged to seek out new information and make connections among dispersed media content' (Jenkins 2006: 12).

Participatory culture is necessarily associated with convergence media, as convergence does not occur through media appliances, however sophisticated they may become. 'Convergence occurs within the brains of individual consumers and through their social interactions with others. Each of us constructs our own personal mythology from bits and fragments of information extracted from the media flow and transformed into resources through which we make sense of our everyday lives' (Jenkins 2006: 13).

The participatory rationale in a convergent media ecology clashes against a rigid regulatory framework that defines who gets to see/read/listen to what, when and where. Even though media industries and their overwhelming power try to keep control of how their products circulate, the intellectual property protection scheme that has operated efficiently throughout most of the 20th century proves to be completely inefficient when extended to the digital domain, where content is separated from its technical form and transformed into bytes of information available to copy and share. The everyday media practices, in which new media affordances are put into play, transform massive media consumption into massive media production (Manovich 2008).

## Shaping digital culture

Abigail De Kosnik states that piracy is the future of television: global, participatory, fan oriented, with no timetables (De Kosnik 2010); hence, there is a lot to learn from the pirate function in the digital media ecology.

In the distribution circuit of TV series and movies, the Internet has expanded the boundaries of what we get to see. Even though the power of agenda setting of corporate media is evident, we no longer depend on a programming menu to watch a movie or a TV series.

If the movie industry has never considered distributing films other than Hollywood productions and a few European or Asian movies in Latin America, the Internet provides a window into a much wider menu. In this, as in many cases, so-called digital piracy covers a market failure and expands our cultural experience.

'Digital piracy' fosters transformations in the media landscape, even when regulatory tendencies seem to push in the opposite direction. These are some preliminary hypotheses about the impacts of 'digital piracy'/sharing culture in the audiovisual digital landscape upon which further research is needed, both for improving distribution systems and for expanding the audiovisual cultural offerings with a global reach.

Piracy practices seem to be pushing the traditional movie and TV market to expand distribution, rethink programming and risk more in terms of creativity and storytelling. The success in any given platform of an audiovisual content might trigger new content or aesthetic experiences on other platforms. In Argentina, the experience shows that innovative endeavours were not attached to legal regulation or at least operated in the grey zone that lies where there are no clear regulations.

Also, audiovisual pirate platforms provide access to global content – or at least a more global content than the one formal actors provide – and in many cases, this content is curated by participatory networks in which audience/user/produser–prosumer agency is a key component.

As Larkin proposes, piracy is much more than a legal affair. As a socio-technical structure, it reflects how we watch, share and participate around TV and movies in this digital era. And it places us – users, produsers, prosumers – in a much more active role that is worth exploring.

## Notes

1 See Snickers and Vonderau (2009) (editors), *The YouTube Reader*, National Library of Sweden.

2 Conten ID is the system created by You Tube for intellectual property rights holders by which they can identify and manage their content on the platform. Every uploaded video is analysed and checked against an archival database with information about the proprietary content. The rights holders decide what happens when a coincidence between any video content in YouTube and a work that belongs to them is detected. When this happens, the video receives a Content ID claim. To see more YouTube regulations about intellectual property rights, access https://support.google.com/youtube/answer/2797370?hl=es-419 (accessed on 25 March 2020).

3 A virtual public network (VPN) is a technology that enable users to mask their computer's IP address and circumvent geo-blocking technologies that are frequently used by streaming service providers in order to comply with intellectual property regulations. For a more detailed discussion about geo-blocking strategies, see Lobato and Meese (2016), Theory on Demand #18, Geoblocking and Global Video Culture.

4 Cyberlockers provide a service to store archives online. Megaupload provided such a service, also known as cloud storage services, and gained enormous popularity worldwide. It was dismantled in 2012 by the FBI because of intellectual property rights infringements.

5 B. Larkin (2007), *Pirate Infrastructures, in Structures of Participation in Digital Culture*, SSRN, 74.

6 It is frequent that media associations and alliances equate music and video downloading or streaming on sites that are not under the control of formal media actors with regular theft. This has also been the case with the copying of VHS or DVDs. In fact, in Argentina, many films on VHS or DVD opened with institutional advertising showing a purse or a car theft and eventually stating that you would be doing the same if you copied the film. This perspective is also present in educational campaigns led by major networks. For example, FOX Latin America launched the Anti-Piracy League. With the slogan 'Defending your fun', they visit primary schools and give talks associating illegal copying, downloading and sharing with the theft of ideas or of creative works.

7 The 2017 report, in which Argentina is listed on the Priority Watch List, states that 'While optical disc copyright piracy is widespread, online piracy continues to be a growing concern and criminal enforcement for online piracy is nearly non existent. As a result, IP enforcement online in Argentina consists mainly of right holders trying to convince cooperative Argentine ISP storage to take down specific infringing works, as well as attempting to seek injunctions in civil cases. Right holders also cite widespread use of unlicensed software by Argentine private enterprises and the government'. See: https://ustr.gov/sites/default/files/301/2017%20Special%20301%20Report%20FINAL.PDF, p. 51 (accessed on 9 August 2017). In previous years, the Report noticed an almost 100% rate of digital piracy. For example, in 2015, the Report said: 'Internet piracy rates approach 100 percent in several content areas. For example, Argentine-run

notoriousMarket cuevana.tv – offering pirated movies and TV shows – is the 75th most popular website in the country, with an estimated 150,000 visitors each day. As a result, IPR enforcement in Argentina consists mainly of rights holders trying to convince cooperative Argentine online providers to agree to take down specific infringing works, and attempting to seek injunctions in civil cases. Criminal enforcement is nearly nonexistent'. See: https://ustr.gov/sites/default/files/2015-Special-301-Report-FINAL.pdf, p. 56 (accessed on 9 August 2017).

8 Interview in Página/12 newspaper, 2 December 2011, available at www.pagina12.com.ar/diario/sociedad/3-182543-2011-12-02.html (accessed on 11 April 2019).

9 Film historian Fernando Martín Peña describes in chronological order the history of the cinema industry and distribution in Argentina, pointing out how a true and powerful film industry was born, consolidated and then almost destroyed. See F. Peña (2012), *Cien años de cine argentino*, Buenos Aires, Biblos-Fundación OSDE.

10 The documentary film 'Un importante pre estreno' (An important pre release) (Calori 2015) shows how local cinephilia managed to distribute and release international films that were prohibited by dictatorships in Argentina. The film parallels the history of local cinephilia with censorship and shows how piracy was the only strategy against authoritarianism.

11 The metaphor of ecology, as defined by anthropologist Mimi Ito, emphasises the characteristics of an overall technical, social, cultural and place-based system in which the components are not decomposable or separable, in which everyday practices – Ito analyses those of the young in the United States[1] – existing structural conditions, infrastructures of place and technologies are all dynamically interrelated (Ito 2009: 31). Content – video, audio, texts; self produced or produced by others – flow throughout devices, adding in this path different prints from different users that participate in some way or the other in this flow.

12 Fansubbing (fan and subtitler) is a very interesting phenomena of participatory and sharing culture. Remotely distributed, they manage to translate, subtitle and share the entire translation and subtitles of movies or TV episodes, integrating a large network of amateur translators. To explore this phenomena, see Díaz-Cintas and Muñoz Sánchez (2006), 'Fansubs: Audiovisual Translation in an Amateur Environment', in *The Journal of Specialised Translation*, Issue 6.

## Bibliography

Benkler, Y. 2006. *The Wealth of Networks How Social Production Transforms Markets and Freedom*. New Haven and London: Yale University Press.

Bunz, M. 2007. *La utopia de la copia – El pop como irritación*. Buenos Aires: Interzona.

Bunz, M. 2014. *The Silent Revolution. How Digitalisation Transforms Knowledge, Work, Journalism and Politics without Making Too Much Noise*. New York: Palgrave Macmillan.

Bury, R. 2018. *Viewer and Fan Engagement with Digital TV*. New York: Peter Lang.

Bury, R. and J. Li. 2013. 'Is It Live or Is It Time Shifted, Streamed or Downloaded? Watching Television in the Era of Multiple Screens', *New Media & Society*, 17 (4): 592–610.

Calori, S. 2015. *Un importante pre estreno*. Tiratruenos, Instituto Nacional de Cine y Artes Audiovisuales (INCAA). Buenos Aires.

Castells, M. 1997. *La era de la información. Economía, sociedad, cultura, Vol. I: La sociedad red*. Madrid: Alianza.

Castells, M. 2011. *Communication Power*. New York: Oxford University Press.
Correa, C. 2016. 'Innovation and the Global Expansion of Intellectual Property Rights: Unfulfilled Promises', Research Paper 70, South Centre. Available at: https://www.southcentre.int/wp-content/uploads/2016/08/RP70_Innovation-and-IP-Unfulfilled-Promises_EN-1.pdf.
Curran, J., N. Fenton and D. Freedman. 2012. *Misunderstanding the Internet*. New York: Routledge.
De Kosnik, A. 2010. *Piracy Is the Future of Television*. MIT: Convergence Culture Consortium.
De Kosnik, A. 2016. *Rogue Archives: Digital Cultural Memory and Media Fandom*. Cambridge, MA: MIT Press.
Diaz-Cintas, J. and P. Muñoz Sánchez. 2006. 'Fansubs: Audiovisual Translation in an Amateur Environment', *JoSTrans: The Journal of Specialised Translation*, 6: 37–52.
Doueihi, M. 2010. *La gran Conversion Digital*. Buenos Aires: Fondo de Cultura Económica.
Drahos, P. 2010. *The Global Governance of Knowledge: Patent Offices and Their Clients*. New York: Cambridge University Press.
Drahos, P. and J. Braithwaite. 2002. *Information Feudalism: Who Owns the Knowledge Economy?* London: Earthscan Publications.
Drahos, P. and R. Mayne. 2002. *Global Intellectual Property Rights: Knowledge Access and Development*. Hampshire and New York: Palgrave Macmillan.
Fredriksson, M. and J. Arvanitakis. 2014. *Piracy: Leakages of Modernity*. Sacramento, CA: Litwin Books.
Gillespie, T. 2007. *Wired Shut: Copyright and the Shape of Digital Culture*. Cambridge: MIT Press.
Gitelman, L. 2006. *Always, Already, New: Media, History and the Data of Culture*. Cambridge: MIT Press.
Jenkins, H. 2006. *Convergence Culture: Where Old and New Media Collide*. London and New York: New York University Press.
Jenkins, H., S. Ford and J. Green. 2013. *Spreadable Media. Creating Value and Meaning in a Networked Culture*. New York: New York University Press.
Johns, A. 2010. *Piracy: The Intellectual Property Wars from Gutenberg to Gates*. Chicago & London: University of Chicago Press.
Karaganis, J. 2011. *Media Piracy in Emerging Economies*. SSRC. Available at: http://piracy.ssrc.org/
Karaganis, J. and L. Renkema. 2013. 'Copy Culture in the US and Germany'. Available at: http://piracy.americanassembly.org/wp-content/uploads/2013/01/Copy-Culture.pdf
Larkin, B. 2007. 'Pirate Infrastructures', in J. Karaganis (ed.) *Structures of Participation in Digital Culture*. SSRC. Available at: https://s3.amazonaws.com/ssrc-cdn1/crmuploads/new_publication_3/structures-of-participation-in-digital-culture.pdf
Liang, L. 2005. 'Porous Legalities and Avenues of Participation'. Available at: www.stephenmclaughlin.net/ph-library/articles/liang/Liang%202005%20-%20Porous%20Legalities%20and%20Avenues%20of%20Participation.pdf
Lobato, R. 2012. *Shadow Economies of Cinema. Mapping Informal Film Distribution*. London: Palgrave Macmillan, BFI.
Lobato, R. and J. Meese. 2016. *Geoblocking and Global Video Culture, Theory on Demand #18*. Amsterdam: Institute of Network Cultures.

Manovich, L. 2008. 'The Practice of Everyday (Media) Life'. Available at: http://manovich.net/content/04-projects/059-the-practice-of-everyday-media-life/56_article_2008.pdf

May, C. 2006. 'Social Limits to the Commodification of Knowledge: Ten Years of TRIPs', *Journal of Institutional Economics*, 2 (1): 91–108. https://doi.org/10.1017/S1744137405000226.

Mizuko Ito, Sonja Baumer, Matteo Bittanti, danah boyd, Rachel Cody, Becky Herr Stephenson, Heather A. Horst, Patricia G. Lange, Dilan Mahendran, Katynka Z. Martínez, C. J. Pascoe, Dan Perkel, Laura Robinson, Christo Sims and Lisa Tripp. 2009. *Hanging Out, Messing Around, and Geeking Out. Kids Living and Learning with New Media*. Cambridge, MA & London: MIT Press.

Peña, F. 2012. *Cien años de cine argentino*. Editorial Biblios – Buenos Aires: Fundación OSDE.

Philip, K. 2005. 'What Is a Technological Author? The Pirate Function and Intellectual Property', *Postcolonial Studies*, 8 (2): 199-218.

Sadin, E. 2017. *La humanidad aumentada. La administración digital del mundo*. Buenos Aires: Caja Negra Editora.

Sell, S. 2003. *Private Power, Public Law: The Globalisation of Intellectual Property Rights*. Cambridge: Cambridge University Press.

Sell, S. and C. May. 2006. *Intellectual Property Rights: A Critical History*. London: Lynne Rienner Publishers.

Snickers, P. and P. Vonderau. 2009. *The YouTube Reader*. Stockholm: National Library of Sweden.

Stiegler, B. 2009. 'The Carnival of the New Screen', in P. Snickers and P. Vonderau (eds.) *The YouTube Reader*, pp. 40-60. Stockholm: National Library of Sweden.

Wu, T. 2010. *The Master Switch: The Rise and Fall of Information Empires*. New York: Alfred A. Knopf.

# 11 Listening global

## Sonic texts, technologies and the new listening subjects

*Ratheesh Kumar*

Revisiting the sites of sound cultures and their corresponding socialities, in times of relentless upgradation and transformation of global media technologies, would enable us to address the domain of the transformed *listener*. How are sounds and sonic regimes appropriated by and incorporated into different social and political categories of identity, community, region and nation? Cultural mediations enable connections between sounds and images, and the corresponding identifications are often translated into a process of homogenisation, essentialisation and freezing these sounds within fixed spaces and bodies. In times of new media and digital technologies, the cultural dynamics of production and distribution of sonic texts offer a conceptual ground to approach the new listening subject beyond the thesis of 'culture industry' and frameworks of hegemony and control.

By centring some of these interconnected issues in hearing cultures, this chapter seeks to trace the shifting borders in production, listening and appreciation of popular soundtracks, music compositions and their rerecorded, dubbed and technologically tilted versions. The focus here is on the new listening habits and techniques at the crossroads of digital recording technologies through reading – with ears, of course. It also attempts to chart how the genre of film music and music makers negotiate and respond to the notions of boundaries, purity, tradition and authenticity in contemporary Indian music that simultaneously transcends and re-presents particular social and geographical locations, communities and the nation itself. Against this backdrop, the chapter navigates through distinct episodes of sonic reconfigurations accompanied by major shifts in auditory technology and the technologies of power and control. These episodes locate the listening subject in two different historical contexts; first in the 1950s, where radio broadcasting became a trigger in post-independent India to disciplining not only the music genres but also a mechanism of controlling listening habits. Second, it traces the experience of the listening subject in the past two decades amidst the rapid shifts and ruptures in the sonic field in the time of emerging digital formats, mobile and internet music. The chapter is organised in a sequence of issues and events that marks the ways in which sonic texts are perceived and consumed. In the first part, it problematises the methodological traditions on the study of the sonic field, the approaches to musical compositions, composers and genres in particular. The second focal point is on the technological shifts in the making and hearing of sonic texts at different historical junctures, with an emphasis on the digital era of sound recording and listening. Finally, the chapter underlines the newness in listening practices and habits that creates a new listening subject in the emergent global soundscapes.

## Sonic texts and the public discourse[1]

An expedition into the literature on sound and music in India would reveal the predominance of certain conventional access points through which the auditory domain of the subcontinent was mapped for intellectual as well as for public scrutiny. The literary and the poetic portions of sonic texts, nature and boundaries of genres – classical, light, folk, film music – and the artists situated in and around those genres and their identities altogether constitute the conventional and the most prevalent entry points (Ranade 2006; Booth 2014; Subramanian 2008). Evidently, fixation of such earmarked gateways impedes other possible openings into the auditory field.

Discussions of the works and lives of composers and technicians of sound and music predominantly tend to linger around the question of the artists' identity, region and cultural location (Booth 2008; Weidman 2006). Presumably, the focus gets dragged down to the question of who they are and where they come from. This mode of inquiries into identity and sound cultures limits the significance of transforming technoscapes, restructured genres and new listening habits and subjectivities inaugurated by the global digital media (Schafer 1994; Attali 1985; Sterne 2003; Erlmann 2004). Against this backdrop, the attempt here is to trace how patterns of sound mixing in popular mediascapes (Appadurai 1990) engage with the intelligibility and rationality of the listeners and the reconfiguration of old and new modes of listening.

By centring global technological shifts, including recording technologies; instrumentations in recording; sound output and circulation; composition of the audience and listeners' choices in the time of mobile, portable and container technologies, it is imperative to navigate through certain contemporary sonic texts and technologies in order to make sense of the formation of a new listening subject. The attempt here is to provide a critique of the predominant scholastic view trending the confinement of auditory experiences into certain methodological convenience inaugurated by the European enlightenment project, which heavily rested upon the dominance of the visual/scopic regime and in the subsequent reduction of the auditory sense (Seremetakis 1994; Schafer 1994; Hirschkind 2001, 2006; Sterne 2012).

The changing nature of the sound text – soundtracks, songs, music compositions and modes of listening – is normally featured in every decade or at any crucial juncture of formulaic shift in composition, arrival of new composers and sound designers or in the wake of technological innovation in recording and reception. As a response to the technological shifts, including the recording technologies, instrumentations in recording, sound output and circulation, composition of the audience and their modes of listening also get transformed, thereby inaugurating new dimensions of auditory experiences. The technologically enhanced listener transgresses the state of *passivity* in the act of hearing assigned to her by the regime of the sensorial hierarchy entangled in the discourse of modernity (Seremetakis 1994). Before examining the agential potentials of this listening subject in the global soundscape, I would like to begin with the constraints in the narrowed tracks that conventionally guided inquiries into the sonic texts and their possible *hearing*. An unravelling of auditory production and circulation governed by technologies of ideology and technologies of rule has to be enunciated through sketching certain crucial moments of historical and political significance.

## Sounds of *Slumdog Millionaire*[2]

> *I come from a country and a civilisation that given [sic] the universe a word; that word is preceded by silence, followed by more silence; that word is 'om'. So I dedicate this award to my country.*[3]

Excited Rasul Pookkutty at the Kodak Theatre Dias while receiving the Academy Award, pitching the 'sound of the nation' becomes a critical note that one can hit to ponder the political character involved in it. I recall this auditory episode of celebration, not just to limit this 'sound narrative' as a predicament at the negative end or reinventing one more positive stereotyped 'non-Hindu' Indians at the crossroads of identity politics. Rather the negotiating tendencies and complicities involved in this political game unlock certain issues to fathom.

The 2008 Oscars marked the deciding moment for Indian music/sound as it had arrived on the global scene in distinctly new ways. While in the case of Rasul Pookkutty, it was the first ever international achievement for an Indian in the field of film sound (sound mixing), one can see *Slumdog Millionaire* also made possible A. R. Rahman's original foray into international production of music. His earlier international ventures, *Bombay Dreams* and *Lord of the Rings*, were stage productions, and other ventures like *Elizabeth* and *Warriors of Heaven and Earth* did not have songs like in the Bollywood music tradition but were limited to background music.

The nature of discussion during the post-Oscar celebration evidently marked the overtone of religious (Muslim) and regional (south Indian) identity when the artists and their works are cited in the larger public domain. Rasul's words 'provisionally' established the gestures of a 'true' Indian and a 'good' Muslim, and, along with A. R. Rahman, he pulls the pan-Indian to proclaim, 'These Muslims made our country proud'. A popular cross-reference to this take – 'they are Indians rather than Muslims' – unravels certain situational identity remarks and their political undertones towards scrutiny. It's also interesting to note that many accounts of Rahman's musicography stress the spiritual side of his life while describing his practice of composing and recording with mastery over the emerging technoscapes in sound production. I refrain from taking this debate forward in this chapter, as it draws on a different vantage point and can offer a separate project altogether. My concern here is to place the nature of discussions that eventually slip away from the central trope in the whole discourse – the auditory dimension of production and experience – and completely shift into the terrain of identity (here religious) of the performer. This identification in myriad subtle ways indicates the potential audience for the performers who belong to specific cultural and geographic locations.

Post-Oscar debates and discussions in India went around the question of the artists' identity rather than the soundscapes that they created and the technology they engaged with, the genres that they attempted to restructure and the new listening habits that they inaugurated. Why did such analysis of sound and music and their interface with everyday life, sociality and public sphere become an absence? How did the patterns of sound mixing in popular cinema engage with the intelligibility and rationality of the audience? How does it consistently track the shifting tendencies of hearing the symbolic in contemporary sociality in which the text is constructed and circulated? The logical connect that is established between the sonic and the figural is articulated at least in three aspects: 1. to cater to the existing sound sensibilities, 2. to generate new listening habits and 3. to challenge and resist the conventional practices and frozen sound structures and their corresponding meanings. Cinema soundscapes constantly connect with the social world and everyday life in conceiving sonic representations and meanings. All these aspects are not merely internal to the text but are embedded in the sociality that constantly engages with the text. In another sense, one could 'hear' through the burden of sociological and anthropological conventions to heavily rely on the conceptual orthodoxy translated into the frames of community, class, religion, gender and other forms of identities (Erlmann 2004).

A possible debate on sound and technology in contemporary India seems to have been reduced to a discourse on identities that mark religion, region, gender, ethnicity and nationalism, which in turn tends to probe the cultural location of artists. Rather than opening a discussion on the analytic scope of sound and technology, formal complexity, compositional strategies, audience and genres, the focus was dragged down to the question of where these artists are culturally located. This dominant mode of inquiry on the identity of the artists/performers hijacks and distorts the possibility of understanding what they are doing with sound, music and technology and, most importantly, how they are connecting with particular kinds of audiences and inaugurating new listening cultures. Such an attempt at analytical rigour becomes a lack in the public and intellectual spheres to a great extent (Manuel 1993; Weidman 2006; Kumar 2011). In a normative account, auditory texts in comparison with written texts do not equally qualify to be treated as an intellectual enterprise. This tendency has its roots in the dominant epistemological traditions of modernity that are born out of a particular geopolitical history. However, I have no plan to chart this complex domain of modernity with reference to the hierarchy among the senses (Seremitakis 1994; Schafer 1994; Hirschkind 2006). On the other hand, I wish to focus on the construction of the 'listener-citizen' in the frame of the nation-state and how this subject gets released from the insulated space of auditory experience in the time of global digital technologies. In a pedagogic sense of the term, 'the listener' is a passive entity carved out from its subject position, and it further entails the idea of its agency only in the act of listening, a state of 'silence'. Therefore, it is inscribed in the body of the listener, the absence of 'doing'. What the listener *does* while transforming her into an active subject, rejuvenating her agency in a digitally enabled sonic world, is the central question that I pose here.

## The auditory domain and the technologies of rule

Music broadcasting and listeners' choice of music were always part of the cultural politics of ruling. When radio broadcasting was considered a potential and powerful medium of communication from the time of World War II onwards, nation states in postcolonial times actively entered the field. The redesign of the field of broadcasting became a priority agenda in most states around the globe in the second half of the twentieth century (Lelyveld 1990; Subramanian 2008). It will be worthwhile to take a look at the policies and programmes on broadcasting of music in India during the early years of the post-independent nation.[4]

David Lelyveld gives an account of the politics of Indian music in the twentieth century and its adaptation to radio broadcasting in particular, both as a technology and as an institution, during the last decade of British rule in India and the first decade of the post-independent nation. He explores the social location of music, the economics of performance and the profile of the musicians, what they were instructed to play and who the potential listeners were, as all these domains were imbued with authority, power and control in the contours of both modern and traditional institutions of polity and culture. However, Lelyveld argues 'beyond context, the actual content of the music and the technical principles of its form are at the heart of how one relates social arrangements to cultural understandings' (Lelyveld 1995: 51).

The concern over musical genres and cultures, predominantly Western and Indian/Eastern, and the subsequent qualifications of hierarchy, purity and notions of performance rituals and boundary maintenance became points of tensions and contestations in the time of redesigning broadcasting in India. However, musicologists like John Foulds, who was appointed at All India Radio's Delhi station to oversee music programming in the 1930s, had a passion for creating a synthesis of Indian and Western music.[5] It was Foulds who began to release instrumental music from its subordinate position to vocal music and provided it with an independent identity, thereby enabling it to exploit specific technical resources. In his approach to music, Foulds was committed to preserving the intonations of Indian music, which led him to ban harmonium from the radio – except using it as background score in radio drama – for the reason that its well-tempered scale would tamper with the central feature of Indian raga-based music, the micro-tonic intervals[6] (Lelyveld 1995: 53).

However, such creative convergence of genres and mutual respect were rarely available to the experience of music and sound cultures of the Subcontinent. An examination of traditional notions about music in India would signify a downbeat outlook towards Western music and a growing anxiety over its spread (Keskar 1967; Lelyveld 1995; Kumar 2005). In the larger commonsense, Western music becomes a homogeneous and monolithic form of art, representing the shadow of the imperialist rule. This commonsense entails certain myths about the Western forms and practices of music, which situates them with a sense of uniformity, thereby neglecting the heterogeneous identities of those musical genres and their historically and politically loaded internal contradictions and tensions. In another sense, Western musical genres, irrespective of their uniqueness and differences, are construed as invading force, the spectre of colonising and threatening 'European other' as against the 'soothing and melodious' musical traditions in India. While Western music signifies the loudness and cacophony of sound, its Indian counterparts characterise soft and gentle musical expressions as part of the aforementioned commonsense (Kumar 2005; Weidman 2006).

When the idea of the West itself collapses into the signifiers of imperialism and cultural invasion in the frame of mind, the musical forms and genres of those regions are conveniently categorised as equivalent to the 'colonial master'. Binary constructions of musical genres such as Western and Indian, classical and folk, pure and contaminated become anchoring points of value judgment and hierarchical ordering of both performance and listening cultures. Indian classical versions of Carnatic and Hindustani traditions of music, in this xenophobic understanding, become the only available 'pure' and 'authentic' modes of musical expression. Western music genres such as rock, jazz, pop, hip-hop, country and so on are not only considered 'impure', but their increasing popularity in the Subcontinent can create a threat and ultimately endanger the 'native' musical traditions, especially the classical genres (Weidman 2006; Kumar 2011; Kumar 2005).

This common belief about the music genres of the occidental region stems from apathy and a steadied blindness towards the history and politics of music in the Western world. Non-classical musical forms like jazz, rock, reggae, rap and hip-hop evolved through various forms of resistance and critique against the power dynamics embedded in Western classical music, as well as the Eurocentric construction of hegemonic knowledge over art and culture (Attali 1985; Middleton 1990; Sterne 2006; Kumar 2005). The language of resistance and critique that the aforementioned genres inaugurated has been misheard in the essentialising notion about the West as a uniform entity of polity and culture. Against that backdrop, the politics behind the assumptions related to music genres need to be unpacked beyond the dichotomous constructions of music as Western and Indian or pure and impure.

The recent controversy over t-shirts with Bob Marley's image that erupted in the state of Kerala illuminates the xenophobic 'mishearing'. Bob Marley t-shirts were construed in the cultural parlance as a dangerous and threatening symbol to the middle-class morality in Kerala's public sphere in the recent past. In some cases, the state police even arrested young men who grew long hair and wore Bob Marley t-shirts as the symbolism, in that particular commonsense, represented crime, drug addiction and immoral activities among the youth, the ill effect of the 'west', in other words labelled the 'new generation' in a depressing sense.[7] Needless to say, this morality consciousness has nothing to do with Marley's music, life and politics, but it has more to do with the signified in that image, more or less equivalent to the racial stereotyping of men with dark skin and long hair. Here, one can observe how the state (reading the previously mentioned police act) is compelled to become a gullible entity, falling in tune with the popular imagery of racial stereotyping. The state's interventions in the field of art and music are extensions of such calculations about music and morality and reflected heavily in the policies and programmes of broadcasting in the national media. The early trajectories of this commonsense can be traced back to the 1950s, when radio broadcasting in India became an instrument to engage with such anxieties over the music of the 'other'.

As part of the post-independence project of salvaging Indian music and Hindu tradition, music broadcasting was subject to a radical redesign in the 1950s. B. V. Keskar, the then-minister of information and broadcasting (from 1950 to 1962), was dismissive of British-administered broadcasting in India, especially in the context of broadcasting Indian music. He was the chief designer of the musical ideologies and policies of All-India Radio. Keskar believed that, primarily through radio broadcasting, the musical heritage of India could be resurrected. This imagination signifies the crucial role of the state post-independence in repairing the damage done to Indian music under Muslim and British rule (Keskar 1967; Lelyveld 1995: 55).

The reorganising of broadcasting was attributed to the endangered condition of Indian/Hindu music traditions due to the spread of Western, Persian and Sufi forms of music and art during colonial and pre-colonial times (Keskar, Lelyveld). Keskar had serious concerns about reviving the music traditions rooted in 'Indian culture' and Hindu civilisation. The reforms in broadcasting that Keskar proposed were to 'purify' the Indian classical music, especially Hindustani and Carnatic classical music, as the former was subjected to severe contamination during the Mugal and British rule in India (Keskar 1967; Lelyveld 1995). Accordingly, Carnatic and Hindustani vocal music programs were aired with a greater priority. New ways of classifying music genres became part of the redesign, as classical, light and folk music genres were identified with strict separation in the timing of broadcasting and in the identification of different target audiences for these genres. While making the imagined boundaries of listening cultures, Keskar must have imagined who can listen to what kind of music. This gets reflected in the identification of groups such as 'students', 'rural uneducated', 'urban educated', 'rural women' and 'urban women' as audiences with specific listening capacities and tastes for different genres. This design also entails a pedagogic communication of music meant for specific audience groups, not based on their experience and exposure to different genres of music but more related to their class, region and cultural locations. Another concern of broadcasting was over the precise scheduling of music genres in appropriate slots according to the choice and desires of different audience groups (Lelyveld 1995:53).

As a result of these interventions, film music, which is considered an 'impure' combination of Western orchestrated and erotic Urdu lyrics in Keskar's version, had disappeared from All India Radio (hereafter, AIR) for a brief period.[8] The idea of listeners according to Keskar was straitjacketed, as he believed 'simple people living in the villages have simple music and enjoy simple songs. . . . The more developed people, who read and write will have complex feelings and will require a more complex vehicle to express it' (Lelyveld 1995: 56; Keskar 1967: 2). Creating an alternative popular form for film music had become a pressing need, as the classical versions could not be appreciated by a larger audience, as it requires cultural capital, taste and training. The idea of introducing 'light music' against the 'contaminated and impure' film music became a priority in order to produce a popular alternative. However, the absence of film music from AIR triggered the erosion of a large number of audiences, who shifted to listening to Radio Ceylon.[9] This trend of listeners' responses compelled Keskar to re-introduce film music, but he devised it through separating the genre from mainstream broadcasting. Vividh Bharati, a separate radio station only for film music, was opened with national coverage based in Delhi, with a thick balance of recorded film songs, all detached from the main program channels (ibid.: 60).

Whatsoever the refashioning of programmes in AIR, in the early 1970s, new technologies like cassette recorders began to undermine the dominance of broadcasting and enabled a large number of production units, both legal and otherwise, and mostly localised, to initiate new audiences and settings for a variety of decentralised and diverse auditory culture (ibid.: 60). The story became radically unique in the 1990s and after listening cultures started shifting from one platform to the other at lightning pace. This summarises the narrative of listening from the hegemonic and well-controlled broadcasting scheme owned by the state to decentralised private owners coming onto the scene when cassette and CD and DVD cultures, and most recently formats like MP3, iTunes and Blu-Ray, become part of everyday life. As a container technology of recorded sound, the MP3 represents the idea of portability and exchange as its central characteristics (Sterne 2006, 2012). As Jonathan Sterne argues with the case of the MP3 as a technology of psychoacoustics, digital audio cultures work according to logics somewhat distinct from digital visual culture (Sterne 2006: 825).[10] Sterne treats the MP3 as a cultural artefact in his analysis that tracks the possibility of going beyond the technological traits and the material dimension and to trace the psychoacoustic and the auditory dimension in the making of new listening practices inaugurated by it (Sterne 2012). The forthcoming section will take a look into the technological dimensions of the sonic field and the changing patterns of listening practices.

## Digital technologies and portable sounds: reconfiguring the auditory field

A few months ago, a film song titled '*Jimikkikkammal*', from a Malayalam movie became a sensation on YouTube, not simply through its popularity but by simultaneous reproduction and circulation of it in multiple versions, representing a range of music genres worldwide.[11] These rerecorded versions of the song varied from the Caribbean rap style to the Carnatic *Ragamalika* style of rendition, produced and performed by relatively unknown artists – individuals and groups. One cannot say that '*Jimikkikkammal*' is the first of its kind to experience such a multitude of re-produced versions from different regions and genres. When one searches similar musical compositions from Indian albums or films, it results in spotting a few others, in which a prominent trendsetter titled 'Why This *Kolaveri Di*' would surface instantaneously.[12] A. S. Ajith Kumar finds how the '*Kolaveri Di*' music video initiated the possibilities for dialogue and multiple musical engagement among the different stakeholders, including composers, technicians, editors, marketers and listeners alongside a range of activities (Kumar 2011). Exploring the possible ways of engaging with the '*Kolaveri Di*' song, Ajith Kumar writes: 'The "listener" is more visible now, and has more powers. He/she shares, likes, comments, makes his/her own videos and broadcasts them by herself/himself' (Kumar 2011: 1). Kumar claims that it was not his attempt to jump into any sort of technological determinism by making such a claim on the listening act but to underline the crucial shifts taking place in the domain of music making, sharing, broadcasting and reproducing. It also accounts for the new ways in which the listener's potential is discovered in the medium of Internet and mobile music (Leyshon 2009; Kumar 2011; Jeffrey and Doron 2013; Gopinath and Stanyek 2014).

Technology, Walter Benjamin claimed, would allow the audience to control the conditions of its own experience in radically new ways (Benjamin 1936). Manuel Castells places a different layer in the understanding of the social structure and its potential transformation that is technology (Castells 1996, 2000). He writes: 'There is another layer that is folded in production/consumption, experience, power, and culture. This is technology. Technology is embodied in technical relationships, which are socially conditioned, so in itself it is not an independent, non-human dimension' (Castells 2000: 7). Castells calls for integrating 'technology in its own ground as a specific layer of the social structure' (ibid.: 8). He stretches a sociological concern by raising the question of 'how the technological arrangements through which humans act upon matter (nature), upon themselves, and upon other humans' (ibid.: 9). Castells borrows here the term 'technological paradigm' from Christopher Freeman to signify the shift from the industrial age to the information age, where digital technology and microelectronics take centre stage (Freeman 1982; Leyshon 2009). In this backdrop of a paradigm shift, how can we make sense of the unprecedented magnitude of technological mediation that reconfigures our everyday life, economy and culture, the manifold challenges that globalisation inaugurates and cultural responses to this process? Moreover, how might culture itself be mediating this progression, becoming simultaneously a subject and an object? With the flow of cultural technologies, life ways, values, symbols and ideals get altered, and individuals' expectations, aspirations and perspectives are being transformed. John Tomlinson centres the question of how routine practices and experiences with digital and electronic media technologies renovate the surface of everyday life in the time of globalisation (Tomlinson 2007). The field of digital audio technologies in the last decade itself witnessed radical alteration, which literally enunciated the idea of 'global immediacy', reflected in Tomlinson's account (Tomlinson 2007; Held and Moore 2008; Slobin 2008)

With the advent of digital sound technologies, we entered a world with an acoustic environment which is relatively unfamiliar and radically different from the past (Erlmann 2004; Leyshon 2009; Sterne 2012). Presumably, the new media invents the listening subject to act up on a multitude of platforms. A.S. Ajith Kumar notes how the ringtone was a new form of music that came with the spread of mobile phones. When music composers like A.R. Rahman started making ringtones, they no more remained an alert of a call but came to be considered music pieces (Kumar 2011: 2). Airtel, one of the leading mobile service providers in India, claimed in 2009 that its users completed over 200 million music downloads. This happened at a time when film songs were the most popular music form in the Subcontinent. A few years later, Nokia launched a music album titled 'Connections' composed by A.R. Rahman (Kumar 2011). With the arrival of mobile music, the idea of sharing became the central aspect of listening. Kumar attributes this shift in contrast with the listening practices and audio space of the music hall, radio, television and other analogue technologies. The YouTube audiovisual space created a different set of multilingual audiences. It offers unique opportunities and possibilities among different people to connect and interact with each other (Kumar 2011).

MP3 and other portable and container technologies of the new media platforms offer immense possibilities for listeners to create their own music and ringtones and share them among fellow listeners distributed worldwide. For about a decade or more, the MP3 has occupied centre stage in the domain of digital audio formats and as an effective apparatus for file sharing and portability (Sterne 2012).[13] Langdon Winner writes that technological artefacts 'embody specific form of power and authority' (Winner 1986: 19). He distinguishes the politics of technologies in two categories. First, a format like MP3 needs to be understood as a crystallised set of social and material relations embedded in its formation. It is a device that works for and is worked on by a group of people, technologies, ideologies and other cultural and material facets. In that sense, Sterne aptly puts it in the form of a 'tour guide for social, physical, psychological and ideological phenomena through which people organise their everyday life' (Sterne 2006: 825). It is then important to place the listening subject in the debate on MP3 beyond its legal and economic dimensions, and the cultural and aesthetic factors need to be foregrounded in order to understand the shifts in listening practices channelled through the container technology. Shifting the substantial question of MP3 from law and economy to the technological form and a sonic object would yield a more context-specific understanding, especially while linking it with the users and their preoccupations of sharing and inaugurating new listening practices. The users of MP3s tend to reconfigure their listening practices and choices frequently in a mode of distraction against the notion of concentrated listening, as the idea of hearing is located not in any fixity but 'on the move'. As Sterne rightly states: 'the anticipated praxeology of listening encoded in each MP3 emphasises distraction over attention and exchange over use' (Sterne 2006: 827).

The discussion here intends to underline one among several audio formats in the digital world of communication and entertainment in order to suggest how those formats and devices invent new modes of listening in the way of their functioning. The reference of MP3 as a cultural artefact enables us to raise larger questions in the making of new listening subjects, whose possibilities are reflected not only in the use of digital audio formats but also in the creation of innovative audio content. Presumably, how does one take an account of the shifting terrains of listening beyond its passivity attributed in conventional auditory fields? Charles Hirschkind, in his engagement with the notion of the figure of the listener in the episode of *The Storyteller* in Walter Benjamin's account (1969), illustrates the sensorial capacity of the listener beyond the experience of individual senses in the act of hearing. In this context, he writes: 'within the model of absorptive listening figured in *The Storyteller*, it is in some sense the body in its entirety that constitutes both the medium of expression and the organ of audition. For these listeners as well, the organ of audition is the human sensorium in its entirety, not the narrow passageway of the ear and its cognitive functioning' (Hirschkind 2006: 28). The interface among different senses in parallel ways enables one to extend the idea of connectivity of listening spaces beyond geopolitical and cultural boundaries (Slobin 2008; Booth 2014). In other words, how does the new listening subject transcend the spatial and geopolitical configurations of region, nation, language and culture? The following episode will illuminate this aspect transcending the cultural boundaries of listening practices.

## *Chackocha* song and its phonemic presence

Almost a decade ago, a music video became widely popular among the Malayali audience around the world. This can be considered one of the early 'viral' video songs circulated among Malayali audiences on YouTube in 2007, when the usage 'viral' itself gathered little attention in the new media parlance. The song is a Russian folk song with a peculiar set of subtitles. The song is titled 'Brows' by Ivan Kupala, from the album 'Kostroma'. One would become curious about the popularity of a Russian song and its unusual circulation among a large number of Malayali audiences. The popularity factor can be unfolded only through a discussion about the peculiar set of subtitles that I mentioned earlier. Interestingly, the Russian song on YouTube carries its subtitles in Malayalam. However, the subtitles were not meant to serve its usual purpose, which is to provide the exact translation of the content in a different language, the language of the target audience. Here, the creators of the YouTube video claim in their edited version of the song: 'This is not a translation, this is how it sounds in Malayalam' [This is what I believe the song sounds like in Malayalam – inspired by 'Buffalax'].[14] The song begins with '*O Chackocha*' in Malayalam – which means 'hey, brother Chacko', and then it proceeds with funny combinations of Malayalam words.

The subtitles follow then, and the Malayalam equivalents of the Russian words/sounds were arranged line by line, which has nothing to do with the lyrics of the song in the original. This is a peculiar kind of auditory experience, commonly known as *soramimi* in Japanese, which actually means 'mishearing' or 'fancy hearing'. It normally implies musical lyrics when they are misheard as nonsensical forms in clusters of sounds equivalent in a different language. 'Mondegreen' is the English equivalent of *soramimi*, whose literal meaning is mishearing or misinterpretation of a sound piece as an outcome of near-homophony. Mondegreen is often created by individual listener(s) when they are unable to make sense of the actual meaning in the original language while listening to a song or any other sonic text. In such situations, the listener(s) improvise(s) by attaching similar sound content/lyrics to the sound text. In this process, a word from a foreign language is translated homophonically into a language of one's own in order to create a set of meanings which is not available to the listener in the first instance.[15]

In the case of this Russian song, the Malayalam sequence of lyrics, or the 'sounding track', produces another lyrical effect of humour and creativity. There are at least two levels of auditory impact of humour that one can hear through the song. First, there is a significant amount of humour inscribed in the entire act of this 'misheard' translation and the newness of it to a large number of audiences. Second, the Malayalam-sounding words in the Russian language and their sequence of arrangement offer another poetics of humour and satire in its own terms. The whole episode of this sonic innovation, which entails a unique auditory experience, must have evolved from the imagination of a single listener or a small group of listeners, who created this refurnished sound text. It is really hard to convey this sonic experience to those readers who are outside of the language discourse and those who are unable to listen to the music video by following the subtitles. Given this analytical constraint, my emphasis here is on the transformation of the passive listener (in the time of old media) to the 'producer listener' (in the time of new media), who is not only technologically enabled but also imaginatively positioned to deploy the craft of 'recomposing' a song for a different set of audiences.

Here, the act of listening gets destabilised in its conventional time and space. At one level, music compositions and genres transgress the boundaries of regions and communities in the advent of a new mediascape (Appadurai 1990). And in another dimension, the listener transforms herself into an active subject who re-creates the compositions and customises them to a unique listening experience.

I wish to conclude this chapter by citing another interesting episode of music genres becoming global with little notification and in the absence of signboards holding them anymore. The story here is of a song from the Dominican Republic titled '*Kuluki Takatha*', which recently became amazingly viral among the audience in the regions of South India, especially Tamil Nadu and Kerala. Many of its listeners were unable to recognise the origin of the song, and many others confused it with a local song created by some amateur artist, composed in the home-video style, since the initial parts of the lyrics sound like the Malabari dialect of the Malayalam language. A local television channel's survey among its audience revealed a similar trend of identification of this particular song. The song was originally composed by Tono Rosario for an album titled *Grandes Exitos* (2010). Rosario has been a household-name musician in the Dominican Republic since 1978, as he popularised the Latin American dance music genre called the merengue. Surveys reveal that the most-valued merengue music videos on the market are of Rosario's compositions. And the recent unplanned eastward journey of the song '*Kuluki Takatha*' to South India becomes a moment of excitement for both the composer and the listeners, as in the case of '*Jimikkikkammal*''s westward travel, which are enabled by the digital enabling of listening possibilities in a global context.

Through these citations of travelling music, I do not wish to celebrate the idea of the choices available to a liberated listener who seemingly exercises free will in the act of listening. Users and listeners of digital audio sources are now situated across a wide range of sociocultural and economic settings. Since smart phones have become part of common peoples' everyday lives, conventional categories of 'listeners' such as 'urban', 'rural', 'educated and 'uneducated' have become more or less redundant. Listeners are exposed to different auditory texts and genres at random, irrespective of the acoustic and aesthetic qualifications determined by their sociocultural locations. In the age of cell phones enabled with digital technology (Jeffrey and Doron 2013), internet users are no longer confined to the old class of computer literates. When the audio and visual content of the internet reaches the domain of mobile phones, it traverses the borders of conventional usage. Here the praxeology of listening and auditory perception gets transposed to a terrain of powerful and significant aesthetic experience; at times, it celebrates the limit of the human ear (Sterne 2006). The idea of 'distorted' listening and the 'casual' listeners of digital audio cultures share the promise of exploring distinct sonic experiences. This underlines the changing dynamics of power and control, where the listening subject can negotiate with the notions of boundaries, authority and control in the practice of hearing and shaping distinct auditory frameworks.

## Notes

1 I prefer to use the term 'sonic text' in the context of this chapter, which represents wide-ranging forms of sound content. Though the discussion is on musical content in most instances of the chapter, they do not strictly fall into the conventional genres of musical compositions, songs and instrumental music; rather, they include new forms of sonic expressions, recreated and rerecorded by composers and individual consumers and shared on new media platforms. However, the audio contents in the form of speeches, talks and conversations are not considered for analysis within the scope of this chapter. In that sense, speech dialogues, voice text and conversational content as exclusive genres of auditory expression will be beyond the scope of my analysis.

2 'Slumdog Millionaire', Dir. Danny Boyle. 2008. www.imdb.com/title/tt1010048/ (accessed on 21 March 2020).

3 From the acceptance speech delivered by Rasul Pookkutty after winning the Oscar for sound mixing for *Slumdog Millionaire* at the 81st Academy Awards in 2009. www.youtube.com/watch?v=8In11J6U2Iw (accessed on 21 March 2020).

4 For a detailed account of the history of radio broadcasting in India, see Lelyveld 1990. See also Avasthy 1965.

5 The appointment of two European musicologists, John Foulds in Delhi and Walter Kaufmann in Bombay, to the radio stations of All India Radio in the 1930s was a crucial moment in overseeing the Western music programming and experimentation in the shifting terrains of Indian music genres. See Fielden 1936; Lelyveld 1990, 1995. Also see Bakhle 2005.

6 Microtones are any intervals smaller than a semitone. They occur in certain exotic scales, and they also have been exploited by some late nineteenth- and twentieth-century composers. Microtonal music is often produced by bowed and wind instruments when a note is played from the previous one through smooth transition without having an audible break between notes. Raga-based Indian vocal music is a perfect example of the production of microtones in regular intervals in a composition.

7 'New generation' became a coinage to signify a particular lifestyle among youth in Kerala, who follow a freak way of life, challenging the existing moral framework; 'freekan' is another term used in a similar way in the local language. However, the term is not used in any sense of concrete meaning in tune with empirical sense making of the term. It becomes an attribute of a different lifestyle among men and women who grow out of the existing middle-class morality.

8 Lelyveld notes that in 1954, the State's negotiations with the Film Producers Guild of India for rights to film songs and on the question of rationing did not work out so that for a short time, they virtually disappeared from AIR programming, and the listeners of film music had to reach out to either independent broadcasting from Goa or the high-power commercial broadcasts of Radio Ceylon. See Lelyveld 1995.

9 When film music was virtually absent from AIR programs, a survey was made to collect information about listener preferences, and it revealed that out of ten households with licensed radio sets, nine were tuned to Radio Ceylon and the tenth set was broken. See Lelyveld 1995. See also Mitchell et al. 1997.

10 MP3 stands for MPEG-1, Layer-3. MPEG (Motion Picture Experts Group) is a consortium of engineers and others formed with the support of the International Standards Organization (ISO) and the International Electrotechnical Commission. MPEG started functioning in 1988 as an ad hoc group with an aim to evolve a standardised data compression scheme in the broadcast telecommunications and consumer electronic industries. For a detailed account of the technical dimensions of MP3, see Sterne 2006, 2012.

11 '*Jimikkikkammal*' was composed by Shaan Rahman for the Malayalam film *Velipadinte Pusthakam*, Dir. Lal Jose. 2017. www.imdb.com/title/tt6789174/?ref_=nm_flmg_dr_2 (accessed on 24 April 2018).

12 '*Why This Kolaveri Di*' was composed by Anirudh Ravichander, for the film *3*, Dir. Aishwarya Dhanush 2012. www.imdb.com/title/tt2123129/fullcredits?ref_=tt_cl_sm#cast (accessed on 21 April 2018).

13 Jonathan Sterne examines the design of the MP3 from both industrial and psychoacoustic perspectives to demonstrate how MP3s are so easy to exchange and share among a wider audience. As a container technology for recorded sound, the MP3 shows that the characteristic of 'portability' is crucial to the history of auditory representation. As a psychoacoustic technology, the MP3 showcases that digital audio culture works according to logics that are distinct from digital visual culture. MP3s contain within them a whole world of audition and a praxiology of listening. They occupy minimal space compared to other kinds of digital recordings, and when they are listened to, they are experienced as music, not as file formats. For a detailed account of this, see Sterne 2006, 2012.

14 Buffalax is the YouTube user name of Mike Sutton, who popularised the art of picking a non-English video song in order to give a 'sonic translation' of it in English. See www.wired.com/2009/04/buffalax-is-bac/ (accessed on 21 April 2018).

15 The YouTube video of the Russian folk song titled 'Brows' by Ivan Kupala, from the album *Kostroma*, with Malayalam 'sub-titles' can be found here: www.youtube.com/watch?v=_zEbRrV-flw (accessed on 13 April 2018).

## References

Appadurai, Arjun. 1990. 'Disjuncture and Difference in the Global Cultural Economy', *Theory, Culture and Society*, *Sage*, 7:295–310.

Attali, Jaques. 1985. *Noise: The Political Economy of Music*. Manchester: Manchester University Press.

Avasthy, G.C. 1965. *Broadcasting in India*. Bombay: Allied Publishers.

Bakhle, Janaki. 2005. *Two Men and Music: Nationalism in the Making of an Indian Classical Tradition*. New York: Oxford University Press.

Benjamin, Walter. 1969. *Illuminations: Essays and Reflections*. New York: Schocken Books.

Booth, Gregory. 2008. *Behind the Curtain: Making Music in Mumbai's Film Studios*. New Delhi: Oxford University Press.

Booth, Gregory. 2014. *More Than Bollywood: Studies in Indian Popular Music*. New Delhi: Oxford University Press.

Castells, Manuel. 1996. *The Rise of Network Society*. Oxford: Basil Blackwell.

Castells, Manuel. 2000. 'Materials for an Exploratory Theory of the Network Society', *British Journal of Sociology*, 51 (1): 5–24.

Erlmann, Veit. 2004. *Hearing Cultures: Essays on Sound, Listening and Modernity*. New York: Berg.

Fielden, Lione. 1936. *Indian Listener I*, 14, July 7: *Report on the Progress of Broadcasting*, 21–24.

Freeman, Christopher. 1982. *The Economics of Industrial Innovation*. London: Pinter.

Gopinath, Sumanth and Jason Stanyek. 2014. *The Oxford Handbook of Mobile Music Study*, Vol. 1 and 2. New York: Oxford University Press.

Held, David and Henrietta Moore. 2008. *Cultural Politics in a Global Age: Uncertainty, Solidarity and Innovation*. London: Oneworld.

Hirschkind, Charles. 2001. 'The Ethics of Listening: Cassette-Sermon Audition in Contemporary Egypt', *American Ethnologist*, 28(3): 623–49.

Hirschkind, Charles. 2006. *The Ethical Soundscapes: Cassette Sermons and Islamic Counterpublics*. New York: Columbia University Press.

Jeffrey, Robin and Assa Doron. 2013. *Cell Phone Nation: How Mobile Phones Have Revolutionized Business, Politics and Ordinary Life in India*. Gurugram: Hachette India.

Keskar, B.V. 1967. *Indian Music: Problems and Prospects*. Bombay: Popular Prakashan.

Kumar, A.S. Ajith. 2005. 'Jipsikalumnomadukalum: adipolisangeethathintebhoothakalangal' ("Gypsies and Nomads: The Past Times of Fast-Beat Music"), *Pachakuthira*, DC Books, August, 1(8): 13–18.

Kumar, A.S. Ajith. 2011. 'High Theory, Low "Kolaveri Di": Why I Am a Fan of This Flop Song. Kafeela Web Portal'. Available at: https://kafila.online/2011/12/08/high-theory-low-kolaveri-di-why-i-am-a-fan-of-this-flop-song-a-s-ajith-kumar/ [Last accessed September 13, 2017].

Lelyveld, David. 1990. 'Transmitters and Culture: The Colonial Roots of Indian Broadcasting', *South Asia Research*, 10 (1): 41–52.

Lelyveld, David. 1995. 'Upon the Subdominance: Administering Music in All India Radio', in Carol A. Dreckenridge (ed.) *Consuming Modernity: Public Culture in a South Asian World*, pp. 49–65. Minneapolis: University of Minnesota Press.

Leyshon, Andrew. 2009. 'The Software Slump?: The Digital Music, the Democratization of Technology and the Decline of the Recording Studio Sector within the Musical Economy', *Environment and Planning A*, 41(6): 1309–31.

Manuel, Peter. 1993. *Cassette Culture: Popular Music and Technology in North India*. Chicago: Chicago University Press.

Middleton, Richard. 1990. *Studying popular music*. Philadelphia: Open University Press.

Mitchell, J.L.et al. 1997. *MPEG Video Compression Standard*. New York: Chapman & Hall.

Ranade, Ashok. 2006. *Hindi Film Song: Music beyond Boundaries*. New Delhi: Bibliophile South Asia.

Schafer, R. Murray. 1994. *The Soundscapes: Our Sonic Environment and the Tuning of the World*. Rochester: Destiny Books.

Seremetakis, C. Nadia. 1994. *The Senses Still: Perception and Memory as Material Culture in Modernity*. Chicago: Chicago University Press.

Slobin, Mark. 2008. *Global Soundtracks: World of Film Music*. Middleton, CT: Wesleyan University Press.

Sterne, Jonathan. 2003. *The Audible Past: The Cultural Origins of Sound Reproduction*. Durham: Duke University Press.

Sterne, Jonathan. 2006. 'The MP3 as a Cultural Artifact', *Writings on New Media and Society*, Sage Publications, 8 (5): 825–42.

Sterne, Jonathan. 2012. *MP3: The Meaning of a Format*. Durham: Duke University Press.

Subramanian, Lakshmi. 2008. *New Mansions for Music: Performance, Pedagogy and Criticism*. New Delhi: Orient Blackswan.

Tomlinson, John. 2007. *The Culture of Speed: The Coming of Immediacy*. London: Sage Publications.

Weidman, Amanda. 2006. *Singing the Classical, Voicing the Modern: The Postcolonial Politics of Music in South India*. Calcutta: Seagull Books.

Winner, L. 1986. *The Whale and the Reactor: A Search for Limits in the Age of High Technology*. Chicago, IL: University of Chicago Press.

# Index

Note: Page numbers followed by 'n' refer to notes.

For Product Safety Concerns and Information please contact our EU representative GPSR@taylorandfrancis.com
Taylor & Francis Verlag GmbH, Kaufingerstraße 24, 80331 München, Germany

www.ingramcontent.com/pod-product-compliance
Ingram Content Group UK Ltd.
Pitfield, Milton Keynes, MK11 3LW, UK
UKHW020146200926
475702UK00016B/2574
*9780367546878*